Blockchain in Energy

Editor

Jan Veuger

Scientist in Blokchain and Real Estate, and Professor from 2012–2022 at
School of Finance and International Business
Saxion University, the Netherlands
and
Institute for Business Hanze University Groningen
The Netherlands (2012–2022)

CRC Press
Taylor & Francis Group
Boca Raton London New York

CRC Press is an imprint of the
Taylor & Francis Group, an **informa** business
A SCIENCE PUBLISHERS BOOK

Cover credit: kjpargeter Freepik. The image is copyright free.

First edition published 2024
by CRC Press
2385 NW Executive Center Drive, Suite 320, Boca Raton FL 33431

and by CRC Press
4 Park Square, Milton Park, Abingdon, Oxon, OX14 4RN

CRC Press is an imprint of Taylor & Francis Group, LLC

Library of Congress Cataloging-in-Publication Data (applied for)

ISBN: 978-1-032-15240-0 (hbk)
ISBN: 978-1-032-15243-1 (pbk)
ISBN: 978-1-003-24322-9 (ebk)

DOI: 10.1201/9781003243229

Typeset in Palatino Linotype
by Radiant Productions

Preface

The world-wide energy problem is growing very fast. In an European context, the EU is trying to frame and politically manage this, while the market is very intense. This raises questions for alternatives to other sources, other ways of using and reallocating interests in different areas of power, availability, and uses of energy. In addition, the digital world is developing at a rapid pace in many areas. From my expertise around blockchain, there are many possibilities to make the data about the issues transparent, reliable, and unchangeable. With this one has the information that is reliable and of insight for each user. Blockchain can contribute to this, hence this book to share that knowledge in the field of energy and blockchain.

Studies and solutions on how to deal with blockchain and data do not always provide immediate direction on how data can and should be used. In my professorship (Veuger, 2018), the risks of dataism were already discussed: one relies more on data than on our own powers of observation. Gathering a lot of data is often not the problem. The question, however, is what data is needed to answer your question? The inclusion and exclusion of data is essential because that provides the very data that fits the research question. One should establish that the data is FAIR as the meaning of fair is (fair) and Findable Accessible Interoperable Reusable (FAIR). The term FAIR was first launched at the Lorentz workshop resulting in principles of it in the publication of Wilkinson et al. (2016). Regarding data, data lifecycle, its use, its inclusion and exclusion, ethics, working within frameworks, mining, privacy, etc. alone, there are several dissertations to be written, but I have limited myself to a few references (Mannhardt, 2019; Mannhart, 2018; Manhardt, 2019) with which readers of this book can benefit. All of this calls for follow-up research. Hora est: we do not know what we have not yet researched.

References

Mannhardt, F., S.A. Petersen and M.H. Oliveira. 2018. Privacy challenges for process mining in human-centered industrial environments. 4th International Conference on Intelligent Environments (IE), Rome, Italy, 25–28 June 2018. IEEE 2018. ISBN 978-1-5386-6844-3.s. 64–71.

Mannhardt, F., S.A. Petersen and M.H. Oliveira. 2019. A trust and privacy framework for smart manufacturing environments. Journal of Ambient Intelligence and Smart Environments 11(3): s.201–219. https://sintef.brage.unit.no/sintef-xmlui/bitstream/handle/11250/2593828/08595033.pdf?sequence=4&isAllowed=y.

Mannhardt, F., S.A. Petersen and M.F. Oliveira. 2019. Manuel Fradinho. Process Mining and Privacy in Smart Manufacturing. Informatik Spektrum 42(5): s.336–339.

Veuger, J. 2018, Veuger, J. 2020. Blockchain Convergentie (Blockchain Convergence). Deventer: Saxion UAS. https://www.saxion.nl/binaries/content/assets/onderzoek/meer-onderzoek/blockchain/blockchain-convergentie-jan-veuger-2020.pdf.

Wilkonson et al. 2016. The Fair Guiding Principles for Scientific Data Management and Stewardship, Germany, Springer Nature. The FAIR Guiding Principles for scientific data management and stewardship | Scientific Data (nature.com).

Contents

Chapter 1
Introduction about Blockchain and Energy

Jan Veuger

1. Introduction

The world-wide energy problem is growing very fast. In an European context, the EU is trying to frame and politically manage this, while the market is very intense. This raises questions for alternatives to other sources, other ways of using and reallocating interests in different areas of power, availability, and uses of energy. In addition, the digital world is developing at a rapid pace in many areas. From my expertise around blockchain, there are many possibilities to make the data about the issues transparent, reliable, and unchangeable. With this one has the information that is reliable and of insight for each user. Blockchain can contribute to this, hence this book to share that knowledge in the field of energy and blockchain. As an introduction the case of the Dutch energy sector and second an overview of all contributions with a summary to give an impression of the chapters and finally: hora est!

2. Case as introduction : the Dutch energy sector

Many European countries want to eliminate Russian gas, but with advancing insight it turns out that—especially Gazprom—is in many capillaries of the European economy than was usually assumed (Het Financieel Dagblad, 2022). Interests in the largest gas producers in

Scientist in Blockchain and Real Estate, and Professor (appointed from 2019–2022), School of Finance and International Business, Saxion University, the Netherlands; and Institute for Business Hanze University Groningen, the Netherlands (2012–2019).
Email: j.veuger@corporaterem.nl

the Dutch sea—for example, Wintershall North Sea (15% market share in the Dutch North Sea) where 50% of the shares are owned by Gazprom—are held by Russian oligarchs, among others. Incidentally, these interests in Wintershall North Sea are frozen (Dijk and de Groot, 2022) (Figure 1.2). Gas extraction in the Netherlands is becoming increasingly important because the extraction of gas from the Groningen gas fields (See Figure 1.1) has been phased out due to the problem of earthquakes and, as of October 2022, can only be used as a reserve supply. The gas extracted by Gazprom in this case is a surplus on top of the 5 billion cubic meters of gas that Russia supplies annually to the Netherlands, being 10 to 15% of the total gas consumption in the Netherlands. The dependence on supplies of gas by Russia is thus high and in other European countries even higher. Incidentally, the United Kingdom and the United States do have a policy on this. Besides gas, the Netherlands also has a business relationship in other energy areas such as oil. About 600,00 barrels per day—is 13% of Russia's total oil exports—are delivered to the Netherlands with a value of US$ 9.4 billion. About 20% of all oil processed in refineries comes from Russia and products such as diesel and gasoline are also developed as for example in the Zeeland Refinery where Russian Lukoil has a 45% stake (Dijk and de Groot, 2022).

The major energy contracts of municipalities in the Netherlands are with Gazprom Energy, about 38%. The reason is that the price was/is the main criterion in European tenders for gas supplies. The municipality of Utrecht stated that the supplies were about 20–45% cheaper than comparable suppliers. Not entirely unimportant is that Gazprom has a contract to use 40% of the storage of gas in, for example, Bergermeer, a commercial underground storage between the municipality of Bergen and Alkmaar.

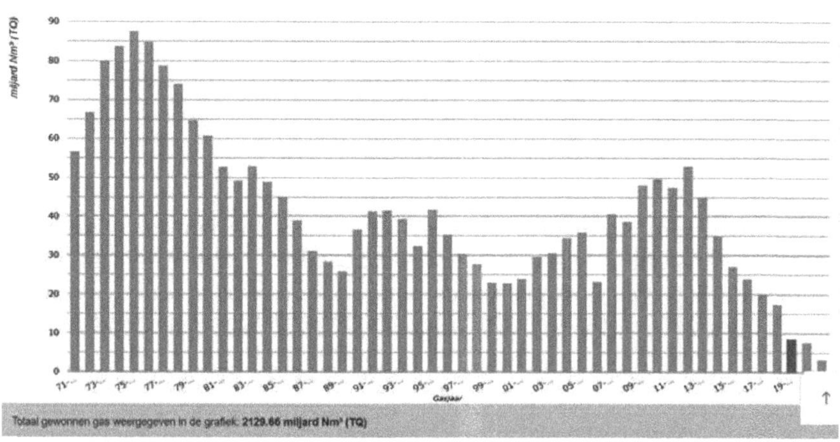

Figure 1.1. Total gas extrachted from Groningen gas field. *Source: NAM:* Gas-en olie productiecijfers | NAM.

2.1 Facts in The Netherlands

Places	Facts
Amsterdam	Amsterdam is a major supply port for Russian raw materials and oil products.
Municipalities	About 120 municipalities in the Netherlands purchase gas from Gazprom through Gazprom Energy. These include the municipalities of The Hague, Utrecht, and Nijmegen. The Russian company won many tenders as it offered the cheapest offer. Several universities (including the University of Twente) and water boards also have energy contracts with Gazprom.
Habor Rotterdam	Petroleum and fuels make up about 80% of the goods Russia exported in 2019. Altogether, that part had a value of over US$ 35 billion. Some 62 million tons of transshipment in Rotterdam is "Russia-oriented". That is 13% of the total 470 million tons of goods handled by the Port of Rotterdam last year. About 20% of Rotterdam's handling in coal and oil products comes from Russia. For liquefied natural gas it is 25% and for crude oil even 30%.

Figure 1.2. Facts. Source Dijk and de Groot, 2022.

2.2 Alternative gas from other countries

There are alternatives to gas suppliers other than just Russia. After Russia and Iran, Qatar has the largest gas reserves in the world. Germany, for example, is 49% dependent on Russian gas, which is more than the European average of 40% (Dohmen, 2022) and therefore much lower than the Netherlands as just described above. However, it is not a simple solution to just do business with other countries for the supply of gas as other issues such as democracy, corruption or human rights are also need to be considered. An example of ranking is the Freedom House. In addition to political ecosystems, it is challenging to replace Russian gas with other countries. To give an indication of this: Russia supplied 155 billion cubic meters of gas to the European Union in 2021. Alternative energy sources are also not a short-term solution (yet). For example, 70% of solar panels come from China and 12% of the world's uranium supply is in Kazakhstan (Dohmen, 2022).

2.3 Changes in the Netherlands

The only Liguedfied Natrual Gas (LNG) terminal in the Netherlands that was built in 2011 had hardly been used by 2022 (Heijn, 2022). The importance of this terminal became clear after the Russian invasion on February 24, 2022. Inspecting the Groningen gas field in the Netherlands, which is a major consumer of gas for industry and individuals. In all, 44% of the energy used in the Netherlands comes from natural gas (Figure 1.3).

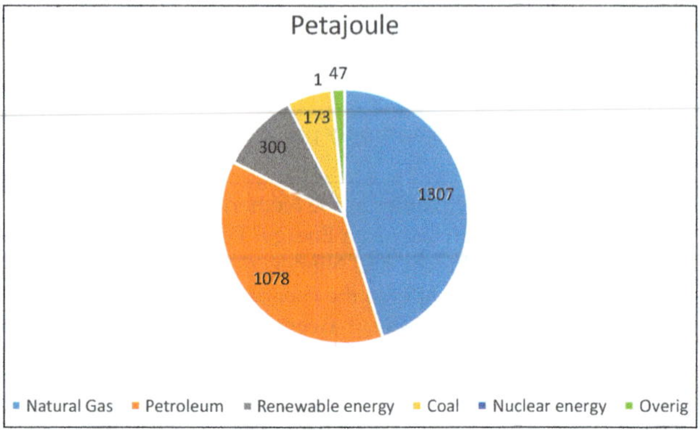

Figure 1.3. Dutch energy consumption 2022 (Source: Elsevier 2022: 14).

In 2012, the Netherlands produced as much energy—especially gas—as it used. The Netherlands had a good position at that time but, due to the reduction of gas production in Groningen due to earthquakes, it became different. By 2022, energy production is only one-third of consumption. In time—around 2050—the Netherlands could become energy independent with wind turbines in the North Sea, replacing Groningen's gas production. To increase the resilience of gas supplies, the use of LNG is relevant. The LNG terminal in Rotterdam is in full operation and can annually convert 12 billion cubic meters of gas, which is 30% of Dutch consumption. In time, the terminal will be expanded to 20 billion cubic meters. Extracting gas from the North Sea is also an alternative according to Shell and NAM, but the permit terms in the Netherlands are very high: 7 to 8 yr where, in addition to the long procedures, it is also a politically sensitive issue (Heijn, 2022). In the United Kingdom it is 3 to 4 yr.

Nuclear power is also an option for energy supply, but its construction takes 10 to 12 yr with costs around 10 billion euros. Electricity plants at Eemshaven and Amercentrale in the Netherlands were both coal plants and now run largely on biomass. Ecologically, there are several discussions about this. Strengthening the energy position in the Netherlands therefore lies mainly in the North Sea: in addition to oil and gas extraction, Shell and Neptune Energy will focus on wind turbines, hydrogen, and CO_2 storage under the seabed: from drilling platforms to pipelines.

3. Overview contributions

Chapter 2: Blockchain in Energy and Sustainability: Q & A by ConenSys Software Inc

Energy companies, ranging from utility providers to oil and gas enterprises, are recognizing the transformative impact of blockchain technology. However, there are a number of critical questions to ask such as (1) How will blockchain benefit the energy industry? (2) How does blockchain impact wholesale electricity distribution? (3) How does blockchain impact peer-to-peer energy trading? (4) How does blockchain impact electricy data management? (5) How does blockchain impact community trading? (6) How does blockchain impact utility providers? (7) How does blockchain impact the oil and gas industry? (8) How does blockchain impact the upstream oil and gas segment? (9) How does blockchain impact the midstream oil and gas segment? and (10) how does blockchain impact data management? All these questions will be answered in this chapter.

Chapter 3: Peer-to-Peer Energy Marketplaces by Sasa Pesic, Dragan Boscovic, and Milenko Tosic

Distributed energy generation and management technologies such as microgrids, domestic solar installations, community solar installations, and electric vehicles enable energy consumers to also act as providers of energy, or so called 'prosumers'. However, most utility companies' traditional energy pricing models are subscription-based, where the utility provider predetermines the price of energy sold and consumers have no say in it. Furthermore, most traditional energy marketplaces limit the involvement of individual households to consuming electricity. In this chapter, the organization and blockchain-based designs of peer-to-peer energy and auxiliary service marketplaces will be discussed. Next, the potential of blockchain technology to manage real-time and future peer-to-peer energy marketplaces will be examined. Such marketplaces are capable of handling transactions in a distributed and heterogeneous system, in which energy resource and storage owners are involved in the energy price decision. Finally, peer-to-peer smart grids flexibility management, aggregation and trading inside will be explored.

Chapter 4: Using Blockchain to Support the Energy Transition and Climate Markets by the World Bank Group

Results and lessons form a pilot in Chile. Countries can achieve a successful energy transition and participate effectively in the climate market by applying available knowledge, good practices, and lessons learned. This chapter provides an example of how blockchain technology contributes to these goals by linking energy and climate sectors, businesses, and customers. It assesses a pilot blockchain project undertaken in Chile to support distributed generation and carbon markets. Recommendations for scaling up innovative technologies to advance clean energy and climate change mitigation agendas are adduced.

Chapter 5: The Potential of Sustainable Blockchain Technology for Decentralized and Open-Science to Boost the Economic Growth of the Deep Technology Start-Up Industry. Putting Power Back into the Hands of Academics, Scientists, and Engineers by Stephen G. Gray

Recent slanders in the world of crypto currency have inadvertently caused an issue for blockchain technology and start-ups in general. The most important component of blockchain has never been the digital asset or currency replacement. It is the software built into blockchain technology that creates the real value. The public might need a year or longer to believe in blockchain and cryptocurrency, but that does not mean what has been destroyed in the realm of FTX does not lead to real creation in the blockchain sector. Perhaps the time is now for young entrepreneurs to dig deeper into the world of blockchain, look away from crypto and NFTs. What is on the back end? What can be done to create real value in our world. Blockchain in its simplest form is the tracking and tracing of data with a viable stamp of approval. One is entering a world where data is going to be the new gold rush, so therefore one needs real blockchain start-ups to form.

Chapter 6: Smart Main Contracting by Wilfred van der Plas and Dion Franken BBA

Smart main contracting focuses on the application of emerging technologies in real estate exploitation in order to achieve a sustainable and future-proof physical living environment. During a workshop, the participants were asked a few questions about smart contracts and maintenance. Eighty-five percent of the participants face challenges in performing maintenance on their buildings or the maintenance they perform. Shocking! Two important points they mentioned are trust and the ongoing discussion about what was been done versus what is being invoiced. Is a smart contract a possible solution? Seventy percent of the participants are not familiar with the term. Thirty percent who do know the term have done little or nothing with it. However, after some introduction to the topic, 75% do think that a smart contract could be one of the solutions for daily maintenance tasks. Fear of the unfamiliar? In the first part of this chapter, the emerging technologies will be discussed in more detail. The exploitation of real estate will then be examined. Following that, one will create the application. The chapter concludes with an integrated application of emerging technologies in real estate exploitation.

Chapter 7: Blockchain Technology for Decentralized Energy Production and Consumption: The Case of an Emerging Economy by Ridoam Karim and Imtiaz Sifat

The purpose of this chapter is to review the basic principles underpinning blockchain technology in the energy industry. After a thorough analysis of literature and existing stylized facts, the study scrutinized contemporary blockchain applications employed in the energy sector and connected them to the prospects and challenges of introducing this technology in the energy production and consumption in the context of Bangladesh. Using qualitative research techniques and semi-structured interviews of seven experts, the study underscored prospects and possible limitations of introducing blockchain technology in the energy sector of Bangladesh. As the technology is still in a nascent stage in Bangladesh empirical elements such as field survey were not considered in this research. The review of the study identifies emerging Peer-to-Peer (P2P) applications for energy trading and application of Internet of Things (IoT) to decentralized marketplaces as key areas of interest. It should be noted that blockchain technology has tremendous potential to deliver substantial advantages in the energy sector, which, when combined with smart contracts, would allow new management applications. This study contributes to business economics and energy literature by offering a comprehensive overview of blockchain activities and initiatives in the energy industry in Bangladesh. The chapter further highlights challenges associated with regulatory and policy implementations which have not been academically discussed in scholarly contributions.

4. Hora est!

Studies and solutions on how to deal with blockchain and data do not always provide immediate direction on how data can and should be used. In my professorship (Veuger, 2018), the risks of dataism were already discussed: one relies more on data than on our own powers of observation. Gathering a lot of data is often not the problem. The question, however, is what data is needed to answer your question ? The inclusion and exclusion of data is essential because that provides the very data that fits the research question. One should establish that the data is FAIR as the meaning of fair is (fair) and Findable Accessible Interoperable Reusable (FAIR). The term FAIR was first launched at the Lorentz workshop resulting in principles of it in the publication of Wilkinson et al. (2016). Regarding data, data lifecycle, its use, its inclusion and exclusion, ethics, working within frameworks, mining, privacy, etc. alone, there are several dissertations to be written, but I have limited myself to a few references (Mannhardt, 2019; Mannhart, 2018; Manhardt, 2019; Petersen, 2018) with which readers of this book can benefit. All of this calls for follow-up research. Hora est: we do not know what we have not yet researched.

References

Dijk, B. en G. de Groot. 2022. Probleem: Russen zitten 'overal' in Nederlandse energiesector [Problem: Russians are 'everywhere' in Dutch energy sector] in Het Financieel Dagblad. Amsterdam: Het Financieel Dagblad.

Dohmen, J. 2022. Europa: van fout gas naar iets minder fout gas [Europe: from faulty gas to slightly less faulty gas] in Het Financieel Dagblad. Amsterdam: Het Financieel Dagblad.

Heijn, J. 2022. Zo wordt Nederland weer baas over zijn energie [This is how the Netherlands regains control of its energy] in Elsevier 2022, 11, March 26th.

Mannhardt, F., S.A. Petersen and M.H. Oliveira, Privacy Challenges for Process Mining in Human-Centered Industrial Environments. 2018. 4th International Conference on Intelligent Environments (IE), Rome, Italy, 25–28 June 2018. IEEE 2018 ISBN 978-1-5386-6844-3. s. 64-71.

Mannhardt, F., S.A. Petersen and M.H. Oliveira. 2019. A trust and privacy framework for smart manufacturing environments. Journal of Ambient Intelligence and Smart Environments 11(3): s.201–219. https://sintef.brage.unit.no/sintef-xmlui/bitstream/handle/11250/2593828/08595033.pdf?sequence=4&isAllowed=y.

Mannhardt, F., S.A. Petersen and M.F. Oliveira. 2019. Manuel Fradinho. Process Mining and Privacy in Smart Manufacturing. Informatik-Spektrum 42(5): s.336–339.

Sobah, A., S.A. Petersen, F. Mannhardt, M. Fradinho and H. Torvatn. A Framework to Navigate the Privacy Trade-offs for Human-Centred Manufacturing. 2018. PRO-VE 2018. Retriewed October 23, 2022: https://sintef.brage.unit.no/sintef-xmlui/bitstream/handle/11250/2576522/_472393_1_En_8_Chapter_Author%2b-%2bfinal%2bproof.pdf?sequence=2&isAllowed=y.

Veuger, J. 2018, Veuger, J. 2020. Blockchain Convergentie (Blokchain Convergence). Deventer: Saxion UAS. https://www.saxion.nl/binaries/content/assets/onderzoek/meer-onderzoek/blockchain/blockchain-convergentie-jan-veuger-2020.pdf.

Wilkonson et al. 2016. The fair Guiding Priniciples for Scientific Data Management and Stewardship. Germany, Springer Nature. The FAIR Guiding Principles for scientific data management and stewardship | Scientific Data (nature.com).

Chapter 2
Blockchain in Energy and Sustainability#

*ConsenSys Software Inc**

1. Introduction: how will blockchain benefit the energy industry ?

Blockchain technology has the potential to transform the energy sector. The energy industry has been consistently catalyzed by innovations including rooftop solar, electric vehicles, and smart metering. Now, the Enterprise Ethereum blockchain presents itself as the next emerging technology to spur growth in the energy sector through its smart contracts and systems interoperability. However the many use cases for blockchain,[1] energy and sustainability are often less recognized. The World Economic Forum, Stanford Woods Institute for the Environment, and PwC released a joint report identifying more than 65 existing and emerging blockchain use-cases[2] for the environment. These use cases including new business models for energy markets, real-time data management, and moving carbon credits or renewable energy certificates on the blockchain.

Distributed ledger technology has the potential to improve efficiencies for utility providers[3] by tracking the chain of custody for grid materials. Beyond provenance tracking, blockchain offers unique solutions for renewable energy distribution.

Consensys Mexico, knowledge partner Blockchain.

* Corresponding author: Julieta C. Herrero: Julieta.herrero@consensys.net

This report is published before at: Blockchain in the Energy Sector | Real World Blockchain Use Cases | ConsenSys.

[1] Blockchain Use Cases in 2021: Real World Industry Applications | ConsenSys.

[2] WEF_Building-Blockchains.pdf (weforum.org).

[3] For Utilities Exploring Blockchain, There's Beauty in the Mundane | Greentech Media.

Legacy energy sectors, such as oil and gas also stand to benefit from the implementation of Enterprise Ethereum solutions. Complex systems with multiple actors could benefit from blockchain technology. For example, petroleum is one of the most traded commodities and requires a network of refiners, tankers, jobbers, governments, and regulatory bodies. The complex network of participants suffers from siloed infrastructures and numerous process inefficiencies. Large scale oil and gas conglomerates are seeking to invest in and implement blockchain technology because of its ability to lower costs and reduce harmful environmental impacts.

Oil and gas companies are particularly concerned about privacy and trade secrets. These private blockchain networks offer data permissioning and selective consortium access to pre-approved parties. Private and consortium blockchains provide an interim solution until public blockchains can implement the necessary privacy features businesses demand. The main benefits of blockchain in the energy sector are:

- Reduced costs
- Environmental sustainability
- Increased transparency for stakeholders while not compromising privacy

But what are the blockchain-use cases in energy? ConsenSys Solutions works with a range of blockchain products that can be tailored to address various energy or sustainability applications, including the following Q & A.

2. How does blockchain impact wholesale electricity distribution ?

Companies looking to implement blockchain technology into wholesale electricity distribution focus on connecting end-users with the grid. Blockchain technologies combined with IoT devices enables consumers to trade and purchase energy directly from the grid rather than from retailers.

Grid+[4] is a blockchain energy company focusing on wholesale energy distribution. The firm has identified retailers as the driving source of inefficiency in the consumer electricity market. Retailers own very little of the grid infrastructure. Instead, they only manage the kinds of services that blockchain technology can replace, such as billing and metering usage.

Supplementing retailers with a blockchain-based platform has the potential to reduce consumer bills by around 40%. By connecting users

[4] GridPlus.

directly to the grid, Ethereum allows users to buy energy from the grid at a cost they desire. The result is a more equitable and stable energy market with lower electricity costs.

3. How does blockchain impact peer-to-peer energy trading ?

While wholesale energy distribution is a primary application for many companies, it is not the focus of all energy firms. A Blockchain In Energy report[5] by Wood Makenzie shows that 59% of blockchain energy projects are building peer-to-peer energy markets. A peer-to-peer energy market is a shared network of individuals who trade and buy excess energy from other participants. These energy markets benefit the masses because they reduce control from central authorities, such as wholesale entities.

Most firms are using enterprise versions of Ethereum. For example, the Energy Web Foundation[6] uses Ethereum, Truffle developer tools, and Gnosis multi-signature wallets to build out their platform. As more and more countries reach energy parity the cost of renewable energy becomes equal to or lower than traditional retail energy. Individuals who produce their own energy will have the ability to trade it with their neighbors and peers. The Australian-based company, Power Ledger, has connected communities to one another to create "microgrids". Microgrids are a group of interconnected loads and distributed energy resources. Microgrids currently exist as a layer on top of the national grid; however, theoretically, they can be separate and self-sustaining. Many blockchain energy companies imagine a future with larger and entirely distributed peer-to-peer grids.

4. How does blockchain impact electricity data management ?

Blockchain can provide consumers greater efficiency and control over their energy sources. Additionally, an immutable ledger provides secure and real-time updates of energy-use data. Various types of energy data include market prices, marginal costs, energy law compliance, and fuel prices. In April, 2018, the Chilean National Energy Commission (CNE) announced it had launched a blockchain project focused on energy. The governmental department will use the Ethereum blockchain to record, store, and track energy data.

---

[5] Blockchain for Energy 2018: Companies & Applications for Distributed Ledger Technologies on the Grid Report I Wood Mackenzie.

[6] Energy Web - Energy Web.

Data is often intentionally manipulated or unintentionally misreported and omitted. The financial costs of intentional corruption and accidental clerical errors can be detrimental to businesses and governments. In the spirit of transparency, the CNE will allow the public to access the records of transactions and prices. The transparency of public blockchains further reduces the chances for monetary or data exploitation.

5. How does blockchain impact commodity trading ?

The gas and energy commodity trading industry is another realm of potential disruption using blockchain technology. Companies have invested millions in building proprietary trading platforms tailored to the unique energy trading industry. Significant costs are required to maintain, update, and secure these systems. Commodities trading requires maintaining a massive ledger that records trades and commodity prices during specific occasions. Applying blockchain technology to commodity trading would be cheaper and more efficient than existing proprietary systems. Immutability, security, and immediacy can all be programmed in the blockchain removing the slow adaptability of large-scale proprietary systems.

6. How does blockchain impact utility providers ?

Electric power providers are large and complex firms that generate energy from power plants, solar farms, and various energy sources. Utility providers do not compete with one another in the same respect to financial services or the banking industry. These firms are more willing to share information and data, that presents a unique opportunity for the blockchain's shared ledger.

Greentech Media, a leading clean energy market analysis firm has identified three ways in which utility providers can benefit from distributed ledger technology. Enterprise Ethereum can process and validate data from many devices at the grid edge before securing the data on the blockchain. Secondly, energy providers can utilize the blockchain to create a system for transactions of data which is critical to distribution. Lastly, distributed ledger technology can be used to develop a system for transacting energy among a diverse set of actors.

7. How does blockchain impact the oil and gas industry ?

The implementation of blockchain technology in oil and gas trading can lower costs associated with the maintenance of various trading systems. Furthermore, blockchain can also reduce costs associated with labor, data management, data visibility, settlement delays, and inter-system communication. The BTL Group, an enterprise blockchain company, recently completed a pilot project with ENI, BP, and Wein Energie. The pilot demonstrated that the use of blockchain technology to facilitate and track gas trades reduced overall costs by 30–40%. The company plans to test the platform with other resources besides gas. Instead of building a system for each commodity, Enterprise Ethereum enables fast integration of new commodities by re-programming the original smart contract.

The oil and gas industry comprises of thousands of companies. These firms are roughly split into three categories: upstream, midstream, and downstream. The journey of one drop of resource can include hundreds of separate entities, companies, processes, and legal agreements.

8. How does blockchain impact the upstream oil and gas segment ?

Upstream refers to the parts of the industry that involves resource exploration and extraction. The upstream oil and gas segment is dominated by four key stakeholders: majors, NOCs (National Oil Companies), independents, and oilfield services. Majors are large, oil and gas companies that manage or own oilfield and well activity. Upstream requires the involvement of dozens of stakeholders, all of whom rely on the data provided by other firms. Blockchain technology optimizes wide-scale, multi-party data coordination.

9. How does blockchain impact the midstream oil and gas segment ?

Midstream refers to parts of the industry involved with storing and transporting resources once they are extracted. Midstream also includes the management of vast transportation networks and substantial regulation. The midstream oil and gas segment can benefit from disaster mitigation and infrastructure maintenance. The heavy regulation and asset intensity require oil and gas companies to focus on risk mitigation. Consequently, these firms can uniquely benefit from sharing information with others in the industry. Blockchain technology excels at providing multi-stakeholder information sharing, especially for asset tracking.

10. How does blockchain impact electricity data management ?

Downstream refers to companies that refine resources into multiple final products or sell products to end users (i.e., gas stations). Furthermore, downstream includes the management of dozens of different products. These products are directed towards different customers, have different environmental regulations, and require various methods of transportation.

Blockchain-enabled supply chains optimize wide-scale and multi-product coordination. The ability of a blockchain technology platform to record and track supply chains could stop a large amount of waste.

Moreover, a platform that utilizes smart legal contracts can replace time, energy, and money currently required by all involved energy companies. An immutable ledger can help manage and track data that is necessary for all stages of oil and gas production. This would further save both time and money by ensuring nothing is misplaced or lost.

Chapter 3
Peer-to-Peer Energy Marketplaces

Sasa Pesic,[1,2,*] *Dragan Boscovic*[1,2] and *Milenko Tosic*[2]

1. Introduction

Few people understand that the transition from fossil fuels to renewable energy sources is only the beginning of a period of significant market disruption. The disruption will remake the composition of energy systems and offer unprecedented choices for customers. Moreover, the interruption will cause the energy system to shift away from the outdated utility monopoly model and introduce distributed generation, decentralization, digitalization, and disruptive technology, potentially putting users in charge and allowing them to reap the economic benefits. Blockchain technology has tremendous potential to revamp the energy sector's service offerings. This can be seen through five important supporting pillars of transactive energy grids: (1) Transparent user accounting and billing, (2) Energy tokenization and secure transacting, (3) Energy origin certificates (4) Increased operational security and (5) Tight privacy control.

Retailers can handle (1) user accounts and payments using blockchains. End-users can be connected with the grid using a wholesale energy marketplace implemented using the blockchain. Energy generated or consumed is a commodity asset that can be accounted for by the blockchain. This asset can be tokenized and tracked through its life cycle using devices connected to the grid. This approach would enable consumers to trade

[1] School of Computing and Augmented Intelligence, Arizona State University, Tempe, Arizona.
[2] VizLore Labs Foundation, Novi Sad, Serbia.
* Corresponding author: spesic@asu.edu

and purchase energy directly from each other rather than from retailers. The addition of Distributed Energy Resources (DERs) is a demanding task, and it leads to new challenges in the management and operation of electricity systems. For example, these are difficult to predict and depend on weather conditions. They also need adaptable methods like the integration of energy storage services and responsive supply and demand management (Aman et al., 2015).

Blockchains have the potential to provide a promising solution for controlling and managing trading energy surplus or elastic demand on a Peer-to-Peer (P2P) basis due to their intrinsic nature. Commodity trading (2) on an autonomous energy marketplace can be secured and recorded using immutable, transparent, and tamper-proof smart contracts. By adopting and using local energy marketplaces enabled by P2P energy trading, one can achieve improved control of decentralized energy systems. This design would increase independent energy production and consumption (after the meter activities), impacting revenue and tariffs (Andoni et al., 2019). Blockchains can also assist in managing flexibility trading platforms, offering the grid operators and managers a unique set of services to balance the grid.

Blockchain-based systems can also help with (3) tracing the origin of produced energy. Energy consumers are often prepared to pay more when buying green energy. However, usually there is no guarantee about the origin of energy purchased. Blockchains can enforce transparency on the origin of the energy purchased such as its type, generating unit, and exact production location (Knirsch et al., 2020).

Furthermore, blockchain, combined with committed hardware components, (4) secures communications between industrial control systems and other operational technology and protocols (e.g., MODBUS, DNP3, BacNet) by including an advanced crypto-signature that assigns a data signer and time of signing. This signature is represented by the hash of the data contained in the signature. The integration of DERs without appropriate cyber-security measures including trustworthy communications and monitoring could potentially destabilize the power grid and create outages and reliability problems for customers. Combining cryptographic signing events and distributed infrastructure helps increase the accuracy of data and reliability of real-time energy exchanges for micro-grids and P2P energy generation and sale (Mylrea and Gourisetti, 2017). Increased data precision indirectly helps to detect cyber-attacks and increase the resiliency of DER-grid integration (Mylrea, 2017).

Finally, companies in the energy sector are concerned about the (5) privacy of data, data ownership, access control, as well as membership of the network. Due to such concerns, public permissionless blockchains are incapable of handling strict privacy and regulatory requests (e.g., GDPR). Hence, private, consortium blockchain solutions are an ideal choice for implementing energy marketplaces for two main reasons: data permissioning through access control and selective membership to pre-approved parties (Gai et al., 2019).

The chapter is organized as follows. First the global energy landscape is described. Next the blockchain technology is introduced, the third discusses its potential use-cases for revamping the energy sector. Finally, P2P energy marketplaces are discussed at length and offer two blockchain-based case-study designs for (1) real-time energy trading and (2) flexibility aggregation.

2. Blockchain technology

The technological architecture and protocols that allow simultaneous access, validation, and record updating in an immutable way across a network that spans numerous entities or places are referred to as Distributed Ledger Technology (DLT). A blockchain is a type of DLT with a specific technological foundation. After a consensus approves all the data, the blockchain establishes an unchangeable ledger of records maintained by a decentralized network. The cryptographic signature and linking of groups of entries in the ledger that creates a chain is a fundamental difference between blockchain and DLT.

The blockchain allows network parties to manage transactions without having to trust each other. The lack of a dependable intermediary allows for faster reconciliation between transacting parties, and the extensive use of cryptography enhances the network's authoritativeness (Maheshwari and Maheskwari, 2019). The blockchain represents a change in architecture, from a centralized trust system to a decentralized one, and with that change, there is an associated change in the market and payments format and structure. The low cost of transacting, security and integrity of data, verifiable transactions and identities, transparency and traceability create fertile grounds for a new wave—a decentralized economy. With built-in cryptocurrencies, blockchains provide a way for participating devices to engage in economic transactions while at the same time incentivizing them (Vasek, 2015).

Every transaction on a blockchain is digitally signed and timestamped, allowing participants to track transactions back to specific dates and, if necessary, identify the corresponding party on the blockchain. This characteristic is related to a critical information security attribute known as non-repudiation, which ensures that no one can imitate the legitimacy of their signature on a file or the authorship of a transaction they initiated. As every transaction is cryptographically associated with a user, this out-of-the-box intrinsic functionality of the blockchain boosts the system's trustworthiness by detecting tamper attempts or fraudulent transactions. Any new transaction made to a blockchain will alter the ledger's global state. Every new iteration of the system simultaneously retains the previous state, a completely traceable history log is available. The blockchain's audit capacity offers enterprises a high level of transparency and security over all business interactions. From a cybersecurity perspective, this provides entities with extra assurance that the data is authentic and that no tampering has occurred (Dai et al., 2017).

The blockchain is a peer-to-peer (P2P) framework with the capability to dis-intermediate central entities or processes within a given business workflow, hence improving efficiencies, and creating an immutable audit trail of transactions. It will shift business models from a human-based trust paradigm to one based on algorithms. The practicality of the blockchain comes due to the fact that it shifts trust from people and institutions to technology. There are three types of blockchains that handle trust and access control in different ways: (1) Public, (2) Private and (3) Consortium blockchains.

1) Public blockchains can be thought of as an open access system. Public refers to blockchain systems such as Bitcoin or Ethereum, where anyone can become a member, and every transaction is public. Public blockchain often comes with inherent cryptocurrencies, or digital money that can be used to settle payments between users. All nodes inside a public blockchain network are anonymous. A public blockchain scales up and becomes more secure as more nodes are added to the network. However, the size of the blockchain network impacts its performance. This can cause large transaction processing times (e.g., a few seconds on Ethereum and up to few minutes on Bitcoin blockchain), rendering the public blockchain infrastructure incapable of handling industrial use-cases where fast execution time is important.
2) A private blockchain is operated and controlled by a single organization. This organization owns all the nodes, while also controlling the governance of the blockchain. For example, a private blockchain can be used to co-ordinate and synchronize data in the supply-chain of a company between various departments. However one concerning aspect of private blockchains is that they allow the middleman back in. The users submitting transactions have no control over ownership of the data. Finally,
3) Consortium blockchains (permissioned) operate under the leadership of a group of entities, thus enabling collaborative transformations involving multiple organizations. The participants' identities are not anonymous. Each transaction being submitted needs to be

signed by the participant key which keeps track of provenance within the blockchain. Consortium blockchains enable a trusted business environment between potentially suspicious participants (e.g., competitors). However they can adopt a governance model that can help them establish trusted agreements as well as handle disputes efficiently. These blockchain infrastructure are built for industrial use-cases, as they bring transaction privacy through subsetting communication channels on the blockchain. Consortium blockchains, such as Hyperledger Fabric of Quorum, keep most of the public blockchain features in terms of security, transparency, auditability and traceability, often without involving cryptocurrencies. Nodes are typically invited to join, and consensus is often not achieved in a resource-demanding manner (i.e., through mining). This increases the transaction throughput to potentially several thousand transactions per second.

The blockchain has prominent applications in many industries, from agriculture to accounting. Activities associated with blockchain technology can be classified into three categories from the standpoint of accessibility and organization: (1) first-generation public blockchain (1.0), (2) second-generation public blockchain (2.0), and (3) third-generation private/consortium blockchain (3.0). Within blockchain 1.0, cryptocurrencies are used in applications relating to financial transactions, such as currency transfers, settlements, and digital payments. Smart contracts for economic markets and financial applications are included in blockchain 2.0. This category is responsible for more than just financial transactions. It expands to assets like bonds, stocks, mortgages, loans, titles, smart properties, and so on. Blockchain 3.0 is applicable to a broader range of applications than just currency, finance, and markets. This includes applications in health, literacy, culture, governments, culture, etc. (Vasek, 2015).

The business logic in blockchains is captured in smart contracts. A smart contract is a self-executing piece of code on the blockchain that eliminates the need for manual intervention to execute transactions. Smart contracts can be used to facilitate, verify, or enforce rules between parties, allowing for straight-through processing and interactions with other smart contracts. Smart contracts comprise conditions that must be met for autonomous transacting. They are stored and run on a blockchain, which makes them decentralized and secure. Smart contracts provide a necessary framework that enables executing transactions between human and physical world in a secured and scalable ecosystem, thus also attending to many of the security challenges that the Internet of Things currently faces (Pass, 2015).

3. Blockchain and the global energy landscape

The energy sector has been going through an intensive digitalization process for the last 30 yr. Recently the focus is put on applying technologies which can efficiently deal with the ever increasing distributed nature of the energy markets. One of the main technologies that is being heavily tested for application in the energy sector is the blockchain. As the data layer/architecture foundation on which information, value and energy are exchanged, blockchain technology has the potential to play an important role in the transformation of the power sector. Its influence begins with niche uses and spreads with stakeholder awareness and acceptance following some effective real world and market validations. The European Union, the US and China are spearheading the developments and validation efforts in applying blockchain technologies in the energy sector. There are important initiatives in Japan, Qatar, Australia and South Africa as well.

There are five key challenges that need to be addressed before the blockchain technology uptake in the energy sector is able to live to its expectations. To begin with, **(1) governance obstacles** such as standards and regulations for applying DLTs in the energy sector are still to be defined and executed. **(2) Performance and energy footprint** of public blockchains raises concerns that application of blockchain technologies would introduce new energy efficiency challenges to be solved. Next, **(3) technology complexity and limited interoperability** with expensive legacy digital systems is hard to solve. Furthermore, **(4) data privacy** is a large concern and the immutable nature of most blockchains clashes with most privacy protection regulations (e.g., the right to be forgotten and the right to own/update your data as prescribed by GDPR). Finally, **(5) Scalability** is questionable since large public blockchains introduce large transaction validation times which is unacceptable for energy grids.

Nevertheless, there are strong global initiatives promoting uptake of blockchain technologies in the energy sector. **INATBA** (International Association for Trusted Blockchain Applications) launched a Task Force with Global Observatory on Energy Trading. Next, the **European Blockchain Partnership** is planning a pan European regulatory sandbox in cooperation with the European Commission. The **European Blockchain Services Infrastructure** (EBSI) puts specific focus on energy-related use cases. There is also the **Energy Web** (EW) Foundation, a global non-profit organization leveraging blockchain to achieve a more transactive energy system. Finally, there is **Alastria** (Spain) a non-profit consortium that aims to accelerate digital transformation through a blockchain.

3.1 Practical blockchain use-cases

Use-cases residing in the energy sector can benefit from functionalities of both public and private blockchains. Still, the inherent necessity of storing and exchanging sensitive data streams (e.g., smart meter readings, energy profiles) puts a higher emphasis on private blockchains that are more capable in handling such data. Where payments need to be made, public blockchains might be used. However, this is not the only possibility. Nowadays one sees more use-cases where tokenized valuables (e.g., time, discounts, service vouchers) are exchanged in contrast to resorting to public blockchain cryptocurrency payments.

The main energy domain use cases where blockchain technologies can provide added value are summarized in Figure 3.1. There are five relevant groups of practical initiatives: (1) P2P energy trading, (2) Grid management, (3) Electric mobility, (4) Management of renewable energy certificates and (5) Financing renewable energy development.

1) **P2P Energy trading** is one of the main applications for DLTs in the energy sector and is presented in detail in this chapter. Major initiatives and market leaders in this area include: Brooklyn microgrid (LO3 Energy - US), the first blockchain based P2P electricity market; Enerchain/PONTON (Germany) P2P local community, distribution flexibility and wholesale trading; Power Ledger (Australia) platform based on Ethereum for energy trading and improving energy market efficiency; KEPCO (Japan) together with Power Ledger demonstrate surplus power trading in P2P manner.
2) **Grid management** and the system operation include several critical services towards the grid. One such service is flexibility

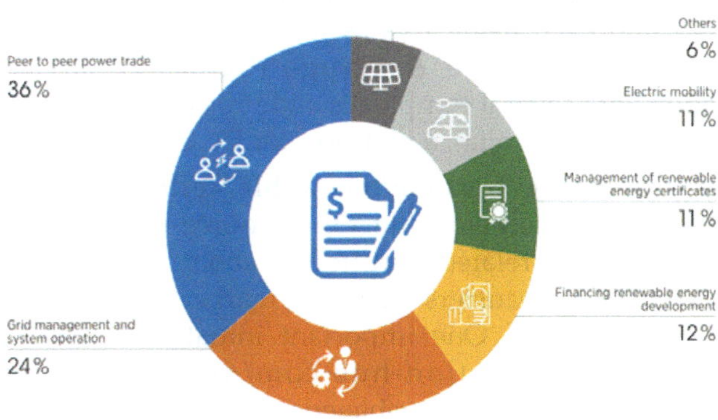

Figure 3.1. Global distribution of blockchain use-cases.[1]

[1] Greenberg, Maurice R. "Applying Blockchain Technology to Electric Power Systems." Center for geoeconomic studies. Accessed December 3, 2021. http://www.ourenergypolicy.org/wp-content/uploads/2018/07/Discussion_Paper_Livingston_et_al_Blockchain_OR_0.pdf.

aggregation. The demand side flexibility aggregation can benefit from P2P approaches in local energy communities. The DLT-enabled transaction tracking and confirmation ensures that the provided and utilized flexibility resources are correctly recorded and can be audited for fair reimbursements. The main initiatives in this area include: Enerchain/PONTON (Germany); Equity (Europe) a crowd balancing platform for grids; JRC (Italy) testing demand-response flexibility services provided by electric vehicles and storage units. Next, energy profiles exchange and scheduling covers P2P data exchange which provide insight into energy consumption patterns and requirements of consumers and producers. This is key for efficient management of micro grids and wider DSO infrastructure. The DLTs can be used for facilitating distributed mechanisms for incentifying profile data sharing between energy market stakeholders. Moving ahead, the energy supply chain management has use cases that largely rely on DLTs to improve transparency in transaction management, reduce transaction costs and improve performance with process automation relying on smart contracts. Finally, energy metering and billing management includes paying energy bills using cryptocurrencies as well as enabling customers to transact using verifiable identities to record and manage metering data, retailer-to-customer settlements, or customer switching between energy providers (retailers). The key initiatives in this area include: PROSUME (Italy), providing real-time monitoring of prosumers' energy consumption, production, and expenditures; Bankymoon (South Africa) integrating BTC payments into smart meters.

3) **Electric Vehicles (EV) charging and e-mobility** use-cases focus on applying cryptographic identities to track and manage EV charging processes and even using EVs as mobile energy storage. The main initiatives include: Share & Charge (Germany), an independent foundation with several companies and projects in the EV and energy sectors; Everty (Australia), a platform for EV charging.

4) **Energy provenance tracking/renewable certificates** includes any approach that documents the exact source of renewable energy generation, issues related certificates about green attributes and tracks ownership transfers between market participants for their green energy claims. One important initiative is GREENCHAIN. https://www.imnovation-hub.com/digital-transformation/greenchain-blockchain-renewable-energy/ (Spain).

5) **Financing renewable energy resources** can be based on many designs. Loyalty or incentive tokens bring distributed mechanisms for rewarding certain kinds of behavior on local energy networks. The incentive tokens can be minted and distributed by energy community

managers, DSOs, or other entities. The tokens can be exchanged within the established community for various services and benefits. Next, investments in renewable energy enable all stakeholders to directly participate in investment programs for building renewable resources in their communities. The investments are tracked in a transparent way and ROI is typically related to reduce CO_2 footprint of communities and reduce bills. The key initiatives and market leaders include: Wepower (Estonia), a platform for renewable generators and investors; NRGcoin (issued by Enervalis - Belgium), an incentive and reward mechanism for more efficient use of renewable energy at a local level; Sun Exchange (South Africa), a crowdfunding platform for solar projects; Efforce (Italy), a platform for trading energy efficiency products worldwide.

3.2 Initiatives of the European Commission

The European Commission (EC) and its Directorate General for Energy (DG ENER) have invested significant resources into research and innovation projects in the domain of energy services, smart grid management, boosting use of renewable energy and decentralizing energy markets. The main goals of DG ENER are: (1) pursuing the European Green Deal objectives and boost Europe's economic recovery; (2) Decarbonizing economy; (3) Boosting energy efficiency; (4) Ensuring energy security and (5) Promoting interoperability across energy markets and regulatory domains. Starting from the "New Deal For Consumers" published in 2015, the EC is introducing new regulations that empower end consumers to act as true prosumers in their energy markets giving them the freedom to choose how and with whom they will transact as energy consumers and as producers. This sets the course for uptake of blockchain technologies in the energy sector and paves the way for true decentralization of the energy markets on local and regional levels.

The European Commission developed the BRIDGE Initiative to bring together Horizon 2020 Smart Grid, Energy Storage, Islands, and Digitalization initiatives in order to create a systematic picture of cross-cutting challenges that appear in demonstration projects and may be an impediment to innovation. The BRIDGE working group on business models puts specific focus on P2P marketplaces relying on distributed ledger technologies.

Some of the key EC funded projects dealing with application of blockchain technologies in the energy sector are:[2] PLATOON, Platone, PARITY, FlexiGrid, Flex4Grid, P2P-SmartTest, FleXunity, BRIGHT

[2] "Business Models." Bridge. Accessed December 3, 2021. https://www.h2020-bridge.eu/working-groups/business-models/.

and most recently INTERCONNECT. The InterConnect project[3] (interoperable solutions connecting smart homes, buildings and grids) is a project funded under Horizon 2020 Innovation Action program (grant No. 857237). The project brings together 50 European institutions to develop and showcase sophisticated technologies for connecting and integrating digital homes and buildings with the electricity sector. Chapter editors directly participate in this project. The project places the foundation for the future of smart energy management solutions by seven connected large-scale test-sites in Portugal, Belgium, Germany, the Netherlands, Italy, Greece and France. Energy and IoT domain convergence through semantic interoperability is at the forefront of the InterConnect project. The InterConnect project introduces the Interoperability Framework as a set of tools and software components that will allow stakeholders to interconnect their semantically interoperable solutions into interoperable ecosystems which are the basis for developing innovative services, use cases and business models. The interoperability framework features P2P marketplace enablers based on DLTs.

3.3 *Privacy concerns*

The main privacy sensitive data that is specific to the energy systems/electric markets are data related to energy consumption. This mainly includes data collected by metering systems. By collecting and analyzing energy consumption data from smart meters, one can receive a detailed model of energy consumption habits of a consumer or a household. Energy consumption patterns are well correlated with living habits of individuals (e.g., when users leave home, when they eat, when they sleep, when they have guests, when they are working, etc.). This is why the privacy protection of any and all energy consumption related data is top priority for energy systems (Doci et al., 2015).

One of the main challenges in applying blockchain technologies in any sector is the distributed and immutable nature of data storing. This raises concerns with respect to data privacy protection since node maintainers are not necessarily trusted or compliant data storages especially in public blockchain networks. Additionally, the immutable nature of the blockchain data storing clashes with the main directives of data privacy protection regulations. For example in the European GDPR directive there are two important rules that blockchain technology is not in line with: (1) the right to be forgotten and (2) data ownership. To begin with, users/participants in digital systems must be able to request from the

[3] "Interconnect Project." Interconnect. Accessed December 3, 2021. https://interconnect project.eu/.

system to delete any and all data related to them. The immutable nature of most blockchains cannot support this. Private, permissioned blockchains could support this feature, but as the system complexity increases this becomes more challenging. Furthermore, users in digital systems must have the right to update or transfer their data collected by one system to another. Again, immutability of blockchains limits this fundamental requirement. To correctly address these challenges, blockchain technology in the energy sector should be combined with advanced data anonymization techniques and with off-chain data storage systems allowing further data manipulation.

4. Peer-to-peer energy marketplaces

Proliferation of distributed energy resources (photovoltaic panels, electric vehicles, smart appliances, and battery storage systems) paved the way for P2P energy marketplaces. The goal is to enable energy prosumers, consumers, and other stakeholders to negotiate and exchange excess energy resources and fulfil their energy needs. In theory, the P2P energy marketplace would allow for lower pricing, reduced monopoly of large energy retailers, flexibility in choosing from whom and what kind of energy is bought or sold.

With the democratization of the energy markets, both in terms of production and consumption, new business models appear. The Peer-to-Peer (P2P) electricity trading is established as a result of the growing deployment of distributed energy resources connected to distribution networks, and the desire to give more incentives to encourage future deployment of these resources

P2P energy trading is a business concept built on an interconnected platform that functions as an online marketplace where customers and producers connect to exchange electricity directly without the need of a middleman. P2P energy trading is sometimes referred to as the *AirbnB* of energy since it provides a platform that allows local distributed energy producers to sell their electricity at the desired price to users willing to pay that price. This electricity is generally exchanged between platform users (buyers/sellers) who also become members of the platform by paying a monthly membership fee, as an example. Suppliers seek the best possible price while keeping their costs and gains in mind. Customers choose the cheapest option depending on their needs and preferences. When the supply and demand offers are matched, a transaction occurs.

A major driving point of P2P energy marketplaces is the reduction of monthly costs of electricity usage. Prosumers, who both generate and use electricity, frequently sell excess electricity to the grid at a buy-back rate. Consumer energy prices for purchasing that energy, on the other hand, are often substantially higher than the buy-back rates that prosumers can get by selling electricity to the utility. The electricity purchased from a prosumer would be lower than when purchasing from the utility since the former takes into account: (1) the additional benefits that distributed energy resources offer to the electricity grid and (2) network's reduced congestion and transmission losses. Thus, P2P energy trading is already naturally incentivized. Furthermore, around 41% of the average electricity bill is spent on monitoring and maintenance of the poles and wires that transport power from generators to consumers' homes.[4] In a P2P approach, some of these expenditures could be avoided.

Prosumers can change roles between buyers and sellers to purchase or sell power in P2P energy trading. Furthermore, they are allowed to directly trade energy with other users in order to reach a win-win situation by seeking a better conclusion than the comparatively high tariffs and low buy-back prices. A P2P trading model can be developed among neighbors in a small community, as well as on a wider scale among many communities (European Parliament, 2018).

Producers will be able to make greater use of their DERs through the P2P energy trading platform, while also making renewable energy more accessible to consumers. It makes the community more robust to outages during crises and, in certain situations, improves energy availability. Decentralized P2P energy trading systems can assist the main power grid in balancing and grid flexibility. These may be summed up in four main advantages of peer-to-peer energy trading for power sector change. These benefits can be summarized through three key pillars:

1. **The empowerment of consumers and prosumers has resulted in increased renewable deployment and flexibility.** This transformation is supported by legislation throughout the world allowing co-ownership of distributed renewable energy resources as well as smart micro-grids allowing localized and efficient energy exchange. This also leads to improved energy access for consumers in mini-grid set-ups (Buonocore et al., 2019; Duscha et al., 2016).
2. **Better functioning of distributed energy resources can help with balancing and congestion management.** Multiple studies have shown that P2P electricity trading helps to balance local generation and demand.[5] It could allow communities to resist power shortages or transmission network damage, improving energy access. To capitalize

[4] "What Makes up the Cost of Your Electricity Bill". Aurora Energy. Accessed December 3, 2021. https://www.auroraenergy.com.au/what-makes-cost-your-electricity-bill-pie-graph.

[5] "Peer-to-Peer Electricity Trading - Irena.org." Accessed December 3, 2021. https://irena.org/-/media/Files/IRENA/Agency/Publication/2020/Jul/IRENA_Peer-to-peer_trading_2020.pd.

on this, penalty functions can exist as incentives for peers to participate in power loss reduction and congestion management, although this model is only theoretical at this point (Nasimifar et al., 2019).

3. **Auxiliary services to the main power grid operator are provided.** DER with P2P energy exchanges create a perfect setup to enable better continuous forecasting of supply and demand management of the grid's flexibility and peak-shaving capabilities. Furthermore, both TSOs and DSOs use various services for congestion management, grid constraints, voltage control, and phase balancing. Both types of operators should have support for extreme events (islanding, blackstart, emergency load control, and backup generation capacity) (Razeghi et al., 2018; Gatis and Giannakis, 2012).

4.1 Marketplace types

The energy market is made up of two short-term forward markets that are linked together. The first, known as the "day ahead" market, requires producers to commit to provide energy 24 hr ahead of schedule, depending on the expected demand. The second market, known as the "real-time" or "hour ahead" market, commits producers to supply energy 1 hr ahead of schedule, based on an updated demand projection. The day-ahead market, on the other hand, sets a timetable for which power plants should be ready to produce energy, whereas the real-time market adjusts those schedules based on a better estimate of electricity demand (European Parliament, 2019).

The day-ahead energy market creates a place where individuals and businesses may buy and sell electric energy for the next day at financially binding, or day-ahead, prices. The day-ahead market, also known as energy futures, guarantees that both buyers and sellers could protect themselves against price swings and volatility in the real-time energy market by locking in energy prices before the following business day (Jasanoff, 2018). For both the sale and purchase of energy, the day-ahead energy market has a financially enforceable schedule of obligations. In some cases, the energy futures market can be expanded to involve contracts that extend to a longer period of time (Burke and Stephens, 2018). An energy's future contract is similar to a wholesale bilateral contract between two (or more) entities trading energy. The definition of a bilateral contract states that it is an agreement between two entities to exchange electric power under a set of specified conditions such as amount of electricity, time of delivery, duration and price (Morstyn et al., 2016). It can be either physical or financial. A physical contract states the electricity transacted must be self-generated and self consumed on specified network buses (Kockar and Galiana, 2020). A financial contract states electricity transacted is based on net metering. This contract ensures the difference between the contract price and the utility price and has no physical transmission implications (Ilic et al., 2011).

Real-time energy marketplaces are financial markets where consumers, businesses, and energy distribution companies may buy and sell energy in real-time, generally 1 hr (sometimes less) before delivery. On the real-time market, auctions take place every K minutes (typically 15 or 30 min), and energy pricing could alter throughout the day. Introducing a set of business rules into the system is required to enable real-time energy transactions. Choosing the Market-Clearing Price (MCP) for energy is a crucial part of such a system. Despite the fact that there may be several asks (sell offers) and bids (buy offers) at varying prices for any particular time period, all energy is sold at a single price, known as the MCP (Hasankhani and Hakimi, 2021).

Typically all real-time energy markets are operated as uniform price auctions. Producers submit supply offers to the marketplace operator, and the marketplace operator selects the lowest-cost supply offers until supply equals demand. This is referred to as clearing the market. The "marginal unit," which is the last energy producer considered, determines the MCP. When it comes to P2P energy trading markets, both the demand and supply side must be taken into account when formulating the MCP, as well as the buy and sell prices of the retailer (as a P2P deal should never be less favorable than the retailer price).

Figure 3.2 shows P2P energy marketplace clearing. Different market scenarios need to be discussed to become familiar with how the clearing mechanism works. Consider scenario 1 (marked as black square): there is 1000 kWh to sell for 30 cents per kWh. At the same time, the demand at that price is 5000 kWh. There is a shortage of 4000 kWh because more consumers would want to buy cheaper energy. From the producers point of view, in the next bidding cycle: (1) Most likely prices are going to increase since there is shortage and (2) Quantity supplied will increase as well since producers would want to sell more at a better price. Now, consider scenario 2 (marked as black circle): suppliers of energy have 7000 kWh to sell for 41 cents per kWh. At the same time, the demand at that price is only 700 kWh. There is an excess of 6300 kWh because less consumers would want to buy energy at such a high price. In the next bidding cycle, two things are likely to occur: (1) Producers will decrease prices and quantity in order to sell more and (2) Demand will increase since prices are lower. This is how one realizes a price where the quantity supplied (Qs) equals the quantity demanded (QD), and this is referred to as the MCP.

When there is no grid congestion, the MCP is paid to every producer that "clears the market". This is why, in a uniform price auction, low-cost producers, also known as inframarginal providers, may be enormously

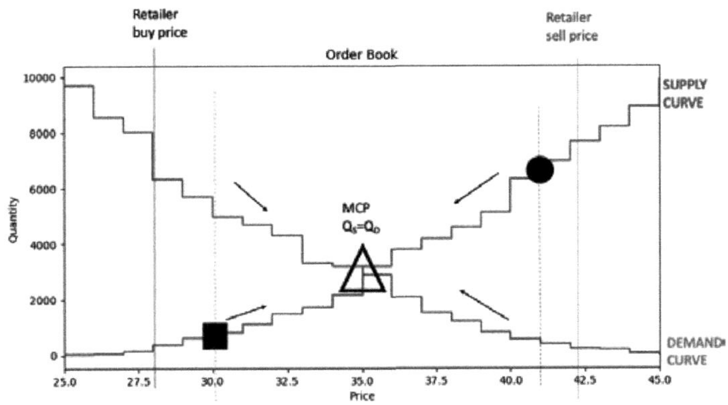

Figure 3.2. Market clearing mechanism.

lucrative. However, when there is transmission congestion, things get more difficult since the market is segmented as a result of the congestion. Some parts of the market are on one side of the restriction, while a few are on the other side, and no further deliveries can be made between them. When demand on one side of the restriction rises, a producer on the other side of the restriction should be sent to supply the demand. If demand grows on the opposite side of the restriction, a different producer could be dispatched on that side. As these producers' costs and supply offers differ, the marginal cost of satisfying demand in one region may vary from the marginal cost of the meeting demand in another. These costs, that are dependant on the location of the producers and consumers, are referred to as Locational Marginal Prices (LMP) (Papavasiliou, 2018). Real-world electricity grids are massive—for example, PJM, an US-based Regional Transmission Organization (RTO) calculates LMPs for over 40,000 different sites every 5 min.[6] Forecasting of MCP, congestion region and severity (Ostadi et al., 2018), as well as LMPs (Alharbi et al., 2020) are important auxiliary services for the grid and marketplace operators, and trending research topics.

Both day-ahead and hour-ahead markets have their advantages and disadvantages. The day-ahead energy market allows individuals and businesses to buy or sell electricity 24 hr before the start of the business day, guaranteeing that they are not negatively impacted by market volatility. However, this might mean that a buyer or seller in the day-ahead energy market misses out on a good financial bargain in the real-time market, since they have already committed to a specific price a day in advance. Energy futures contracts also aim at liberalization of the energy bidding

[6] "EBF 483: Introduction to Electricity Markets". Accessed December 3, 2021. https://www.e-education.psu.edu/ebf483/node/508.

and matching process by eliminating the MCP. The real-time energy market, on the other hand, allows market participants to sell and purchase electricity at any moment of the day, with no fixed or agreed-upon prices. The real-time energy market produces prices that reflect market demand by calculating pricing based on day-ahead commitments and real-time energy consumption. Buyers and sellers that trade in the real-time energy market risk being negatively impacted by real-time demand, but they may also respond more quickly to lower prices and perhaps achieve better bargains than those available on the day-ahead market.

4.2 *Common actors and relationships*

Many of the projects and initiatives that deal with P2P energy trading marketplaces have a different set of actors based on the real-world application and goals of the marketplace. Furthermore, one actor often encompasses multiple roles defined below, depending on the regulation, country, etc. In European P2P energy marketplaces one usually sees the following actors listed below.

A **Distribution System Operator (DSO)** is the legal entity responsible for operating, maintaining, and developing a transmission system and, where applicable, its interconnections with other systems, as well as ensuring the system's long-term ability to meet reasonable demands for electricity transmission (European Union, 2019).

Within the EU Directive 2019/944 the role of the **Transmission System Operator (TSO)** is defined the same as the TSO. Moreover, a set of responsibilities is defined that is shared between the two. However, there are clear differences in real-world scenarios. DSOs manage network loads and ensure that the distribution network is strengthened and maintained so that electricity could be delivered to customers at all times. TSOs connect with the generators required to serve those customers with electricity and regulate the network's real-time flows.

Consumers, Producers, and **Prosumers** refer to human end-users, their households or others. Consumers only consume energy, producers only produce and prosumers can do both.

The **Metering Data Operator (MDO)** is the person or company in charge of collecting, storing, and disseminating validated smart metering. This responsibility is frequently taken over by the DSO.

The **Market Operator (MO)** is an independent third party that organizes a marketplace for buyers and sellers of flexible energy sources to register their requirements and capacities, as well as promote trade and price formation in local flexibility markets.

In the present generation of the smart grid and smart houses, **Home Energy Management Systems (HEMS)** are a burgeoning industry. HEMS may bring value to both the homeowner and the utility by saving money and energy through a combination of control, scheduling, and user information. HEMS can track the energy use of inhabitants in their homes and advise them on how to change their habits depending on the information they get from the system. HEMS can also help utilities implement Demand-Response (DR) programs to minimize peak demand. Similarly, **Building Energy Management Systems (HEMS)** manage all apartments inside a building, each equipped with a HEMS.

The EU Clean Energy Package has two different statutes that designate energy communities. The amended Renewable Energy Directive (EU 2018/2001) establishes the foundation for **Renewable Energy Communities (REC)**, that are responsible for renewable energy. The updated Internal Power Market Directive (European Parliament, 2019) establishes new duties and obligations for **Citizen Energy Communities (CEC)** in the energy system, which encompasses all sources of electricity. The two types of communities differ by geographical scope, activities, participants, autonomy and effective control. A very detailed report about energy communities in the EU can be found here (Caramizaru and Uihlein, 2020). RECs are composed of **REC Members (households - HEMS, buildings - BEMS)** and a **REC Manager**. RECs are not established everywhere: the majority of current P2P energy trading use-cases look at HEMS/BEMS as individual network participants.

Energy Service Providers (ESP), often also called Retailers, are responsible for buying electricity in the wholesale market and selling it to their customers. They usually take on the role of the Aggregator.

Defined by EU 2019/943 regulation (European Commission, 2019), a **Balance Responsible Party (BRP)** is a designated entity responsible for energy market imbalances. In most cases this is as well an established legal entity. The Renewable Energy Directive (European Parliament, 2018) which sets the framework for Renewable Energy Communities does not contain details on balance responsibility. The Electricity Directive (European Parliament, 2019) which sets the framework for Citizens Energy Communities does contain a provision, namely that "Member States shall ensure that citizen energy communities are financially responsible for the imbalances they cause in the electricity system; to that extent they shall be balance responsible parties or shall delegate their balancing responsibility" (Art.16.3.c). When an energy community or the contracted BRP incurs an imbalance on a quarter-hourly basis, the BRP is subject to the imbalance tariffs to the Transmission System Operator (TSO).

The **Aggregator (AGG)**, often also referred to as the **Flexibility Service Provider (FSP)**, is a third-party legal entity that specializes in demand-side participation in the electricity market. In practice, the Aggregator contracts with separate demand sites (industrial, commercial, or residential users) to aggregate their flexibility resources and deliver them to TSO, DSO, and BRP as a single flexibility supplier. In some models the roles of AGG and FSP are separated: the former entity offers portfolio aggregation and optimization services while the latter is the actual market participant offering the aggregated flexibility to buyers. Aggregators often interface directly with Home Energy Management Systems (HEMS) or Building Energy Management Systems (BEMS) of respective Renewable Energy Communities (REC) in order to aggregate and sell the flexibility available at the community level to BRP or other entities.

Auxiliary Service Providers (ASP) are entities providing DSOs (and/or other entities) with various data analytics services such as production and consumption forecasting (to be utilized for grid analysis and flexibility availability computations), flexibility recommendation services, and so on.

Energy service companies (ESCO), in general, act as project developers for a wide range of Energy Conservation Measures (ECMs) and take on the technical and performance risks associated with the project. ESCOs are distinct from other energy-efficiency improvement firms in that they frequently use a performance-based contracting model. When an ESCO completes a project, the amount of money saved on energy is directly proportionate to the company's pay (Ines et al., 2020).

5. Case study 1: Real-time P2P energy trading marketplace

Real-time P2P energy trading marketplace can support two kinds of producers-to-consumers interactions: (1) direct energy contracts and (2) open auction.

Direct energy contracts are established between one producer and multiple consumers. The selling party in the contract is compelled to deliver energy to the buying parties, at an agreed price, until the contract is cancelled by the selling party. These types of contracts are best illustrated through a simple use-case. Assuming there be three parties: Party A is a household with a PV system, and parties B and C are neighbors of the party A. Part A (i.e., the seller) typically generates more than it uses, thus agrees on selling the excess of that energy to neighborhood buyers (i.e., parties B and C). Parties A, B and C enter into a direct energy contract at an agreed-upon price. From the point the contract is active, whenever there is excess, instead of bidding it on an open marketplace, party A would automatically sell to the buying parties of the contract. At the end of the month, the Retailer takes into account these contracts when calculating the monthly bill of parties A, B and C.

Energy auctions represent open marketplaces where selling parties do not know in advance with whom they will match, i.e., sell their energy. They are typically operated on a predefined time schedule and in an automated manner by the Market Operator (MO), Consumers and

Producers. In general the automated flow consists of several steps that repeat in a cycle of K min s: bidding opens every 60 min, stays open for 15 min, closes, MCP is calculated, energy bids and asks are matched and the cycle is repeated. At the end of the month, the Retailer takes into account these trades when calculating the monthly bill of involved parties.

This design accompanies both of these use-cases in a single marketplace solution. It is important to note that both of these modes of energy trading are supported in parallel and can be carried out independently.

5.1 Actors

- *Prosumers* - end-user's households inside the observed neighborhood. Each household has a smart meter installed.
- *Distribution System Operator (DSO)* - is also the Metering Data Operator (MDO). Thus, it is the ground-truth provider that verifies energy exchanges.
- *Market Operator (MO)* - is an independent entity providing marketplace services and data to 3rd parties (e.g., auditors, Auxiliary Service Companies (ASPs)). It does not trade energy.
- *Retailer* - the entity supplying the given neighborhood with energy. It calculates monthly energy bills.

5.2 Channels

Figure 3.3 shows actors and their relationships as specified by the following channels:

- *Users' management* - before interacting with the rest of the functionalities, every blockchain user must register under its own organization. This channel holds smart contracts that handle registration of new blockchain users and updates of existing ones. All organizations have access to this contract.
- *Smart metering data* - is a channel that holds information about individual households' smart meter readings. As DSO is also the Metering Data Operator (MDO), the DSO organization will collect this data and write it on the ledger. The Retailer has read access on this channel, to be able to calculate monthly bills of its customers.
- *Marketplace management* - is a channel that holds smart contracts that support the two types of energy transacting: (1) direct energy contracts and (2) open auction. Prosumers can create/update energy contracts and offers. The Market Operator performs the auxiliary services of order matching and Market Clearing price (MCP) calculation. Lastly, DSO, which has access to smart metering data will provide the ground truth about the actual energy exchanges/trades that took place.

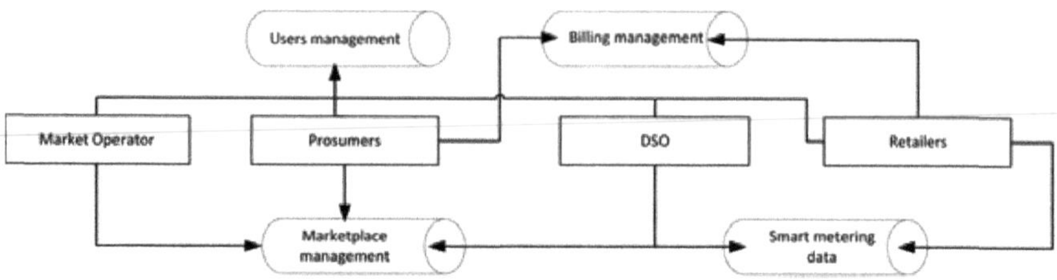

Figure 3.3. Actors and relationships diagram.

- *Billing management* - is a channel that Retailers use to create monthly energy bills that Prosumers can read. Monthly bills are calculated based on general consumption as well as level of participation in the energy marketplaces.

5.3 *Workflows*

There are four important workflows involved in this design: (1) Management of active users; (2) Smart metering data storage; (3) Calculation of monthly bills and (4) Management of energy trading.

Workflows and smart contracts handling use-cases 1–2 are insignificant and involve straightforward Read/Write operations on the ledger. The mathematics behind the calculation of monthly energy bills will not be discussed here, since it is largely dependent on the Retailer (country of origin, etc.). The focal point of this design are the smart contracts and digital assets dedicated to energy trading and support for energy marketplaces. Thus, they will be explained in more detail.

The smart contract handling (1) Direct P2P energy contracts manages three digital assets: (i) Energy Contracts, (ii) Offers and (iii) Energy Exchanges (as show in Figure 3.4). *Energy Contracts* are digitally signed between one energy producer and multiple consumers. It represents a contractual agreement of the producer, to deliver, i.e., sell energy to consumers during the time the contract is active. The workflow starts with a producer offering a consumer or a group of consumers to enter into a contract together. The producer will define a weighting for each consumer inside a contract, for example: consumer A receives 40% of produced energy, consumers B and C receive 30%, respectively. Once consumers have accepted the terms of the contract, the producer will create an *Offer* that has a certain price per kWh. Consumers can accept or decline this offer: only when all of the consumers have accepted the offer, both the offer and contract become active. This can be interpreted as follows: whenever there is an excess of energy created by the producer, it will be sold to the consumers, according to defined weightings. Each time an excess is detected on the side of the producer, a new *Energy Exchange* asset will be created and tied to the active *Offer* of the *Contract*. It will contain

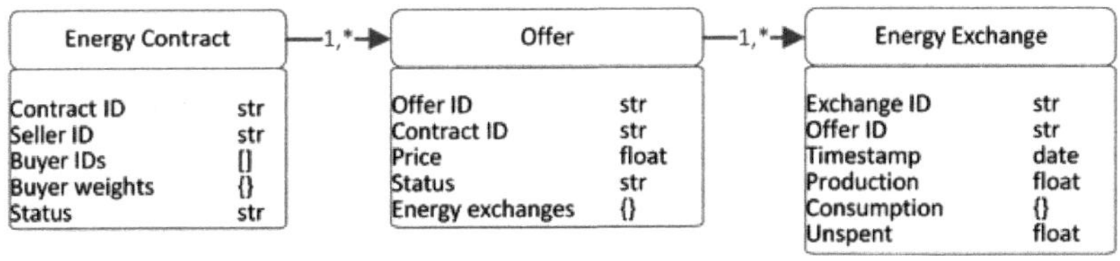

Figure 3.4. Direct energy contracts management.

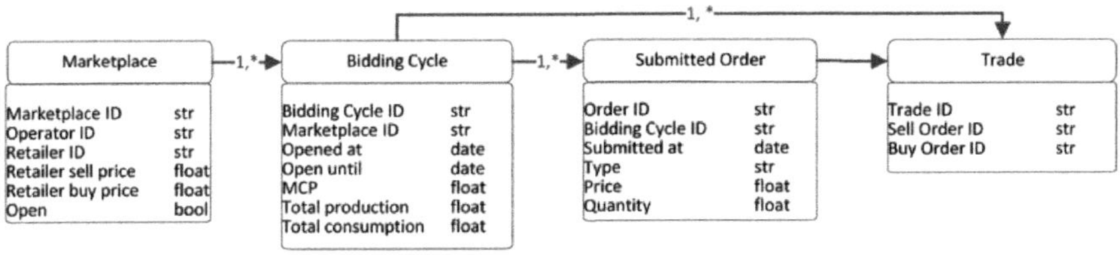

Figure 3.5. Open auction management.

the amount of produced and consumed energy and the approximative excess. The *Energy Exchange* is created/updated by the MDO, which is the DSO in this case. At any point in time, a consumer can leave the *Contract*, thus invalidating it and the last active *Offer*. In that case, the rest of the parties come together and form a new *Contract*. The *Contract/Offer* can also be revoked by the initiating party, i.e., producer.

The smart contract handling the (2) Open auction energy marketplace manages four digital assets: (i) Marketplace, (ii) Bidding Cycle, (iii) Submitted Order and (iv) Trade (as show in Figure 3.5). The *Marketplace* digital asset is created and maintained by the *Market Operator*. On the same digital asset, the Retailer is allowed to set the current buy and sell price. Each time the *Marketplace* is open for bidding, a new *Bidding Cycle* digital record is created. The *Bidding Cycle* is open by the *Market* Operator and the *Market Operator* closes it after a defined period (e.g., 15 min). While the *Marketplace* is open, prosumers can submit new energy orders, yielding the *Submitted Order* digital assets. Every order contains the price, quantity, and type (buy or sell). After the *Marketplace* has been closed, the market clearing price (MCP) is calculated, and the *Bidding Cycle* is updated with information about total production/consumption and the MCP. MCP can be calculated according to various mathematical functions: it can be a range, or a single price (cite). Lastly, *Submitted Orders* can be further matched yielding *Trades*.

5.4 Discussion

This use-case bring a set of important benefits for its actors. First, it makes it easy for prosumers and consumers to engage in P2P energy trading, leaving the interconnection of physical components to energy service providers and DSO. Next, the two marketplace models described above can help Retailers perform the accounting that produces energy bills of its users. At the end of the month, the Retailer will look at every user's activity on both types of markets. It will use this information to calculate the monthly energy bill of users, taking into account the amount of locally produced/consumed energy versus the wholesale market. Furthermore, it allows the DSO to observe individual and group energy profiles (consumption and production), improving their understanding of the local grid, forecasting services, grid balancing and flexibility services. Finally, it allows the Market Operator company to charge a fee for enabling easy access to P2P energy trading.

There are several observations and future work comments to be noted. To begin with, calculating the MCP should be a plug-and-play market component. Thus, supporting easy updates to the way it is calculated is important. Next, instead of giving a single price when submitting an order, a consumer/producer could supply a conditional/limit order, e.g., "buy if price between M and N". Moreover, sometimes, other parties will need information from the marketplace system. These parties, i.e., external actors are entities that do not directly participate in the energy marketplace, but are interested in obtaining some of its data streams for further analysis (e.g., for consumption/production forecasting, official reporting and auditing). Thus, the use-case can be updated to support another actor that can be used to onboard any 3rd party and control its access permissions through smart contracts. Finally, the use-case can be updated with workflows that would enable involved parties to issue and resolve disputes. For example, prosumers can raise a dispute if they think their monthly energy bill has been miscalculated. Retailers would look into this dispute and settle it either manually, or in an automated manner by defining a reactive smart contract function.

6. Case study 2: Flexibility aggregation and trading

The Distribution System Operator (DSO) is a vital player in the creation of a consumer-centric energy system, allowing smart homes, buildings, and communities to offer new standardized flexibility solutions. The large-scale integration of Distributed Generation (DG) based on renewables raises the level of uncertainty in the power system's operation by substituting traditional and controllable generation, diminishing system inertia and making voltage and frequency regulation more difficult. Due to anticipated future flexibility shortages, this creates new system requirements, increasing the complexity of operating both transmission and distribution networks. In this context, the generation-follows-demand design principle must give way to more ambitious design and operation principles focused on local optimization of energy consumption and generation to increase power system efficiency and reduce the need for more costly flexibility solutions.

Renewable Energy Communities (RECs) are key players in enabling DSOs and TSOs access to aggregated flexibility management and activation. Bringing together members over a certain geographical region, and managing and using their joint flexibility eases the collection of flexibility data and flexibility activations. REC Members are compensated fairly for providing flexibility towards the grid through a deduction of their monthly energy bill created by the Retailer. Based on the energy profiles of RECs, external service operators can take part in data analytics for the purpose of recommending appropriate flexibility actions per REC/REC Member and day/time of day, etc.

The dependability of flexibility market solutions is critical, especially when dealing with congestion that has local repercussions. Flexibility is a risk transfer to Flexibility Service Providers (FSPs), who must manage that risk appropriately. It is important to remember that a failure of the flexibility service will result in a network outage that could have been avoided with another solution. Reliability is thus essential for fostering the development of flexibility markets and the transition from experiments to industrial business models. While this use-case does not specifically address risk management, it is vital to keep this in mind.

If the flexibility service is not delivered, penalties can be determined by observing the service criticality, grid status, etc. The penalty must incentivise the FSP to be dependable. It should be high enough so that the FSP will not decide to simply pay the penalty instead of increasing its services' reliability. The reliability concern (technically and/or monetarily) that is the potential failure of flexibility sources within the portfolio must be managed by the FSP. It should not join the market on its own if it cannot attain the needed reliability. A low-reliability service, on the other hand, could be included into a larger portfolio, where reliability can be managed. Typically, this entails assisting in the resolution of difficulties involving higher levels of tension or balancing.

6.1 Actors

- *REC Members* - end-user's households inside the observed neighborhood. Each household has a smart meter installed and a number of smart energy devices managed by the Home Energy Management System (HEMS) of the REC Member.
- *REC Managers* - are local aggregators for the given REC. They are aggregating flexibility bids of their members and requesting flexibility activation from REC Members. They are also aggregating energy profiles of their members, which are used by Service Providers as inputs to various auxiliary services. In this use-case, the REC

Manager is the Flexibility Service Provider (FSP) as well as the Balance Responsible Party (BRP).

- *Auxiliary Service Company (ASP)* - In this use-case the ASP registered consumes aggregated energy profiles of the RECs and creates flexibility recommendations towards the REC.
- *Retailer* - the entity supplying the given neighborhood with energy. It calculates monthly energy bills.

6.2 *Channels*

Figure 3.6 shows actors and their relationships as specified by the following channels:

- *Communities management* - is a channel private to REC Managers and REC Members. It supports the creation of RECs, appointing a Manager. REC Members can then join a REC or leave one. This channel also stores locally aggregated energy profiles that REC Manager aggregates for the REC it manages.
- *Flexibility recommendations* - is used to store flexibility recommendations created by the ASP. ASP creates the recommendations based on the aggregated REC energy profiles.
- *Flexibility activations* - is the channel that serves as a proxy for the REC Manager to issue flexibility activation requests towards the REC Members it manages. The requests can come from two sides: (1) the REC Manager (based on a flexibility recommendation or other locally computed actions) and (2) the DSO.
- *Flexibility activation disputes* - is a channel private to the DSO and REC Manager to resolve eventual disputes and incur penalties for failure to procure flexibility services.
- *Billing management* - is a channel used by the Retailer to calculate monthly bills based on the REC Member's level of activity on the flexibility marketplace.

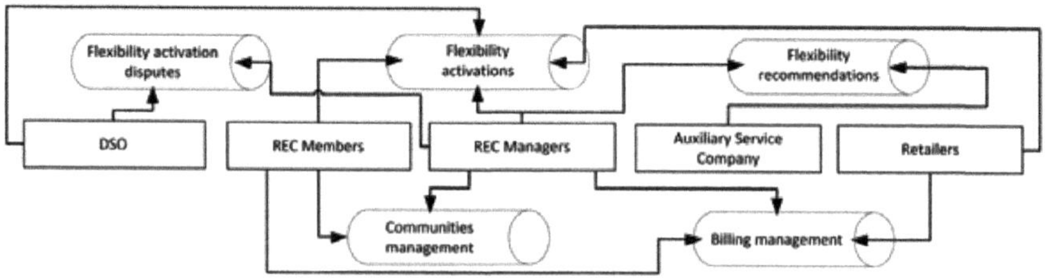

Figure 3.6. Actors & relationships diagram.

Note: users management smart contract is omitted from the design. It provides the same functionalities like in Case Study 1 (energy trading).

6.3 *Workflows*

There are three important workflows involved in this design: (1) Management of renewable energy communities (RECs); (2) Energy profiles sharing and aggregation and (3) Flexibility bidding, aggregation, recommendation and activation.

Management of renewable energy communities (RECs) supports registration of REC Managers, REC Members and the formation of RECs. Once a REC Member registers, it will register its HEMS and smart energy devices. HEMS has a connection towards smart energy devices of the REC Member (see Figure 3.7).

Sharing and aggregation of energy profiles is done on two fronts: (1) REC Members share their energy profiles, privately, with the REC Manager, within the *communities management* channel and then (3) REC Manager aggregates those profiles and shares it with the ASP on the *flexibility recommendations* channel. The energy profile of a REC Member contains information of energy usage per certain time-range (e.g., production and consumption per 15 min).

Flexibility bidding, aggregation, recommendation and activation are the activities that drive this use-case (see Figure 3.8). REC Members share their flexibility bids privately with their REC Manager. The REC Manager will aggregate the bids and can offer that aggregated bid to the DSO or the BRP. ASPs will offer flexibility recommendation bids that might be accepted or rejected by the REC Manager. Every flexibility bid/recommendation is essentially an array of numbers mapped to time and energy availability. Flexibility activations requests are issued by

Figure 3.7. Management of a REC.

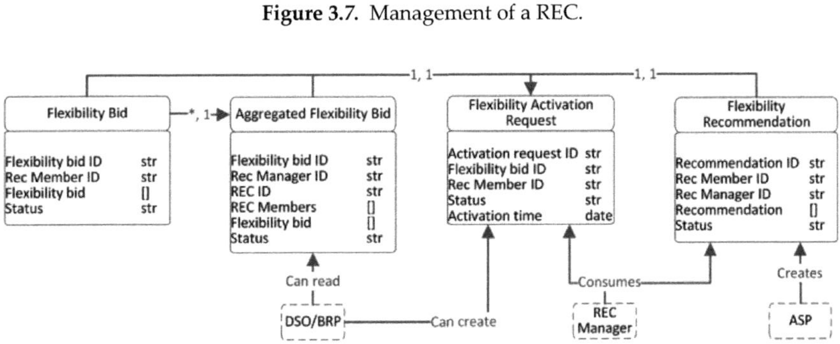

Figure 3.8. Management of flexibility assets.

the REC Manager towards REC Members. The HEMS is the integration point of REC Member towards the flexibility marketplace, and it will be contacted to execute flexibility activation requests. Every REC Member has to report whether its HEMS managed to activate the flexibility package.

6.4 Discussion

This use-case brings a set of important benefits for its actors. To begin with, for individual homeowners there is the benefit of reduction in monthly energy bills based on their active participation in the flexibility bidding market. Next, for a REC, flexibilities are a new instrument for planning and controlling or optimizing grid design for the community's benefit (e.g., the transformation capacity of a primary substation). Finally, for seamless integration with DSOs, it is important to follow existing standardization efforts. This includes choosing the right information model (e.g., for EU markets: CIM, FLEXOFFER, USEF/UFTP AND EEBUS) and more. CIM is officially promoted by the International Electrotechnical Commission (IEC). Putting additional efforts in providing market services that are aligned with existing standards will increase the likelihood for a DSO to participate and effectively contract local flexibility services for congestion management.

There are several observations and future work comments to be noted. First, involvement of other parties, like dedicated Flexibility Service Providers (FSPs) and Balance Responsible Parties (BRPs) are essential. Furthermore, supporting multiple information models and standardized integratory frameworks towards DSOs would provide a good edge for the design of a flexibility marketplace system. Finally, mechanisms for risk management and penalization can be included and operated in an automated manner. If the flexibility service is not delivered, penalties can be calculated by a smart contract observing the service criticality, grid status, etc. This external information should be deterministic across the entire blockchain, thus, one needs to resort using blockchain Oracles (blockchain-based deterministic smart-grid ground truth providers).

Acknowledgement

The work presented in this chapter is in part supported by the InterConnect project which received funding from the European Union's Horizon 2020 research and innovation programme under grant agreement No. 857237.

References

Alharbi, Abdulelah, Shutang You and Yilu Liu. 2020. Correlation between Generator Trips and Locational Marginal Prices (LMPS). 17th International Conference on the European Energy Market (EEM), 2020. https://doi.org/10.1109/eem49802.2020.9221984.

Aman, Saima, Marc Frincu, Charalampos Chelmis, Muhammad Noor, Yogesh Simmhan and Viktor K. Prasanna. 2015. Prediction models for dynamic demand response: requirements, challenges, and insights. IEEE International Conference on Smart Grid Communications (SmartGridComm), 2015. https://doi.org/10.1109/smartgridcomm.2015.7436323.

Andoni, M., V. Robu, D. Flynn, S. Abram, D. Geach, D. Jenkins et al. 2019. Blockchain technology in the energy sector: A systematic review of challenges and opportunities. Renewable and Sustainable Energy Reviews 100: 143–174.

Buonocore, Jonathan J., Ethan J. Hughes, Drew R. Michanowicz, Jinhyok Heo, Joseph G. Allen and Augusta Williams. 2019. Climate and health benefits of increasing renewable energy deployment in the United States*. Environmental Research Letters 14(11): 114010. https://doi.org/10.1088/1748-9326/ab49bc.

Burke, Matthew J. and Jennie C. Stephens. 2018. Political power and renewable energy futures: a critical review. Energy Research & Social Science 35: 78–93. https://doi.org/10.1016/j.erss.2017.10.018.

Caramizaru, Aura and Andreas Uihlein. 2020. Energy communities: an overview of energy and social innovation. Publications Office of the European Union. https://doi.org/10.2760/180576.

Dai, Fangfang, Yue Shi, Nan Meng, Liang Wei and Zhiguo Ye. 2017. From bitcoin to cybersecurity: a comparative study of blockchain application and security issues. 4th International Conference on Systems and Informatics (ICSAI), 2017. https://doi.org/10.1109/icsai.2017.8248427.

Dóci, Gabriella, Eleftheria Vasileiadou and Arthur C. Petersen. 2015. Exploring the transition potential of renewable energy communities. Futures 66: 85–95. https://doi.org/10.1016/j.futures.2015.01.002.

Duscha, Vicki, Arnaud Fougeyrollas, Carsten Nathani, Matthias Pfaff, Mario Ragwitz, Gustav Resch et al. 2016. Renewable energy deployment in Europe up to 2030 and the aim of a triple dividend. Energy Policy 95: 314–23. https://doi.org/10.1016/j.enpol.2016.05.011.

European Commission. 2019. Regulation (EU) 2019/943 of the European Parliament and of the Council of 5 June 2019 on the Internal Market for Electricity. Off. J. Eur. Union 158: 54–124. http://data.europa.eu/eli/reg/2019/943/oj.

European Parliament "Directive (EU) 2018/2001 of the European Parliament and of the Council of 11 December 2018 on the promotion of the use of energy from renewable sources". Official Journal of the European Union, L 328, 21 December 2018. http://data.europa.eu/eli/dir/2018/2001/oj.

European Parliament "Directive (EU) 2019/944 of the European Parliament and of the Council of 5 June 2019 on common rules for the internal market for electricity and amending Directive 2012/27/EU". Official Journal of the European Union, L 158, 14 June 2019. http://data.europa.eu/eli/dir/2019/944/oj.

Gai, Keke, Yulu Wu, Liehuang Zhu, Meikang Qiu and Meng Shen. 2019. Privacy-preserving energy trading using consortium blockchain in smart grid. IEEE Transactions on Industrial Informatics 15(6): 3548–58. https://doi.org/10.1109/tii.2019.2893433.

Gatsis, Nikolaos and Georgios B. Giannakis. 2012. Residential load control: distributed scheduling and convergence with lost AMI messages. IEEE Transactions on Smart Grid 3(2): 770–86. https://doi.org/10.1109/tsg.2011.2176518.

Hasankhani, Arezoo and Seyed Mehdi Hakimi. 2021. Stochastic energy management of smart microgrid with intermittent renewable energy resources in electricity market. Energy 219: 119668. https://doi.org/10.1016/j.energy.2020.119668.

Inês, Campos, Pontes Luz Guilherme, Marín-González Esther, Gährs Swantje, Hall Stephen and Holstenkamp Lars. 2020. Regulatory challenges and opportunities for collective renewable energy prosumers in the EU. Energy Policy 138: 111212. https://doi.org/10.1016/j.enpol.2019.111212.

Ilic, Marija D., Francisco D. Galiana and Lester H. Fink. 2011. Power Systems Restructuring: Engineering and Economics. New York: Springer.

Jasanoff, Sheila. 2018. Just transitions: a humble approach to global energy futures. Energy Research & Social Science 35: 11–14. https://doi.org/10.1016/j.erss.2017.11.025.

Knirsch, Fabian, Clemens Brunner, Andreas Unterweger and Dominik Engel. 2020. Decentralized and permission-less green energy certificates with Gecko. Energy Informatics 3(1). https://doi.org/10.1186/s42162-020-0104-0.

Kockar, I. and F.D. Galiana. 2002. Combined pool/bilateral dispatch. II. Curtailment of firm and nonfirm contracts. IEEE Transactions on Power Systems 17(4): 1184–90. https://doi.org/10.1109/tpwrs.2002.804955.

Krishnamurthy, Dheepak, Canan Uckun, Zhi Zhou, Prakash R. Thimmapuram and Audun Botterud. 2018. Energy storage arbitrage under day-ahead and real-time price uncertainty. IEEE Transactions on Power Systems 33(1): 84–93. https://doi.org/10.1109/tpwrs.2017.2685347.

Maheshwari, Ishan and Piyush Maheshwari. 2019. Beyond bitcoin: the impact of blockchain on the world—a survey. 2019 Sixth HCT Information Technology Trends (ITT). https://doi.org/10.1109/itt48889.2019.9075092.

Morstyn, Thomas, Alexander Teytelboym and Malcolm D. Mcculloch. 2019. Bilateral contract networks for peer-to-peer energy trading. IEEE Transactions on Smart Grid 10(2): 2026–35. https://doi.org/10.1109/tsg.2017.2786668.

Mylrea, Michael and Sri Nikhil Gourisetti. 2017. Blockchain: A path to grid modernization and cyber resiliency. 2017 North American Power Symposium (NAPS). https://doi.org/10.1109/naps.2017.8107313.

Mylrea, Michael. 2017. Smart energy-internet-of-things opportunities require smart treatment of legal, privacy and cybersecurity challenges. The Journal of World Energy Law & Business 10(2): 147–58. https://doi.org/10.1093/jwelb/jwx001.

Nasimifar, Mohammad, Vahid Vahidinasab and Mohammad Sadegh Ghazizadeh. 2019. A peer-to-peer electricity marketplace for simultaneous congestion management and power loss reduction. 2019 Smart Grid Conference (SGC). https://doi.org/10.1109/sgc49328.2019.9056626.

Ostadi, Bakhtiar, Omid Motamedi Sedeh, Ali Husseinzadeh Kashan and Mohammad Reza Amin-Naseri. 2018. An intelligent model to predict the day-ahead deregulated market clearing price: a hybrid NN, PSO and Ga approach. Scientia Iranica. https://doi.org/10.24200/sci.2018.50910.1909.

Papavasiliou, Anthony. 2018. Analysis of distribution locational marginal prices. IEEE Transactions on Smart Grid 9(5): 4872–82. https://doi.org/10.1109/tsg.2017.2673860.

Pass, Rafael and Abhi Shelat. 2015. Micropayments for decentralized currencies. Proceedings of the 22nd ACM SIGSAC Conference on Computer and Communications Security. https://doi.org/10.1145/2810103.2813713.

Razeghi, Ghazal, Fei Gu, Russell Neal and Scott Samuelsen. 2018. A generic microgrid controller: concept, testing, and insights. Applied Energy 229: 660–71. https://doi.org/10.1016/j.apenergy.2018.08.014.

Vasek, Marie. 2015. The age of cryptocurrency the age of cryptocurrency how bitcoin and digital money are challenging the global economic order Paul Vigna and Michael J. Casey St. Martin's. 367 pp. Science 348(6241): 1308–9. https://doi.org/10.1126/science.aab2001.

Chapter 4
Using Blockchain to Support the Energy Transition and Climate Markets[#]

*World Bank Group**

1. Introduction

1.1 The role of emerging technologies in the transition toward low-carbon energy

Energy markets all over the world are undergoing a transformation as new energy and information technologies are emerging and disrupting traditional market architectures. The emergence of blockchain-based utility suppliers, intelligent technology in energy storage, prosumers, and electric vehicles are creating new opportunities for energy generation, distribution, and demand. At the same time, climate change and rapid urbanization are creating critical energy challenges of multidimensional complexity.

The energy transition will play an essential role in reducing the risks and impacts of climate change. To meet the Paris Agreement objective of "pursuing efforts to limit the temperature increase to 1.5°C

Banco Internacional de Reconstrucción y Fomento/Banco Mundial 1818 H Street NW, Washington DC, 20433.

* Corresponding author: J.veuger@corporaterem.nl in licence of World Bank Group 09.09.2022.

This report is published before at: World Bank Document.

above preindustrial levels," annual energy-related carbon dioxide (CO_2) emissions need to fall by more than 70% by 2050 (IRENA, 2019b). The transition towards a low-carbon energy system will require the adoption of clean technologies, the digitalization of the sector, an enabling policy environment, and the identification of synergies within sectors. Experiences from countries that have started this transition can be of use to other countries.

Climate markets and carbon pricing can contribute to a low-carbon energy transition, because they offer the opportunity to scale up the resources mobilized from the private sector, reduce the burden of meeting commitments under the Nationally Determined Contributions (NDCs), and increase global ambition to mitigate climate change. Article 6 of the Paris Agreement recognizes that countries could engage in cooperative approaches, including the use of bilateral agreements, to ensure mitigation outcomes that contribute to individual NDCs.[1]

Emerging technologies can help achieve a low-carbon energy transition while catalyzing the development of climate markets. Technologies such as blockchain are rapidly shaping the society of the future.

Blockchain is emerging as a disruptor of the energy sector, as it can manage complex contracts and facilitate trade among multiple entities and producers. It could be instrumental in managing the growing complexity of the energy sector as well as data security and resource ownership. The sector has been slow to recognize the potential of blockchain, and awareness across the industry is lacking.

One of the uses that is gaining the most attraction is the trading of Distributed Energy Resources (DER). Owners of small-scale generation sell excess generation directly to other consumers. The flow of electricity is coded into the blockchain, and algorithms match buyers and sellers in real time based on preferences. Smart contracts then automatically execute when electricity is delivered, triggering payment from the buyer to the seller. Removing financial transactions and the execution of contractual commitments from central control brings a new level of decentralization and transparency.

Blockchain has the potential to play a significant role in the next generation of climate markets in the post–Paris Agreement era. All markets trading assets associated with emissions reductions, whatever their structure or governance, require centralized registries. The

[1] Article 6 (which has not yet been finalized) recognizes that countries may use Internationally Transferred Mitigation Outcomes (ITMOs) toward their individual NDCs. ITMOs are mechanisms through which countries negotiate bilaterally for climate actions that have mitigation outcomes and can be transferred between cooperative parties. In effect, Article 6 recognizes the exchange of reductions in carbon emissions across jurisdictions

result is a multitude of trading instruments operating within closed technological systems following different rules. Emerging digital innovations (principally blockchain), through the definition and design of new governance structures and operating models, could enable a new architecture for climate markets based on decentralization, transparency, and cost-effectiveness.

Governments and businesses around the world are taking steps to spur the adoption of emerging technologies at scale. The question is no longer whether emerging technologies work, but how they can be integrated into businesses and policies.

1.2 Chile's public solar rooftop program

The Government of Chile, with support from the World Bank and the Partnership for Market Readiness (PMR), kickstarted the entry of disruptive technologies into the energy sector by pioneering the use of blockchain in the electricity sector.[2] Its efforts build on the country's Public Solar Rooftop Program for self-consumption in public buildings and create mitigation outcomes to be recorded in the national registry of Chile's energy sector and reflected in the World Bank's Climate Warehouse for Mitigation Outcomes. This warehouse will provide visibility on mitigation outcome transactions and will enable buyers and sellers to find and compare projects and the associated mitigation outcomes, demonstrating a decentralized information technology approach to connect climate market systems.[3]

The Public Solar Rooftop Pilot has pushed innovation within the Chilean Ministry of Energy. It comes at a very relevant time, as it helps Chile achieve its strategy for a low-emission and resilient energy sector, contributes to the country's NDC goals, and decarbonizes the transition to a greener economy. The Ministry of Energy is committed to the transition toward a low-carbon economy and has played a leading role in Chile's climate change agenda.

1.3 The purpose of this chapter

It provides a timely input for the continued negotiations on international cooperation on carbon markets (Article 6) and the possibility of developing climate markets across national jurisdictions and trade associations. Although the Paris Agreement work program was agreed to at the United Nations Conference of the Parties (COP) 24, in 2018 at Katowice, clarity is still lacking in many areas regarding how to operationalize the next

[2] For information on the Partnership for Market Readiness, see https://www.thepmr.org.

[3] For information on the Climate Warehouse for Mitigation Outcomes, see https://www.worldbank.org/en/programs/climate-warehouse.

generation of climate markets under Article 6. Pilot activities like Chile's public solar rooftop blockchain project could play a key role in testing new operating models and accelerating the development of emerging technologies. The rest of this chapter is classified as follows:

- What Is Blockchain Technology?
- The Energy Transition
- Chile's Energy and Climate Policy
- Chile's Public Solar Rooftop Pilot Project
- Results and Lessons Learned
- Conclusions

2. What is blockchain technology ?

'A blockchain is a shared ledger of transactions between parties in a network, not controlled by a single central authority. One can consider a ledger like a record book: it records and stores all transactions between users in chronological order. Instead of one authority controlling this ledger (like a bank), an identical copy of the ledger is held by all users on the network, called nodes.'[4]

Through a decentralized structure, blockchain technology records information of interest to a given network of participants by sequentially capturing and registering blocks of data. In this way, it constructs a decentralized record-keeping system shared by all members of the network. It is particularly useful for registry functions involving multiple entities or data feeds that require secure and transparent transactions.

Blockchain operates by using programming algorithms to time-stamp blocks of encrypted, mostly transactional data, and link them sequentially. New blocks are added to the blockchain at timed intervals and "chained" together by inserting them into the new block a "hash," or digital fingerprint of the data in the previous block. The new block is then broadcast to all the other computers, or "nodes," that encompass the blockchain network, making the ledger nearly immutable—that is, almost impossible to alter. As the ledger and the number of computers or nodes that support the ledger grow, the security and immutability of the blockchain network increases.

Blockchain technology is best known for its use as the underpinning architecture for cryptocurrencies, such as bitcoin, to facilitate financial transactions. But there are other important functions and reasons for the use of blockchain (including more secure storage/tracking of data such as

[4] OECD Blockchain Primer (https://www.oecd.org/finance/OECD-Blockchain-Primer.pdf).

energy generation, CO_2 emissions, land registry information, supply chain transactions). Blockchain delivers best in synergy with other emerging technologies (such as advanced energy metering infrastructure). The business value of interconnects between new technologies to potentially combine with each other is underlined by their capability to address unmet market needs, create new products/services/solutions due to the uniqueness of their combined potential, and drive unlikely players from diverse industries to work with each other. The World Economic Forum has identified blockchain technology as one of the six megatrends underpinning the transition toward a digital and connected world (WEF, 2015).

Chile's Public Solar Rooftop Pilot Project, described in this chapter, is a blockchain network in which computer servers or nodes capture data from an electricity meter, then store and hash this information in predetermined time blocks to a blockchain created for the project.

Blockchain algorithms can also program transactions or trades across participants with an if-then code. These predetermined commands can be digitally encrypted in a smart meter application or a "smart contract," thereby facilitating trade between consumers or producers. Potential transactions requiring the approval of both parties can be built into the application, with all information pertaining to the transactions recorded securely in the blockchain structure. All nodes within the network will have the same transaction parameters and host the results of the transaction. In this way, blockchains ensure that the same transaction cannot occur twice. These processes can be automated through blockchain applications. Blockchain not only registers data in a secure and transparent way; it also, through applications that use smart contracts, can coordinate multiple trades across many participants in a network, in effect solving the problem of market coordination. For example, a prosumer (an end user who both consumes and produces electricity) can program the sale of excess electricity at a predetermined price, and a consumer can accept energy at this price under certain conditions. If both agree to the trade, the exchange occurs. It is then automatically registered in the shared ledger. This system eliminates the need for a trusted intermediary or centralized registry.

Figure 4.1 and Figure 4.2 presents the blockchain process schematically, beginning with data block number 6. As electricity is generated, data on emissions and solar radiation are recorded through sensors and captured by the network nodes every 15 min and put into a new block. The data collected are hashed and saved to the block, along with the hash of the previous block. In the figure, for example, Data Block 7 has been issued hash number 7657grt64; the block also contains the hash number of the previous Data Block 6 (3457hfg64).

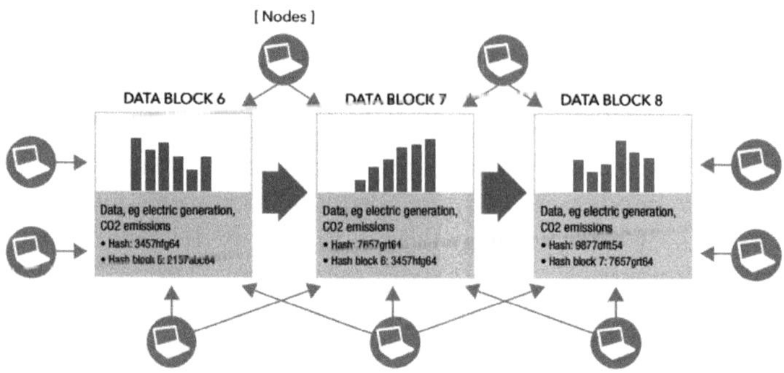

Because it can execute transactions without the need for trusted intermediaries and a centralized registry system, blockchain is usually referred to as a peer-to-peer network (figure 2). Blockchain has the potential to significantly reduce the transaction costs associated with trades or regulated contracts.

Figure 4.1. How blockchain works.

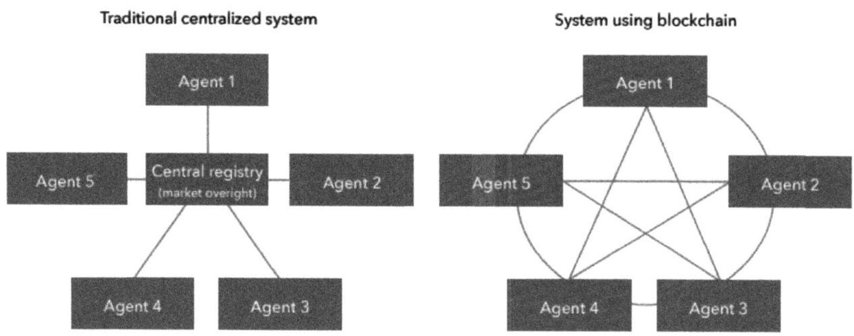

Figure 4.2. Traditional centralized registry system and system using blockchain.

The main advantage of blockchain is that it solves the coordination problem across multiple market participants—without a centralized intermediary that records transactions. Thus, it can facilitate transparency, reduce the costs of each transaction, and reduce information asymmetries in the markets in which it is applied. These benefits are especially relevant for complex transactions with multiple traders that require a tamper-proof system that supports energy trading and carbon markets.

A blockchain system has several variable features, the chief among them is the openness of the platform (public or private) and the level of permissions required to add information to the blockchain. A "public blockchain" is an open network in which anyone can read, write (i.e., generate transactions for the ledger to record), or participate (i.e., verify new blocks for addition to the chain); whereas a "private blockchain" is an invitation only network governed by a single entity. Private blockchains allow organizations to employ distributed ledger technology without making the data public. Similarly, a "permissioned blockchain" needs prior approval before use, whereas a "permissionless blockchain" lets anyone host a node and add data to the ledger.

Each structure has advantages and disadvantages. The decision about which blockchain structure to adopt will depend on the specific objectives of the system to be built, the nature of transactions, and the type of market (Peter, 2019) as well as cost considerations.

In summary, blockchains deliver capabilities that are very attractive to most of the sectors/industries, i.e., data reliability, accurate chain of custody tracking, improved traceability, and product visibility. However, as is the case with any information system, blockchain faces a complex and potentially a controversial array of issues that need to be correctly addressed during the design of the blockchain information system. Among the most important issues are: (i) quality of its data, (ii) regulation and governance; and (iii) potential difficulties with interoperability between blockchains and with existing systems.

3. The energy transition

In the last two centuries, the world has experienced at least two major energy transitions—from biomass to coal, and then from coal to liquid fossil fuels (Kander et al., 2013). There is now evidence that a new energy transition—toward renewable sources, changes in the structure of the energy market, and the emergence of distributed energy resources (DERs) and prosumers—is underway.

3.1 Features of the energy transition

The growing share of renewables

According to the International Energy Agency (IEA), the share of renewables in meeting global energy demand is expected to reach 12.4% in 2023, a 20% expansion from 2018. Renewables will benefit from the fastest growth in the electricity sector, providing almost 30% of power demand in 2023, up from 24% in 2017. During this period, renewables are projected to meet more than 70% of the global growth in electricity generation, led by solar photovoltaic (PV) and followed by wind, hydropower, and bioenergy. Hydropower remains the largest renewable source, meeting 16% of global electricity demand by 2023, followed by wind (6%), solar PV (4%), and bioenergy (3%) (IEA, 2019).

The accelerated pace of renewable energy sources in the energy mix is the consequence of both the concern over climate change and increased rate of technological innovation in the industry. According to the International Renewable Energy Agency (Irena, 2017), the installed costs of utility-scale solar PV projects fell by 74% between 2010 and 2017, from US$4,621 per kilowatt (Kw) to US$1,210. Installation costs for newly commissioned onshore wind projects fell by 22% in the same period (from US$1,913 per Kw to US$1,497) (Irena, 2019a).

The increase in storage capacity

Storage capacity has also increased. According to IRENA (2017) electricity storage will triple by 2030, and costs could fall by more than half. Associated technologies, such as electric cars, could increase the demand for renewable energy sources but also contribute to the development of new energy solutions and the co-management of energy generation and demand.

The advent of "prosumers" and distributed energy resources

The growth of solar panel technology and the increased capacity for storage have created new opportunities for consumers. The availability of smart devices in the home has triggered demand for the continuous monitoring and control of electricity consumption, as consumers are starting to explore ways to optimize and manage their consumption. This development is increasing efficiency, opening an avenue for consumers as producers of energy generation (prosumers).

Utilities' business models have changed as well. One important innovation is DERs—small or medium-size installations connected to the distribution network or near the end user that can potentially provide services to the electric power system (European Commission, 2015). Principally, but not exclusively, DERs generate solar PV power. Distributed solar PV energy is considered one of the most attractive renewable energy resources because of its economy, safety, low infrastructure costs, and low marginal cost. The distributed generation market is expected to exceed US$573 billion by 2025 (Bloomberg, 2018).

DER solutions will play a key role as global urbanization advances. About 55% of the world's population currently lives in urban areas. This figure is expected to rise to 68% by 2050 (UN DESA, 2019). Urbanization will put enormous pressure on energy systems—but it can also facilitate innovative DER solutions.

3.2 *The role of new technologies in the energy transition*

New energy technologies for storage, DER, information technologies, the utilities of the future, and electromobility are among the technologies driving the on-going energy transition. The digitalization of the energy sector, although slow, is especially relevant; it is already causing some large multinational energy companies to introduce major changes to their traditional modus operandi:

- Corporate structures now include digital and data science organizational arms. Corporations are hiring data scientists and cloud architects.
- Corporations are partnering with start-ups to learn more quickly and remain competitive—particularly on data analytics, machine learning, and cloud architecture.
- Corporations are acquiring companies that operate on the retail side, such as aggregation platforms, the Internet of Things (IoT), and machine learning platforms.
- Corporations are introducing digital academies and hubs to bring employees up to speed with ongoing disruptive trends.

In the traditional energy market, energy users buy electricity from power utilities. In a smart grid, energy users are both consumers and suppliers (prosumers) of energy, as surplus renewable energy generation can be traded with utility and other users. The decentralized and secure nature of blockchain technology could mean enabling smart grids and would accelerate the ongoing energy transition to decarbonized and smarter energy systems, addressing some of the challenges the industry is facing.

The energy industry (particularly electricity) is increasingly becoming customer-centric—and customers have shown mounting interest in self-generation and in selling power to the grid. Customers are also demanding energy management services and more transparent energy data from their energy providers, thus increasing their ability to make decisions about their own energy use and about the providers they choose to supply them with energy services. New technologies will power the energy management services demanded by tomorrow's energy customers.

This is the context in which blockchain technology should be understood.

3.3 *The potential benefits of blockchain in the electricity sector*

As blockchain is based on Peer-to-Peer (P2P) transactions, it can reduce the additional and significant regulatory costs of intermediary institutions that regulate contracts. In this way, it provides a feasible means for direct electricity transactions between microgrids. In addition, blockchain can provide a publicly available charging infrastructure for electric cars that tackles the challenge of a limited range by enabling individuals to make their private charging stations available for public use for a fee. Various companies have created a blockchain (Box 1).

Box 1

Examples of the use of blockchain in the energy sector

Enerchain.

In May 2017, the German software company Ponton launched the first platform to trade energy products over the counter using blockchain. Participants in the gas and electricity generation markets can validate and certify transactions without the involvement of a third party, reducing transaction costs, increasing the efficiency of the value chain, and ensuring safe and fast transactions. In the initial (pilot) version, 39 German power and gas generators participated. In May 2019, the platform was officially launched, allowing its use throughout Europe. Participating companies include Iberdrola (a Spanish energy company), Total (a French oil company), RWE (a German energy company), and Enel (an Italian energy company).

The Energy Origin.

TEO is a web platform based on blockchain that improves the traceability of the renewable energy consumed by revealing its origin in real time. Notably, the platform reveals to consumers whether they are using renewable energy. Using blockchain, the system allows producers to connect to the platform and displays the corresponding certificates of authenticity. The platform is currently used by Engie, a producer of renewable energy, and AirProducts, a manufacturer. TEO provides daily, tamper-proof certification and tracks the amount of renewable energy injected into the network (by Engie) and the amount of electricity consumed at the industrial site (by AirProducts).

Greenchain.

ACCIONA Energía, a Spanish renewable energy company, launched the Greenchain blockchain project to improve the traceability of renewable energy generated worldwide. It allows consumers to check, in real time, the origin of the renewable energy they are consuming. Five hydroelectric and wind generators in Spain and four corporate clients in Portugal are piloting the project, which will then be scaled up to countries such as Mexico and Chile.

Powerledger. A software that allows for peer-to-peer energy trading from rooftop solar panels. It uses blockchain technology to empower households to trade their excess rooftop solar power with their neighbours. The technology can also be used to trade renewable energy and environmental commodities.

Bitlumens.

BitLumens is building a decentralized, blockchain-based micro power-grid for the 1.2 billion people without access to electricity and banking. It uses blockchain for transactions and payments through a token. Villagers can buy tokens that are used for pay-as-you-go electricity and rent-to-own equipment. Tokens could also be used for remittance or crowdfunding purchases of electricity on behalf of recipients. The company earns money through sales of equipment.

Sun Exchange.

The business model pertains to funding panel equipment. It purchases solar cells and lease them to schools and businesses in emerging markets. People from around the world can buy panels and lease them to recipients and receive dividends for doing so.

3.4 Blockchain and climate markets

Two conditions must be met for carbon markets to emerge. First, the international climate negotiation framework must recognize that mitigation outcomes can be transferred across jurisdictions. Internationally Transferred Mitigation Outcomes (ITMOs) refer to any carbon-based trades affecting Nationally Determined Contributions (NDCs). ITMOs and market trades of carbon emissions are regulated under Article 6 of the Paris Agreement, the negotiation of which has not yet been finalized

(Box 2). According to one study, effective Article 6 trading rules could save up to $250 billion a year on climate action by 2030.[5]

Second, the significant transaction costs associated with carbon markets must be reduced. In carbon markets, transaction costs are incurred in connection with information asymmetries, coordination, oversight of emissions trading, and the accounting structure through which trades are registered.[6] All these institutional and governance structures, and therefore costs, could be significantly reduced if they are well-designed and agreed among all carbon market parties and complemented by blockchain technology in decentralized carbon markets.

Box 2

The United Nations Framework Convention on Climate Change and the Paris Agreement

The centerpiece of the international climate governance regime is the UN Framework Convention on Climate Change (UNFCCC), adopted at the 1992 Rio Conference. The convention established a broad set of principles, including the principle of common but differentiated responsibilities.

On December 12, 2015, at the Conference of Parties (COP) 21 in Paris, parties to the UNFCCC reached a landmark agreement to combat climate change and accelerate and intensify the actions and investments needed to achieve a sustainable low-carbon future. Builds on the UFCCC, the Paris Agreement established a new framework for global cooperation by all parties to the convention.[a] In that way, it unites all countries in a common cause to undertake ambitious efforts to combat climate change and adapt to its effects. It also provides for enhanced support to help developing countries to pursue those goals.

The basis of the Paris Agreement is a nonbinding bottom-up approach (in contrast to the top-down structure of the Kyoto Protocol). The agreement. It sets a goal of limiting average global warming to 2°C (and identifies the need to confine increases to 1.5°), which it seeks to achieve by requiring all parties to submit plans for their "nationally determined contributions" (NDCs)–country policy commitments that are unilaterally determined, voluntary, and nonbinding–and to make their NDCs increasingly ambitious over time.

The agreement specifies the need for international financial support for developing countries with respect to both mitigation and adaptation. The accompanying COP Decision, also nonbinding, reiterates the goal of contributions of $100 billion for this purpose. The agreement also sets out the need for support for capacity building, technology transfer, and climate education.

Market instruments and carbon pricing have been identified as relevant policy instruments for achieving the Paris Agreement targets. Article 6 of the Paris Agreement (which has not yet been negotiated is especially important, as it gives new life to carbon markets and cooperative mechanisms.

a. In 2019, under President Trump, the United States withdrew from the agreement.

---

[5] See https://www.ieta.org/resources/International_WG/Article6/CLPC_A6%20report_no%20crops.pdf.

[6] A few studies have been conducted on transaction costs in carbon markets, but they center on monitoring, reporting, and verification. Examples include Schleich and Betz (2004); Jaraite, Convery, and Di Maria (2010); Mundaca et al. (2013); Joas and Flachsland, (2014); and Kerr and Dusch, (2015). Michaelowa and Stronzik (2002) reviewed the transaction costs of implementing the Clean Development Mechanism, concluding that they may be considerable. Krey, (2004) reached the same conclusion for India.

In the absence of a structured market,[7] governments must identify a national registry and accounting systems that are secure and can register emissions reductions and trades within a specific market. Maintaining such a registry is extremely costly and involves massive coordination and information security issues, especially across jurisdictions and legal systems. The difficulty of maintaining these registries is one of the principal problems hindering the emergence of integrated carbon markets across the world.[8]

4. Chile's energy and climate policy

4.1 *Climate policy*

Chile has positioned itself as a global leader in the international climate policy. It has committed to phase out coal by 2040 and move toward carbon neutrality by 2050. As the energy sector is the main contributor to greenhouse gas emissions, accounting for 78% of total national emissions (MMA, 2018), and electricity generation is the principal contributor in the energy sector, accounting for 53% of emissions (MMA, 2018), efforts have focused on promoting renewable energy sources, pursuing distributed energy alternatives, incentivizing energy efficiency, and regulating emissions reductions.

Under the Paris Agreement, Chile has committed to reduce the CO_2 intensity of its GDP by 30% by 2030 from its 2007 level. That translates to a reduction from 1.02 tCO_2e/C$ (Chilean pesos) million in 2007 to 0.71 tCO_2e/C$ million in 2030.[9] In addition, and subject to international funds, it has a conditional commitment to reduce the CO_2 intensity of GDP to 35–45% of the 2007 level. Chile has been among the first countries to update its NDC. The updated NDC has a more ambitious mitigation goal, with an absolute goal at 95 Mton by 2030, earlier peak of emissions

[7] Article 6 of the Paris Agreement recognizes the heterogeneity of approaches, providing a basis for countries to voluntarily cooperate with each other to deliver on their NDCs and raise ambition. This Article signals the use of carbon markets globally, allowing for decentralized bilateral cooperation approaches, including through internationally transferred mitigation outcomes. Emerging technologies have enabled increased data availability, systems automation, smart grid applications and data transfer, grid management, technological systems, and diverse governance rules. Information about mitigation outcomes is collected in a variety of repositories, including spreadsheets, databases reflecting pipeline activities, and registries at the country, regional, or institutional level. The new generation of climate markets is likely to develop as a network of decentralized markets, linking at regional, national, and subnational levels, without centralized functions and processes.

[8] It has been argued that one of the principal problems of the Clean Development Mechanism under the Kyoto Protocol were its transaction costs (see Chadwick, 2006).

[9] In addition, Chile has committed to the sustainable development and recovery of 100,000 hectares of forested land area.

in 2025, and lower carbon budget of 1110 Mton for the 11-year period,[10] showing therefore its commitment to the international climate agenda.

In April 2018, the Ministry of Energy launched the Energy Roadmap 2018–2022, which includes climate change as a cross-cutting issue in the roadmap's seven priority areas. In January 2020, the government sent Congress the first national climate change law, legally binding Chile's commitment to achieve carbon neutrality by 2050 and to phase out coal-fired generation by 2040. Chile's present energy grid includes 28 coal-fired power plants, with an average age of 18 yr, which emit 26% of all greenhouse gases while contributing just 4% of the country's power generation. Chile's low-emission energy strategy will make the country a pioneer in the fulfilment of international targets to reduce emissions.

To further advance the energy transition, the government has set a new, more ambitious target of generating 20% of the country's energy and 45% of all electric generation from renewable sources by 2025. To comply with its decarbonization commitment, Chile will phase out eight coal plants through a voluntary agreement with power generation companies. These plants represent 19% of the total installed capacity of coal-fired power plants, with a capacity of 1,047 megawatt tons (MWt). The expectation is to cover the shortfall with renewable energy generation. There is no schedule yet for phasing out the remaining 20 plants.

Chile has enormous potential in renewable energies, particularly solar and wind energy generation. Some estimates suggest that by 2030 up to 75% of electric power generation in Chile could come from renewable sources (PSR and Moray Energy, 2018). The energy transition—and the use of market instruments—may be the key to accelerating Chile's emissions reduction targets.

Chile is also exploring the development of a strategy for participating in integrated carbon markets.[11] It is a member of the Pacific Alliance (a trading association made up of Chile, Colombia, Mexico, and Peru), which has committed to move toward sustainable economic growth, and created a Green Growth Group to discuss mechanisms to advance collaboration in the development of carbon markets. It also belongs to the Carbon Pricing Leadership Coalition, a World Bank–led coalition of countries and corporations committed to carbon pricing, and supports the Carbon Pricing of Americas initiative, an initiative of national and subnational

[10] https://www4.unfccc.int/sites/ndcstaging/PublishedDocuments/Chile%20First/Chile's_NDC_2020_english.pdf.

[11] Integration of carbon markets has proved to be challenging due to their bottom-up nature. Climate markets worldwide have different scopes and approaches, which add to the complexity of market integration and trading across borders. Using the warehouse example, blockchain has the potential to facilitate communication between bottom-up markets, track assets across different systems and avoid double counting.

jurisdictions in the Americas aiming at promoting dialogue on carbon pricing and integrated carbon markets.

Chile implemented a carbon tax in 2017.[12] The tax is significant because it is the only one in the region explicitly based on emissions, not carbon fuel content. It is therefore the most likely tax in the region to support progress toward more sophisticated market instruments.

A tax reform bill currently before Congress proposes a carbon emission offset scheme to compensate for the tax. If passed, it would be the first offset scheme in the region with these characteristics.

In recent years, various jurisdictions in the Western Hemisphere have implemented carbon pricing to support efforts to mitigate climate change. Argentina, Colombia, and Mexico, like Chile, have imposed carbon taxes. In North America, California and Quebec have an integrated Emissions Trading System through the Western Climate Initiative, and the U.S. states in the northeast have an integrated emissions trading scheme for electricity generation companies known as RGGI (see https://www.carbonpricingleadership.org/).

Several continental initiatives seek to promote further links across Latin American jurisdictions and between North and South American jurisdictions. Among them are efforts through the Pacific Alliance and a recent initiative promoting a carbon market of the Americas.

Major bottlenecks remain, such as integrating criteria, methodologies, institutions, and objectives, and dealing with the transaction costs of markets for carbon emissions.

It is not clear how to fully operationalize a market-based offset mechanism in a country like Chile, with its limited financial and human resources and small number of taxable facilities, or more broadly across the region. A new registry system and monitoring, reporting, and verification protocols will almost certainly be necessary.[13] Of concern is how to achieve the necessary level of information security for operation of a tax with offsets or a broader carbon market. According to one study, Chile lacks the capacity to achieve a minimum level of cybersecurity; a carbon market or offsetting scheme would require millions of dollars of

[12] The government of President Bachelet (2014–18) implemented a \$5 per ton tax on CO_2 emissions in 2017 (General Tax Reform Bill, Law No. 20.780) on facilities in various sectors, including food-processing, refining, and electricity. In 2017, 96 facilities were taxed, raising \$191 million in revenue. The CO_2 tax covered about 40% of the country's carbon emissions.

[13] The Ministry of Energy, with support from the World Bank, is now developing such a system.

investment.[14] The transactions cost problem, and the required level of security, could be solved by adopting blockchain technology, as shown in Chapter 4.

4.2 Energy policy

Chile's energy policy was built through a broad participatory process (ChileEnergía, 2050). It establishes guidelines and goals for the development of a reliable, sustainable, inclusive, and competitive energy sector (Box 3). The policy is based on four pillars, each of which has specific goals and targets for 2035 and 2050.[15]

Thanks to Chile's generous endowment of renewable energy sources, the significant decline in installed capacity prices, and a series of innovative policy instruments (see Box 3), the country has experienced a remarkable energy transformation in the last few years. Installed capacity in nonconventional renewable energy sources (excluding large hydroelectric) increased sharply, from practically zero in 2008 to 21% of all energy sold in 2018 (CNE, 2018). Total generation was 76.2 GWh in 2018,

Box 3

Key policy innovations promoting renewable energy in Chile

The Renewable Energy Law (Law 20257).

The first important reform for the renewable energy sector was the approval of a Renewable Energy Law, which included a renewable portfolio standard. An RPS is a quota system that encourages renewable energy generation by setting the proportion of electricity supply that must be produced from eligible renewable energy sources. Renewable energy technologies were first added to the energy mix in Chile in 2008, with the approval of Law 20257, which aimed to support the generation of electricity from nonconventional renewable sources, such as biomass, small hydraulic energy (capacity of less than 20 MW), geothermal energy, solar energy, wind power, and marine energy. This law was amended in 2013 (Law 20698, better known as Law 20/25), which states that renewable energy must make up 20 percent of the energy mix in Chile by 2025.

Restructuring public auctions.

Chile improved the ability of generators of renewable energy to compete in energy auctions. Renewable energy projects without a power purchase agreement used to face significant obstacles obtaining funding from commercial banks. PPAs can be achieved in Chile through bilateral negotiations or participation in power auctions–carried out by the National Energy Commission (CNE)–for regulated consumers served by the distribution grid.

Since 2005, Law 20018 has required electricity distribution companies to contract their energy requirements by means of competitive nondiscriminatory auctions (including renewables). A submitted bid with the lowest price is awarded a long-term contract (typically, a PPA for the project). In 2014 three-time blocks were established in the bidding process, covering 11 pm–8 am, 8 am–6 pm, and 6–11 pm (peak demand). This modification in the structure of the auction scheme greatly favored renewable generators, which can offer power cheaply at the times of the day they produce it.

In the latest and largest energy auction ever, the CNE had the goal of adding generation of 12,430 GWh/year, consisting of five-time blocks for 20 years starting in 2021. This auction covered 30 percent of Chile's energy demand (Ministry of Energy 2016). Wind and solar PV projects were awarded about 40 percent of the energy at the auctions. The efficient and competitive nature of auctions has reduced energy costs, encouraging further investment in the sector.

Energy transmission.

Law 20936 on electricity transmission, adopted in July 2016 aims to create a robust interconnected transmission system that allows the unification of Chile's power grid by connecting the Northern Interconnected System with the Central Interconnected System. The interconnection of the systems will allow two medium-size markets to merge, forming a more competitive marketplace and allowing the energy generated from large solar potentials in the north to be distributed to the central and southern part of the country.

Distributed energy.

The key regulatory instruments for distributed energy are Law 19940 and Law 20571, adopted in March 2004 and March 2012, respectively. Law 19940 grants distribution projects below 9 MW the right to connect to the grid, creating a market for small energy generators (i.e., those with installed capacity of up to 9MW).[a]

Law 20571 authorizes a system of net billing of residential generators.[b] It regulates self-generation of energy based on nonconventional renewable energies and efficient cogeneration. The law gives users the right to sell their surplus directly to the electricity distributor at a regulated price through net billing.

[a] Small energy generators are regulated by D.S. N° 244 of the Ministry of Economy and D.S. N° 101 of the Ministry of Energy.

[b] Net billing pays the retail rate for customer-consumed generation and a below retail rate for exported generation.

[14] Achieving an acceptable level of security at the Ministry of the Environment and the Superintendency of the Environment, the agencies that regulate and operate the current tax, would require an investment of almost $17 million (over a three-year horizon) for the tax currently being implemented (Deloitte, 2017). Moving toward an Emission Trading Scheme (ETS) or an offset mechanism would require even more resources for design and implementation, as well as a significant investment in information security to reach the level of security of banks.

[15] The relevant goals for 2035 include the following: (a) "a fully bidirectional energy system with information technologies allowing both the production and management of energy at all levels"; (b) "at least 60 percent of renewable energy in the national electricity generation"; and (c) for 2050, "greenhouse gas emissions from the Chilean energy sector [that] are consistent with the limits defined by science at the level global and with the corresponding national reduction goal, promoting cost-effective mitigation measures."

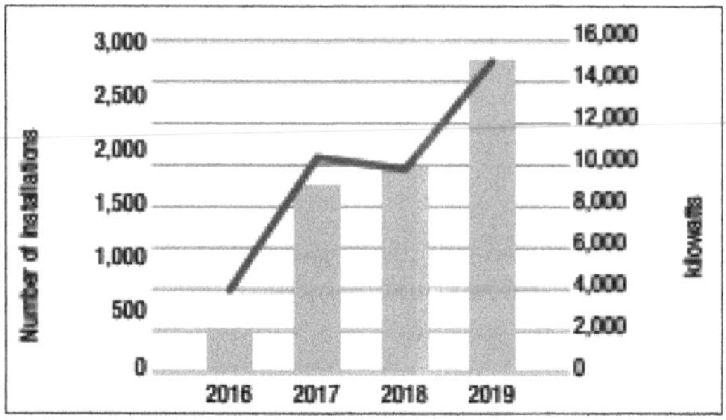

Figure 4.3. Number and kilowatts of distributed energy installations in Chile, 2016–19. Source: Ministry of Energy of Chile.

of which 34 GWh were renewable and 10.8 GWh were nonconventional renewable, principally wind and solar (CNE, 2018).

Chile's policies have been so successful that the government's commitment of decarbonization by 2040 and carbon neutrality by 2050 will be met by renewable energy. Chile has great potential in solar renewable energy, but distributed solar PV generation has yet to take off (Figure 4.3). One reason is the high initial upfront investment (for solar panels, for example) of DER installations. The payback period is estimated at 8–14 yr, depending on the system installed (CNE, 2019). To incentivize investment with such a long payback period, the government has implemented a series of subsidies to support the distributed energy market.

5. Chile's public on solar rooftop project and its blockchain pilot

In 2014, Chile's Ministry of Energy created the Public Solar Roofs Program (known as PTSP, its Spanish acronym) to support the installation of PV systems in public buildings. The objectives of the $13 million program were to reduce the cost of operating public buildings, stimulate the market for PV solutions through the installation of solar panels, and generate free public access to information on the costs and conditions of PV projects aimed at self-consumption.

The project explored the potential of a blockchain-based monitoring, reporting, and verification system that validates and registers electricity generation certificates and, concomitantly, emissions reductions. This exploration led to the implementation of a pilot blockchain project, the goal of which was the creation of an institutional infrastructure to foster the growth of a carbon market capable of generating the funds required for initial investments in DER installations. It is notable that at the date of this report, Chile does not have an emission trading scheme in place through which emission reductions can be traded. The DER market is still nascent and lacks a competitive retail market for trading of distribution resources. The value added of the pilot was limited to testing existing institutional structures and capacity for registration, measurement of data, verification, and certification.

Generating distributed energy resources (DERs) based on renewable energy sources has several advantages:

- It provides a secure and stable source of electricity generation at a low cost.
- It reduces electricity losses and peak demand.
- It has the potential of making a significant contribution to emissions reductions

The scalability of distributed energy generation and the possibility of generating an environmental asset in the form of emissions reductions requires the emergence of a market to facilitate trade across DER installations, sectors and, eventually, jurisdictions. One of the main challenges in creating such a market is the need to validate and consolidate trade in energy generation and emissions reductions among agents. Ensuring the integrity and cost-efficiency of trades requires sufficient market oversight to afford potential market participants certainty with respect to energy supply and emissions reductions. The transaction costs involved in verifying emissions reductions can be extremely high, especially when dealing with multiple trades across many small facilities.

The PTSP program ran from 2015 to 2019 and is expected to be renewed. During this period, it implemented 133 projects, with an investment of about $5 million, reaching about 5 MW of installed capacity.

The pilot was implemented in 10 public facilities selected from the 133 photovoltaic (PV) installations participating in the PTSP. Its objective was to test a blockchain-based system of certification for renewable DERs and emissions reductions. The project installed hardware and developed a blockchain algorithm designed especially for DER installations. The blockchain platform provided information from February 19, 2019 to August 30, 2019.

To validate data, the Public Solar Rooftop pilot initiative used a measurement system independent of the generation plant, which read multiple climatological variables, including solar irradiation. The data was then compared with what was reported on the monitoring platform of the generation plant. If both gave similar results, it was assumed that the information was correct and then emissions reductions were estimated.

Given the characteristics of the pilot, it was assumed that the plants displaced average energy from the grid, and not the last dispatched plant (that is, the PV self generation was not enough to change the national energy mix), so the reduction was calculated as the amount of energy generated by the emission factor of the SEN (National Electricity System).

The main attributes of the pilot are the following: (i) document the provenance of distributed solar PV generation; (ii) track emissions reductions achieved by each unit of distributed PV generation system; and (iii) track ownership transfers between participants.

5.1 *Setting up the pilot*

Preparation and implementation of the pilot involve four steps, as described below.

Step 1: Install and operationalize data loggers

PTSP facilities record information on electricity generation data loggers that do not have a web-based network connection.[16, 17] Independent inspection on the ground is therefore required to verify and certify these data, which is extremely costly. To address the problem, the pilot installed monitoring stations at 10 facilities to capture detailed realtime information on energy generation to determine emissions reductions.[18] PhiNet data loggers are data acquisition systems programmed in Linux, Nginx, and NodeJS that capture relevant information on energy generation and consumption, as well as other control variables, such as temperature and radiation, which can independently verify generation data. The PhiNet stations generate blocks of data (on electric generation, radiation, and so forth), which are uploaded onto the web every 15 min (Figure 4.4)

Step 2: Program the blockchain structure

Phineal, the company that implemented the pilot project, developed a public, permissioned blockchain platform designed specifically to manage energy installations.[19] The platform, GTIME, identifies five data points relevant for energy management and the blockchain identifier. The blockchain platform records the following information:

- Geolocation in Universal Transverse Mercator coordinates
- Time stamp using Coordinated Universal Time

[16] The program received support from the World Bank–managed Partnership for Market Readiness (PMR program).

[17] They are connected only to the central platform of Meteocontrol, the company that provides the centralized registration platform.

[18] Servers were programmed in Linux, Nginx, and NodeJS. Monitoring stations were PhiNet with GHI and connected directly with data logger blue-log.

[19] The blockchain architecture is hybrid. Phineal can authorize other servers to operate as miners, but it did not do so. For a blockchain architecture to be hybrid or open, an Internet connection must be available.

Source: Phineal 2019.

The PhiNet stations generate more data than is strictly necessary. Data on radiation and temperature, for example, are useful for verifying the efficiency of the PV installation, but they are not needed to estimate reductions in greenhouse gas emissions. They were collected because one of the objectives of the project was to verify whether the electricity generation recorded on the registration platform currently operating the PTSP (Meteocontrol) was consistent with the PhiNet record and other control variables.

Figure 4.4. PhiNet data loggers and public solar roofs.

- Environmental data (radiation and ambient temperature)
- Electricity generation (obtained from the billing meter or data acquisition system)
- Identification of the PV facility
- Media Access Control (MAC) address of the facility (unique identifier of the network device).

Every 15 min, the GTIME data block pulls energy and environmental data with a specific ID and time stamp from the PhiNet installation equipment.[20] It also provides a history of transactions—in this case, the energy injected into the network (Soto and Hermosilla, 2019).

As the stations need 5 min to establish machine-to-machine communication over the Internet, every 20 min the PhiNet sends the data and generates the GTIME block, which is "stamped" sequentially in the chain, as shown in Figure 4.5.

Step 3: Operationalize the blockchain

Nodes within the GTIME blockchain were installed in public and private buildings throughout Santiago de Chile to capture data from data loggers. Nodes were required to have an Internet connection and a connection to the mainframe computer (both consuming less than 5 W). After information is captured and stored on the blockchain, the information is made available

[20] See https://gtime.io/.

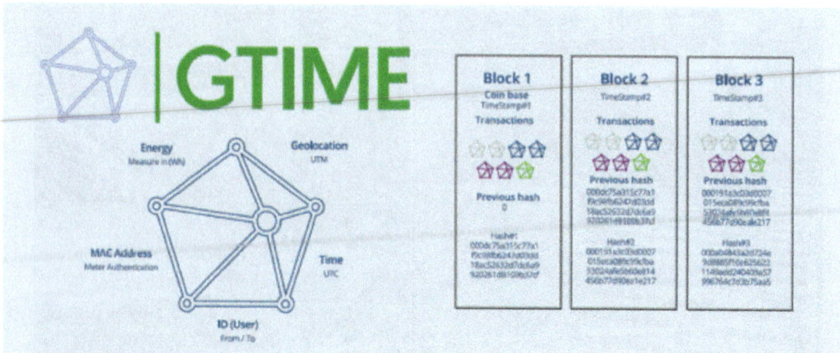

Source: Soto and Hermosilla 2019.

While this phase of the program did not register peer-to-peer transactions, trading could be programmed into a future iteration. This pilot captured only data on PV energy. Additional information could be included in the block for other sources of energy, such as wind patterns, or different types of data could be recorded and transferred (for example, a hash of images associated with reforestation projects).

Figure 4.5. The GTIME blockchain.

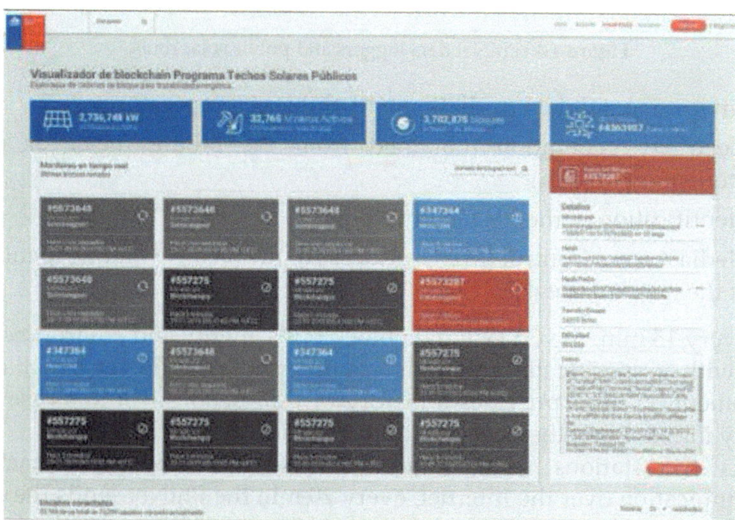

Figure 4.6. Data visualizer. Source: http://gtime.io.4040/.

to interested parties and the general public through a free-access website on which it is possible to visualize the generation of certified energy.

The GTIME blockchain is a dedicated (closed) blockchain network. As Phineal is responsible for vetting each of the participating nodes (through a license that provides access to the network), only Phineal and government servers were allowed to participate. Phineal set up 10 dedicated servers to host the blockchain network. They were installed remotely and operated through the permissioned platform that Phineal set up. The advantage of this approach is the ability to control participation and utilize a low-cost, low-energy consensus mechanism.[21] In this case, the only costs were for Phineal's proprietary programming and the initial investment associated with setting up the data miners.

5.2 Coast of the project

The total cost of the pilot project was about $100,000 (Table 4.1). But this figure does not give a clear picture of the actual or future costs of making this type of project replicable and scalable, for several reasons:

- Phineal donated its proprietary programming, which it had already created. Blockchain architecture is not expensive, but it does require programmers.
- The project involved actions and processes that are not necessary for verification, such as the PhiNet monitoring installations.[22]

Table 4.1. Capital and variable costs of Chile's public solar roofs program.

Item	Capital costs	Variable costs	Total cost
10 monitoring stations	PhiNet station (hardware with data loggers): $4,000	Installation and verification: $10,000 ($1,000 each)	$50,000
Blockchain installation	GTIME proprietary blockchain algorithm: 0 (Phineal had already developed the software)	Programming: 0	0
Blockchain management		Human resources: $10,000	$10,000
Miners (10 miners)	Purchase of 10 servers (20 others were already on hand): $500	5W of energy a day for three years: $500	$5,500
		Human resources: $10,000	$10,000
Visualizer	Dedicated line	Programming: $10,000	$10,000
Other administrative costs			$14,500
Total			$100,000

Source: Phineal 2019; communication with Eduardo Soto, head of the Phineal project.

No legal issues were assessed in the pilot. Similar projects in other sectors and countries could face legal hurdles.

---

[21] Data mining consumes energy. If the mining structure is public and open, an economic incentive must be put in place so that third-party servers can dedicate time and computer memory for mining. This is the approach taken by bitcoin, where mining activity is paid for with bitcoins for each puzzle solved or data block mined. In closed blockchains, the mining is carried out by dedicated servers. The advantage of this approach is that no additional payment for the actual mining is required; the only costs are the initial investment of acquiring and operating the servers and the energy cost of the mining. The mining structure to adopt depends on the specific contractual arrangement the blockchain structure is trying to solve. In the case of this pilot, where the number of facilities was small and there was a role for government-regulated contracts, a hybrid blockchain was more appropriate, with Phineal giving permission for carrying out the mining.

[22] The PhiNet monitoring stations are not strictly necessary in the case of energy distribution, because the energy produced can be captured from a smart meter. The PhiNet monitoring station captured data on solar radiation and temperature; such data are needed to determine the efficiency of panels, but they are not necessary for verifying energy produced.

- Energy, technology, and programming costs are all falling.
- Phineal does not clearly separate its own sunk costs from its operating costs.
- Table 4.1

6. Results and considerations for scale-up emerging from the Chile blockchain pilot in the energy sector

The pilot provides a real-world example of the application of blockchain to the energy sector that could be replicated in other countries or sectors. It demonstrates that a blockchain platform can guarantee the integrity and transparency of the data and bring in participants from the public and private sectors. The project reduced emissions by about 800 tons of CO_2 equivalent a year and saved about $250,000 in energy costs. The project addressed three problems: measurement, registration, and verification.

The measurement problem

The project set up its own web-based measuring systems, the PhiNet stations. However, any web-based stations that are standardized can be used. Distributed Energy Resource (DER) projects in Chile, including those participating in the PTSP, are not required to have a web-based generation metering system (smart meter). Yet web-based smart meters could be made a requirement in future applications, in order to track energy generation efficiently and collect the corresponding emissions reduction data. DER systems not equipped with smart meters will need ground-based inspection with independent verifiers.

The registration problem

Establishing unique protocols for connecting new sources is necessary to register new facilities properly. The pilot has demonstrated the ease of establishing protocols for connecting new sources. PV facilities are identified using their Media Access Control (MAC) address. This is not a problem that blockchain resolves, but a good onboarding process can do the job. If the blockchain network encompasses many solar panels and sensors, then cloud technologies (such as an IoT hub) can be used to identify and monitor these devices.

The verification problem

Blockchain infrastructure ensures the data has not been tampered with, thus facilitating verification, and allowing the certification of offsets. As the project continues or expands, a hybrid or even open source non proprietary blockchain could be explored as the basis of verification. The Ministry of Energy's own Open Energy project may present a better alternative, as it is based on Ethereum, a well-known blockchain platform. While the application of blockchain on climate markets remains nascent, lessons from the pilot, offered below, can help countries replicate and scale up similar projects to other sectors as they search for an integrated approach to energy transition and new carbon markets.

6.1 *An integrated approach can help create incentives for a more decentralized energy system able to absorb more renewable energy*

The pilot helped strengthen and develop the market for small-scale renewable energy generation, which has had difficulties taking off, by creating additional incentives through the potential sale of climate assets. The Ministry of Energy has achieved a great deal in terms of fostering large-scale renewable energy and pricing carbon for large-scale thermal boilers and turbines, but distributed generation development is lagging. Despite the advent of net billing (see Box 3), the regulatory environment and business model are not yet conducive to a strong push for distributed energy.

The development of an MRV system to track production from renewables-based DERs, and the link to a potential climate registry, could help create additional incentives for small-scale renewable energy generators and the development of start-ups as business models. It has helped move the DER agenda forward in an innovative way by using new technologies and linking it to potential future climate markets.

The project also helped establish conditions for a unique combination of private financing incentives for DERs with an innovative and well-designed public program and an MRV system, providing a practical application of the approach known as maximizing finance for development.

6.2 *Blockchain technology acts as an enabler of a well-designed business model*

The benefits of using a blockchain architecture are numerous but scalability and replicability of this and similar pilots remain a challenge. The reason behind this is that it relies less on the digital readiness of public or private entities, and more on the lack of functional business models. For instance, in the energy sector, implementation of smart meters (needed to be able to track transactions of DERs) has been a controversial issue in several countries because of the large up-front capital investments required for full-scale implementation throughout a country (these extra costs are often transferred to end users through electricity bills). However, a well-designed business model that links DERs transactions with the benefits of carbon trading could make the deployment of expensive smart meters profitable due to both selling of energy and climate assets. Therefore, blockchain technology acts as an enabler of a well-structured business model. Looking forward it is crucial to evaluate the operational framework by linking sectors (i.e., bringing climate revenues to the energy sector, which generates approximately 70% of the greenhouse gas emissions worldwide) and identifying technology convergence (i.e., blockchain and smart metering).

6.3 *Blockchain technology can create a secure system for collecting and transferring energy and emissions while reducing transaction costs*

The project developed and generated a shared ledger system of relevant energy generation and emissions reduction data. The blockchain structure ensures that the transferred information from each facility is secure and provides a platform that can support a wide range of applications, including the trading of emissions reductions. Backed by a specific Monitoring, Reporting, and Verification (MRV) system, the blockchain structure allows the Ministry of Energy to better track DERs.

Blockchain reduces the transaction costs of emissions trading by generating a viable and robust system that guarantees the integrity of climate-asset information and makes these assets tradable. The project established a practical and cost-effective MRV system for energy mitigation actions tailored to the needs of Chile's energy sector, which could be expanded to include small-scale power producers.

Chile currently imposes a carbon tax of $5 per metric ton. Congress has recently approved a reform that allows facilities that want to reduce their carbon tax liability to do so by offsetting their emissions by paying a third party to reduce their emissions equivalent. Although technically possible, the high transaction costs of developing and verifying emissions reductions makes it highly unlikely that tax-liable facilities could offset emissions with the emissions reductions of small facilities, such as DER generators. However, a blockchain architecture such as the one proposed by this pilot could be the basis for a broad market in emissions offsets. A blockchain-based trading system, if well designed, could be both economically and technically viable. This blockchain-based trading system would allow facilities affected by the carbon tax to buy offsets from DER facilities, helping these facilities to meet the upfront costs of PV installations and credit subsequent emissions reductions to the facility, enabling it to reduce its carbon taxes. The blockchain structure is well suited as a supportive infrastructure for this scenario.

6.4 The pilot helped build relationships with global initiatives

The project strengthened collaboration between the World Bank and the Ministry of Energy on future climate markets under the Paris Agreement, according to the joint statement released April 11, 2019. The collaboration focuses on the development of mitigation outcomes, the World Bank Climate warehouse, and the piloting of blockchain technology. It provides an important example of supporting trade in climate assets registered through blockchain that could eventually build a Pacific Alliance Emissions Trading Scheme for Latin America and the Caribbean, which could serve as a model for middle-income countries at other locations. The project also provided a replicable innovative framework for generating climate assets and developing efficient market-based mechanisms capable of mobilizing additional finance to drive DER activities.

6.5 Integrated energy policy frameworks

The pilot is implemented in a nascent market segment—distributed energy resources—that is set to grow substantially in the future (most notably in middle-income countries such as Chile). A combination of energy/digital technologies in fact will amplify the scope of DER markets. The "distributed" nature of this market implies multiple transactions (between the prosumer/aggregator and the grid, and among consumers, or peer-to-peer). To date, Chile has a net billing policy that rewards surplus energy injected to the grid at a fixed or regulated tariff. Under these conditions prosumers have no incentive to add battery energy storage (solar-plus-storage), since storing/shifting load is not rewarded by a peak tariff (for example, consuming stored solar energy during peak time would reduce the electricity bill for the prosumers, or storing solar energy for injections during peak time could be rewarded by a higher tariff). If peak tariff were allowed in Chile, solar-plus-storage would have a more strategic impact and higher benefit (i.e., more renewable energy and less emissions reductions) on the grid. Thus, in the future, recording and verifying these more complex transactions with blockchain will be even more important (or justifiable), since the potential for system benefits (deferring generation and network expansion and displacing fossil-fuel peakers) would be—in principle substantially higher.

6.6 Considerations for scale-up

Chile's experience can provide relevant lessons to other countries exploring the use of blockchain to support climate markets. Blockchain could also contribute to the decarbonization goals and climate markets strategy of the country. However, there are some key considerations that the government of Chile could assess further to scale up the use of blockchain on climate and energy markets.

Additional testing

The Public Solar Rooftop program provided relevant insight on the potential of blockchain for the energy sector, but further testing is needed to understand the full potential of the technology and assess the challenges. The potential to support the country's climate strategy will depend on different criteria and the decision to implement a blockchain approach should be based on a thorough evaluation of different factors, such as:

- *Cost benefit analysis*: further analysis is needed to understand the benefits of blockchain application compared to different technologies, and what are the costs associated to running and maintaining a blockchain-based system.
- *Governance*: the decentralized nature of blockchain requires a good understanding of the governance options and of the stakeholders that should be involved in the process.
- *Regulatory framework*: given the rapidly evolving landscape of blockchain technology, it will be important to consider how to comply with rules related to the data managed on the blockchain system.
- *Interconnection with climate policy instrument and tools*: Additional testing should evaluate the feasibility of interconnection with national systems and tools, and how the connection would work given system requirements such as documentation, support tools, and permissions.

Cross jurisdiction interconnections

Given the transparent and decentralized nature of blockchain, the technology could support the development of cross-country linkage. One of the main potentials of blockchain is its ability to connect decentralized systems and help securely track assets across different systems and avoid double counting. This could provide critical benefits for cross-country linkages since connecting diverse market mechanisms through a decentralized, blockchain-based approach could potentially be simpler and more cost-effective, in comparison to a centralized approach. Blockchain technology could allow instant comparison of reliable data across national and sub-national jurisdictions. The experience and lessons learned by the Government of Chile through this program could serve as a starting point for regional coordination and collaborative testing in future years. Other countries in Latin America such as Peru, Colombia, and México are already implementing carbon pricing instruments and could potentially benefit from the application of blockchain technology.

7. Conclusions

Technology can help countries achieve a successful energy transition and meet the ambitious commitments set out in the Paris Agreement. Due to new technologies, standardized protocols, rules, and structured certification systems, the costs of monitoring and reporting progress toward commitments are falling. But authorities still need to deal with the coordination problem associated with centralized accounting and registration systems, as well as verifying energy generation and emissions reductions, both of which involve considerable costs.

These costs can be particularly high when there are many small facilities, such as renewables-based distributed energy projects. For prosumers and carbon emission markets to be viable in such settings, a cost-effective system for verifying energy and emissions is required. In parallel, dealing with climate change mitigation implies significant global costs. The World Bank estimates that global integrated carbon markets could potentially reduce mitigation costs by 54% in 2050, or approximately $3.94 trillion (World Bank, 2016). These costs can be reduced by creating greenhouse gas where mitigation abatement costs are as low as possible, which in turn requires the development of energy and carbon markets.

However, the transaction costs associated with the development of these markets can be extremely high. Their emergence requires an institutional infrastructure that can support the coordination of multiple agents and ensure information security, verify energy and emissions reductions, and register energy and emission trades across different countries and legal systems. The lack of such an infrastructure is one of the principal problems stymying the emergence of integrated energy and carbon markets across the world.

Blockchain technology may provide a solution. A blockchain-based architecture can accommodate data that are captured automatically to support an integrated network of energy and climate markets over time. Furthermore, as the pilot project in Chile shows, although initially complex, blockchain does not require a sophisticated information technology infrastructure. This key disruptive technology, if coupled with a well-designed governance structure and converged with other technologies, could facilitate the development of markets by supporting transactions of all types of energy and emission-related data (facility-level, projects, programs, quantified production, life-cycle attributes) in a shared, globally accessible environment, at a low cost.

Chile taxes carbon at a rate of $5 per metric ton, and a new tax bill has approved a reform to allow for an offsetting scheme—thus providing the basis for a carbon market. Facilities that pay the tax can reduce their tax liability if they can show equivalent reductions elsewhere. However, the high transaction costs associated with emissions trading across small facilities that can reduce emissions, such as distributed energy generators, makes it unlikely that they will become viable market participants. For such trades to be possible, a central authority must register them and account for the energy generated and/or emissions reduced. Doing so is relatively simple for large facilities, but very costly for small ones. By reducing the transaction costs associated with registering trades from small facilities, blockchain may open an immense new market of energy and emissions reductions and generate the upfront investment in distributed energy installations, while having a direct impact on small and medium-size firms, local communities, households, and sustainable consumption practices such as public transport and cycling.

Addressing the transformational energy transition and climate change threats will require the application of diverse and innovative solutions and approaches. Mitigation implies enormous economic costs. Integrated carbon and energy markets support mitigation while reducing overall transaction costs. Blockchain may be just the right technology to facilitate the emergence of the institutional and governance structure necessary to develop and bring together synergies in carbon markets and the ongoing energy transition, at both the local and global levels.

Acknowledgments

This report was prepared by a core team comprised of Patricia Marcos, Florencia Sanchez Zunino, Susan Elaine David Carevic, Rachel Chi Kiu Mok and Rodrigo Pizarro. The authors would like to express their sincere thanks and gratitude to Juan Pedro Searle (Ministry Energy Chile), Francisco Dall'Orso León (Ministry Energy Chile) and colleagues at Phineal for the support and guidance offered in the elaboration of this study, the timely feedback, and the excellent collaboration throughout. The team would also like to thank World Bank colleagues including Marianne Fay, Virginia Brandon, Bjorn Philipp, Chandra Shekhar, Stephanie Gil, Gabriela Elizondo, Stela Mocan, Stephanie Rogers, Janina Franco and Francisco Winter for the advice and guidance provided throughout the elaboration of this report. The team would finally like to thank Nannel Gacitúa, who designed the cover and the layout and typeset the report.

References

Bloomberg. 2018. Distributed Energy Generation Market Size Worth $573.7 Billion by 2025: Grand View Research, Inc. Distributed Energy Generation Market Size Worth $573.7 Billion by 2025: Grand View Research, Inc. - Bloomberg

Chadwick, Bruce P. 2006. Transaction costs and the clean development mechanism. Natural Resources Forum 30: 256–71. Climate Change Coalition. https://www.climatechaincoalition.io/ Climate Ledger Initiative. https://www.climateledger.org/resources/CLI_KeyFindings.pdf.

CNE (Comision Nacional de Energia). 2018. Anuario estadistico de energia 2018. Santiago. https://www.cne.cl/wp-content/uploads/2019/04/Anuario-CNE-2018.pdf.

CPLC (Carbon Pricing Leadership Coalition). 2017. Report of the High-Level Commission on Carbon Prices. https://www.carbonpricingleadership.org/report-of-the-highlevel commission-on-carbon-prices/.

Deloitte. 2017. Informe de diagnóstico de ciberseguridad. Santiago.

European Commission 2015. Study on the Effective Integration of Distributed Energy Resources for Providing Flexibility to the Electricity System. Brussels. https://ec.europa.eu/energy/sites/ener/files/documents/5469759000%20Effective%20integration%20of%20 DER%20Final%20ver%202_6%20April%202015.pdf.

Fujimori, Shinichiro, Izumi Kubota, Hancheng Dai, Kiyoshi Takahashi, Tomoko Hasegawa, Jing-Yu Liu, Yasuaki Hijioka, Toshihiko Masui and Maho Takimi. 2016. Will international emissions trading help achieve the objectives of the paris agreement? Environmental Research Letters 11: 104001.

Global Climate Action Partnership. 2019. Energy 2050: A Participatory Process for a Long-Term Energy Policy and its Role in Climate Change Policies in Chile. Energy 2050: A Participatory Process for a Long-Term Energy Policy and its Role in Climate Change Policies in Chile - Global Climate Action Partnership.

Hof, Andries, Michel G.J. den Elzen, Annemiek Admiraal, Mark Roelfsema, David E.H.J. Gernaat and Detlef P. van Vuuren. 2017. Global and regional abatement costs of nationally determined contributions (NDCs) and of enhanced action to levels well below 2 C and 1.5 C. Environmental Science & Policy March 3.

IEA (International Energy Agency). 2018. Global Energy & CO_2 Status Report 2018. Paris

IEA (International Energy Agency). 2019. Renewables 2018: Market Analysis and Forecast from 2018 to 2023. Paris.

IETA, University of Maryland, and CPLC. 2019. The Economic Potential of Article 6 of the Paris Agreement and Implementation Challenges. Washington, DC.

International Justice Initiative. n.d. Costs for Developing Countries to Develop NDCs. University of Tasmania. https://docs.google.com/spreadsheets/d/1ImW9Y1NL8aSbmF l8qV9ygHtCvr8VxIs4DCQgthw_OQ/edit#gid=0/.

IPCC (Intergovernmental Panel on Climate Change). 2014. Climate Change 2014: Synthesis Report. Contribution of Working Groups I, II, and III to the Fifth Assessment Report of the Intergovernmental Panel on Climate Change, ed. R.K. Pachauri and L.A. Meyer. Geneva.

IPCC (Intergovernmental Panel on Climate Change). 2018. Summary for Policymakers. In Global Warming of 1.5°C. An IPCC Special Report on the Impacts of Global Warming of 1.5°C above Pre-Industrial Levels and Related Global Greenhouse Gas Emission Pathways, in the Context of Strengthening the Global Response to the Threat of Climate Change, Sustainable Development, and Efforts to Eradicate Poverty, ed. V. Masson-Delmotte, P. Zhai, H.-O. Pörtner, D. Roberts, J. Skea, P.R. Shukla, A. Pirani, W. Moufouma-Okia, C. Péan, R. Pidcock, S. Connors, J.B.R. Matthews, Y. Chen, X. Zhou, M.I. Gomis, E. Lonnoy, T. Maycock, M. Tignor, and T. Waterfield. Geneva.

IRENA (International Renewable Energy Agency). 2017. Electricity Storage and Renewables: Costs and Markets to 2030. Abu Dhabi.

IRENA (International Renewable Energy Agency). 2019a. Renewable Power Generation Costs in 2018. Abu Dhabi.

IRENA (International Renewable Energy Agency). 2019b. Transforming the Energy System— and Holding the Line on the Rise of Global Temperatures. Abu Dhabi.

Jaraite, J., F. Convery and C. Di Maria. 2010. Transaction Costs for Firms in the EU ETS: Lessons from Ireland. Climate Policy 10(2): 190–215.

Joas, F. and C. Flachsland. 2014. The (Ir)relevance of Transaction Costs in Climate Policy Instrument Choice: An Analysis of the EU and the US. Climate Policy, December 1 doi:10.1 080/14693062.2014.968762/.

Kander, Astrid, Paolo Malanima and Paul Warde. 2013. Power to the People: Energy in Europe over the Last Five Centuries. Princeton, NJ: Princeton University Press.

Kerr, S. and V. Duscha. 2015. Going to the source: using an upstream point of regulation for energy in a national chinese emissions trading system. Energy & Environment. https:// ideas.repec.org/p/mtu/wpaper/14_09.html.

Krey, M. 2004. Transaction Costs of CDM Projects in India: An Empirical Survey. HWWA Report 238, Hamburg Institute of International Economics. https://www.econstor.eu/obitstream/10419/32919/1/385360975.pdf.

Lee, W., L. Xiang, R. Schober and V.W.S. Wong. 2004. Direct electricity trading in smart grid: a coalitional game analysis. IEEE Journal on Selected Areas in Communications 32: 1398–1411.

Michaelowa, A. and M. Stronzik. 2002. Transaction Costs of the Kyoto Mechanisms. HWWA Discussion Paper 175, Hamburg Institute of International Economics.

Michaelowa, A. and F. Jotzo. 2005. Transaction costs, institutional rigidities and the size of the clean development mechanism. Energy Policy 33: 511–23.

Ministerio de Energía. 2016. Energía 2050. Política energética de Chile. Santiago. http:// www.energia2050.cl/uploads/ libros/libro_energia_2050.pdf.

Ministerio de Hacienda. 2014. Ley N° 20.780. Art. N° 8, Reforma Tributaria. Santiago.

MMA (Ministerio del Medio Ambiente). 2018. Tercer informe bienal. Actualizacion de Chile sobre cambio climático. Santiago. https://mma.gob.cl/wp-content/uploads/2018/12/3rdBUR-Chile-SPanish.pdf.

Mundaca, L., M. Mansoz, L. Neij and G. Timilsina. 2013. Transaction costs analysis of low carbon technologies. Climate Policy 13(4): 490–513.

Nakamoto, S. n.d. Bitcoin: A Peer-To-Peer Electronic Cash System. https://bitcoin.org/bitcoin.pdf.

OECD (Organisation for Economic Co-operation and Development). 1991. Recommendation of the Council on the Use of Economic Instruments in Environmental Policy. Paris. https:// legalinstruments.oecd.org/en/instruments/OECD-LEGAL-0258.

OECD (Organisation for Economic Co-operation and Development). n.d. OECD Blockchain Primer. https://www.oecd.org/finance/OECD-BlockchainPrimer.pdf.

Peter, Viktor. 2019. Blockchain in the energy sector: an introduction to the technology and its potential. In Blockchain Meets Energy Digital Solutions for a Decentralized and Decarbonized Sector. German-Mexican Energy Partnership and Florence School of Regulation.

Phineal. 2019. Proyecto de consultoría para pilotear certificación de generación de ERNC y transferencias de estos resultados de mitigación utilizando blockchain. Ministerio de Energía, AGCID, and the World Bank. http://www.precioalcarbonochile.cl/wp-content/uploads/2019/10/Entrega_-Informe-final-piloto-blockchain.pdf.

PSR and Moary Energy. 2018. Flexibility costs under high variable renewable energy generation: the Chilean case. Flexibility costs under high variable renewable energy generation: the Chilean case . S. Mocarquer, R. Quinteros, S. Binato, M. V. F. Pereira (morayenergy.com).

Schleich, J. and R. Betz. 2004. EU emissions trading and transaction costs for small and medium sized companies. EU emissions trading and transaction costs for small and medium sized companies | SpringerLink.

Smil, V. 2010. Energy Transitions: History, Requirements, Prospects. Santa Barbara, CA: Praeger Publishers.

Soto, Eduardo, and Diego Hermosilla. 2019. Sello Sol & Blockchain GTIME: Electricity traceability system using blockchain. In Blockchain Meets Energy Digital Solutions for a Decentralized and Decarbonized Sector. German-Mexican Energy Partnership and Florence School of Regulation.

UNEP (United Nations Environmental Program). 2020. Designing a Blockchain Model for the Paris Agreement's Carbon Market Mechanism. https://unepdtu.org/publications/designing-ablockchain-model-for-the-paris-agreements-carbon-market-mechanism/.

UNFCCC (United Nations Framework Convention on Climate Change). 2015a. UNFCCCFCCC/ CP/2015/L.9/Rev.1: Adoption of the Paris Agreement UNFCCC, Paris, 1–32.

UNFCCC (United Nations Framework Convention on Climate Change). 2015b. UNFCCC Intended Nationally Determined Contributions (INDCs). http:// www4. unfccc.int/submissions/indc/Submission percent20Pages/submissions.aspx.

United Nations. 2019. World Population Prospects 2019. population.un.org/wpp/publications/files/wpp2019_highlights.pdf.

WEF (World Economic Forum). 2015. Deep Shift Technology Tipping Points and Societal Impact. Survey Report, September. Global Agenda Council on the Future of Software & Society.

World Bank. 2018. Blockchain and Emerging Digital Technologies for Enhancing Post-2020 Climate Markets. Washington, DC.

World Bank. 2019. State and Trends of Carbon Pricing. June. Washington, DC. Doi: 10.1596/978-1-4648-1435-World Bank, Ecofys, and Vivid Economics. 2016. State and Trends of Carbon Pricing 2016. October. Washington, DC: World Bank. 2019. Joint Statement by the World Bank and Chile's Ministry of Energy announcing a collaboration on future climate markets under Article 6 of the Paris Agreement.

Chapter 5
The Potential of Sustainable Blockchain Technology for Decentralized and Open-Science to Boost the Economic Growth of the Deep Technology Start-Up Industry. Putting Power Back into the Hands of Academics, Scientists, and Engineers

Stephen G. Gray[1,*] and *John Zandbergen*[2]

1. Introduction

Recent rumors in the world of crypto currency have inadvertently caused an issue for blockchain technology and start-ups in general (Fortune,

[1] Founder & CEO at NouBio Inc, Republic of Ireland.
[2] CEO Ourobionics, Netherlands.
* Corresponding author: Stephen@ourobionics.com

2022). The most important component of blockchain has never been the digital asset or currency replacement. It is the software built into blockchain technology that creates the real value. The public might need a year or longer to have faith in blockchain and cryptocurrency, but this does not mean what has been destroyed in the realm of FTX does not lead to real creation in the blockchain sector. Perhaps the time is now for young entrepreneurs to dig deeper into the world of blockchain, look away from crypto and NFTs. What is at the back end? What can be done to create real value in our world. Blockchain in its simplest form is the tracking and tracing of data with a viable stamp of approval. One is entering a world where data is going to be the new gold rush, therefore there is a need for real blockchain start-ups to form.

The truth is that the majority of blockchain start-ups and companies are entirely focused on cryptocurrency which is defined as a peer-peer electronic cash system that accepts direct payments without financial intermediation. It attracts investors due to the ability to trade anonymously avoiding higher transaction costs than existing financial assets. What distinguishes the value of cryptocurrency value from financial assets is the fact that it supports a security implemented by an algorithm to track all the verified transactions. Not only is the initial peer-to-peer payments in cryptocurrencies attractive to investors but also speculative behavior is applied as an investment instrument to respond in high volatility, price, and trading volume. Although cryptocurrencies are not as stable as other currencies in financial markets, it is a preferable option to integrate in portfolio diversification and trading strategies. Given the recent price volatility of cryptocurrencies and the risk investors carry for this emerging market, this chapter studies the volatility behavior of the five largest cryptocurrencies (Bitcoin, Litecoin, Ripple, Dogecoin, Stellar), S&P 500 and Gold in order to specify and compare asymmetric volatility before and during the Covid-19 shock.

There are several companies that have pivoted away from this world of crypto and NFTs. Cad Chain focuses on the protection of 3D CAD files. Consensys has its eyes set on changing the world of financial transactions by embracing decentralized finance solutions, enabling fast and secure financial transactions. Unstoppable domains could lead to the next stages in websites that have a real function rather than a business or personal landing page. Brave has built a blockchain-enabled browser to rival Google Chrome with privacy at the center of its technology.

Start-up company Republic wants to modulate the investment sector by allowing new ways to invest in real world assets and companies. Spring laboratories uses blockchain to enable secure information transfer between businesses by making use of blockchains' power of transparency and real-time data ledger technology. Geno bank is using blockchain to track and trace biological samples or the data associated with genetic testing like 23 and me. Vulpine Designs Inc is another start-up company that is working on the feasibility of cloud-based blockchain solutions for the trillion-dollar synthetic biology industry and ecosystem.

It does not stop at the start-up level. IBM has helped more than 220 businesses develop data governance tools that run on blockchain (Daley, 2021). The biggest defense giant, and one of the largest companies in the world Lockheed Martin integrates blockchain into its developmental processes and is using blockchain in cyber security methods while also using the software. Ford Motor company uses blockchain to detect environmental or human rights violations that have occurred in refineries and mines for electric vehicles. Ford is also researching a blockchain system where drivers can transfer data and cryptocurrency between each other (Daley, 2021).

In this chapter, I will focus on the journey of the start-up Cart Allum Blockchain Solutions as an example of a company with its own sustainable blockchain technology and plans to change decentralized science and open science as a whole. A published blockchain technology and a realistic use case. The company started out as a shopping basket application with blockchain inside. It has since then transformed into an entirely different start-up. This goes to show the fluidity of the start-up world. The same way you tube entered the world as a dating app and Facebook was just for high-ranking universities. The start-up serves as the best example of not only a new blockchain technology but the other use cases that young entrepreneurs need to consider. The purpose for this chapter is to move away from the focus on crypto, NFT and banking disruption side of blockchain and focus on the real-world potential of this innovative technology and how it can lead to an ecosystem of start-up companies in this sector.

2. A sustainable blockchain solution for decentralized and open science to boost the creation of new deep technologies and start-ups

As a bioengineering academic I disliked publishing. I preferred to invent and when I invented, I would build, keep a record, and never use it. My issue with publishing is the academic world itself. The journals that scientists and engineers publish make US$6 billion in annual revenue (Buranyi, 2017) while those that do all the research and write all the content get little to no remuneration. In no other industry would such a business model be allowed to exist. There is nothing wrong with journals and their business model but there should be room for change. The vision of Cart Allum Blockchain solutions started out this way: what if data could be protected and academics could share without fear of stolen ideas. Then it ballooned into what if scientists got remuneration for their written work when it is cited or shared? What if we can build a real decentralized peer review system? What if journals could finally protect their articles and reviews from sci-hub with the same technology that rewards those that write in the journals. What if a new open-science and open-sourcing concept existed instead of patenting and publishing certain know-how was hidden behind a blockchain area owned by the inventors? Is not the value of a patent, the trade secrets and protection from others using it. A patent does not last forever and know-how or even minor recipes in protocols are highly valuable.

The reality is that scientific publication and its peer review system strongly rely on major industry players with large paywalls such as Elsevier and centralized metrics (JCR Impact Factor) and databases [Scopus]. The large issues in this system concern fairness, quality, performance, cost, unpaid labor, transparency, and accuracy or unbiased evaluation process (Ambar, 2021). The open access movement has attempted to provide a free access solution but now academics must pay extra to make their article or review open-access so it has already gone in the opposite direction. Blockchain provides the much-needed opportunity to solve this problem at a greater scale but also as a start-up such as Cart Allum Blockchain Solutions. Blockchain can build the decentralized infrastructure that is needed for new models of scientific production, dissemination, and real protection of know-how and intellectual property (Ambar, 2021). This should spawn more sharing of research and data prior to publication or patents based upon what blockchain can build into each file to protect how the file is used, traced, edited, shared, stored, etc. (Ambar, 2021).

Blockchain driven decentralized science [BlockDeSci] can enable a decentralized reviewer reputation system, open-access by-design infrastructure, transparent government process, protection of know-how or patentable information, and full or partial remuneration of the scientists, researchers, and engineers. The details of the technology can be found at the end of this chapter and two proposals of an MVP DeSci technological feasibility of these concepts can be found in the review paper published by researchers unrelated to Cart Allum in 2021—Decentralizing science: towards an interoperable open peer review ecosystem using blockchain (Ambar, 2021). It outlines the concepts but states that architecture is needed to build it, this is the need for the emergence of start-ups like Cart Allum Blockchain Solutions.

Another concept that has been outlined in detail is if decentralized science can actually repair academic working conditions. At present many PhDs and post doctors are struggling to survive financially post the pandemic with reduced availability for research funding, permanent research positions (Sicard, 2022). My personal vision behind Cart Allum Blockchain Solutions is to implement not only decentralized science and more open science but to find new ways for hard-working scientists, engineers, and researchers to find new ways to become self-funded which in turn could boost the deep technology innovation ecosystem. Governing bodies have made significant attempts to narrow social inequalities in research funding distribution, yet it has not considered the importance of academic well-being (Sicard, 2022). In a similar way journals do not consider the knock-on effects of free labor. What if there is a brain drain? Who writes the publications that journals business depend on?

In this context the push of blockchain technology into this sector or ecosystem can push the implementation of systems that mitigate systematic bias and the centralized nature of existing academic auditing for grants, publications, patents and more. Cart Allum are pioneers of this blockchain decentralized and open science fields, but what if Cart Allum opens their technologies to others in this science and engineering industry? Can it implement future-proofing of research funding, academics lives, and more revenue for academics? Scientists and engineers at the frontier of deep technology are paid not just a living wage or a salary like the computer science industry, but maybe even have blockchain funded resources to build what is needed in deep technology without the need for the traditional venture capital route. Or perhaps a way for venture capital groups and angels to fund deep technology in its infancy?

"Blockchain technology arguably could make the digital universe look more like a complex adaptive system of the kinds found in nature, if it becomes the best version of itself. This is a big *if*, and it will be many years in the future, if it comes to pass at all." (Anderson, 2019).

The technological side is a challenge for scalability but the potential of decentralized blockchain systems outside the banking industry can build more disruptive innovations and improvements for academic publishing and peer reviewing. The main issue that Cart Allum encounters as a start-up is not as much on the technological side but more on the adoption side. Will this be a long-term solution adopted by academics? Or will the value of a h-index matter more over time? The common problem of any start-up product market fit. Whatever the outcome this new breed of start-ups could build a new wave of innovation not just in blockchain, open-science, open sourcing, or decentralized science.

3. The dawn of a 3D Bio fabrication and Biomanufacturing Metaverse [Editorial Published October 2021] (Hardle, 2023)

This is taken or modified from an editorial I wrote and published online in October, 2021 (Hardle, 2020) for insight into how the plans of Cart Allum Blockchain Solutions came into existence. Prior to all the news surrounding Facebook's metaverse rebrand and $10 billion investment into the metaverse, the CEO of Ourobionics BV John Zandbergen and the CEO of blockchain company Cart Allum Blockchain Solutions were establishing a partnership in the Netherlands to initiate the development of the first global 3D Bio fabrication & Biomanufacturing Metaverse.

This new network that they envisioned will use blockchain technology to directly reward researchers and developers in cryptocurrency for their designs, protocols, and inventions using any existing 3D bio fabrication or biomanufacturing hardware, software, 3D model database, biomaterial database, or any open-sourced technology database. The start-ups have also developed a roadmap to work together with others and implement blockchain technology platform solutions for supply chain management in the 3D bio fabrication and biomanufacturing industry, stimulating a more circular economy.

Prior to the release of the independent and decentralized blockchain platform technology solutions by 2022, they will have the ability to be connected to all files, databases, and other metaverse platform technologies such as augmented reality, artificial intelligence systems, and gamification networks. The technologies will enable cryptocurrency and metaverse network rewards systems for all researchers and developers that want to open-source their designs, protocols, materials, data, technologies, and for publishing in open science journals. A secondary blockchain system will be developed to repeatedly reward the original inventors and creators further when their open-sourced technologies, 3D files, protocols, data, or open science publications are used by a collaborator for extended research purposes or a start-up/scale-up for commercial purposes.

This "3D Bio fabrication and Biomanufacturing Metaverse" has the potential to spur innovation, unique collaborations, and stimulate potential future biotechnology start-up formation. The concept is inspired by how the RepRap project open-sourced low-cost 3D printers to the public domain and this ultimately led to what one can see now in most of the desktop 3D printing and 3D bioprinting start-up industry. Basic extrusion 3D bioprinting was originally open sourced in 2016 to allow others to build a bioprinter with a RepRap.

If the proposed scientific advances are made in open-sourced technology, 3D bioprinting, regenerative medicine, blockchain, cyborganics, human-machine interfaces, and metaverse technologies it

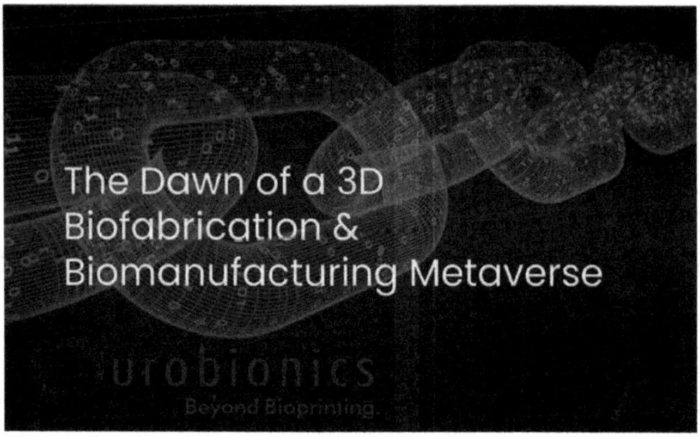

will enhance the strong biotechnology and deep technology ecosystem that currently exists in Utrecht Science Park, Utrecht Region, and start-ups located in other parts of the Netherlands. It has the potential to connect, build, and reward at a global level. On hearing the news, Tech Leap Envoy Prince Constantijn van Oranje, reacted enthusiastically: "This sounds like cutting edge technology development, supported by a solution to fairly rewarding innovators".

Together with other start-ups in the industry, they hope that developing these types of independent and decentralized blockchain technology rewards systems interconnected with existing and emerging metaverse network technologies will encourage academics, entrepreneurs, institutes, and industry professionals to publicly release and share more innovative open-sourced technologies, 3D designs, 3D biomaterials, cyborganics, organ on a chip, or regenerative medicine protocols and increase rewards for open science publications.

Companies in alliance with Ourobionics on the vision behind the need for the development of an open and global "3D Bioprinting & Biomanufacturing Metaverse" to enhance the fourth industrial revolution include the world's first human 3D bioink and biomaterial company Humabiologics; an early stage bio fabrication and biomanufacturing company InvicTech LLC (previously released microfluidic design NFTs); the open metaverse company Beemup paving the way forward in true metaverse interoperability, accessibility and economics, thereby directly providing new revenue models for businesses, brands and creators; and CadChain, a company that has released blockchain technology that provides an integrated and secure software to register authorship, and or ownership of design data, and trust certification for protection of CAD Files, thereby allowing engineers and designers to safely share their design data with stakeholders.

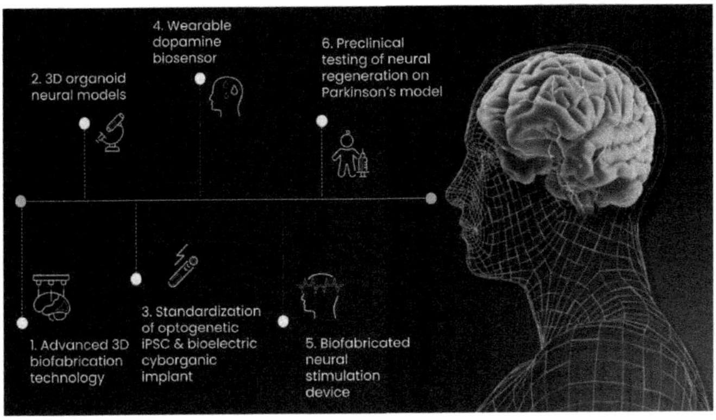

Figure 5.1. The development of a minimally invasive bio fabricated neural regenerative device to treat Parkinson's disease that could be connected to a wearable biosensor with blockchain driven cloud database.

The blockchain and metaverse technologies that have been developed (Figure 5.1) by CadChain and Beemup will be crucial for implementing and enhancing aspects needed for the 3d bio fabrication and biomanufacturing metaverse. CadChain has made some very important steps in using blockchain technology to protect intellectual property. The start-ups will explore forming consortia in the NL, EU, and the USA for non-dilutive funding opportunities to advance the progress of the blockchain-driven 3D bio fabrication and biomanufacturing metaverse. It will be important to ensure that the platforms are decentralized, independent of any one company, allow for new forms of virtual and augmented reality collaborations, and directly reward original inventors, engineers, designers, and researchers. These future technologies should be fully open to the public to ensure the future success and growth of the metaverse.

"After a decade developing new biofabrication technologies and biomaterials and the creation from scratch of a new industry, now the focus is on getting scientific results and procedures that can lead to tissues that can be transferred to specific applications. Any intention to connect the persons working in the field, reward the effort of them using crypto and blockchain and facilitating more resources to speed up the developments is crucial for the success of the field and the impact on the people´s quality of life" said José Manuel Baena, Ph.D. in biomedicine with 10 yr of experience in 3D bio fabrication.

This month a news article was published on the future role of neural interfaces in the metaverse. This directly coincides with the specific focus of the technologies under development at Ourobionics who were recently selected as "Deep Tech Pioneers" for 2021 out of 4,000 applications to the global deep technology organization Hello Tomorrow. Ourobionics are starting the process to raise seed funding alongside multiple funding applications to the Horizon Europe Program (budget of €95.5 billion) on the merging of their advanced 3D bio fabrication and cyborganic technologies to create novel cyborganic and opti-genetic stem cell neural stimulation devices with electronically conductive nanomaterials, bioinks, and biomarker skin sensor technologies for the detection and treatment of Parkinson's disease.

The main goal of Ourobionics is to develop these advanced 3D bio fabrication technologies and applications with the potential to transform the industry of regenerative medicine. Cyborganics itself was published as an emerging industry in 2019 spawned from 3D bio fabrication and biomaterial technologies by the Chief Technology Officer of Ourobionics, Dr. Alireza Dolatshahi-Pirouz. Any advancements made in cyberorganic biosensor and implantation devices could have future alternate uses when interconnected with blockchain technologies and the metaverse as it evolves in parallel with the human-machine interfacing technology industry.

One important factor to make this a success is the abundance of the metaverse, blockchain, augmented/virtual reality, A.I. platform technology, and 3D bio fabrication or biomanufacturing resources and start-ups within this sector that surround Ourobionics, Cart Allum, Beemup in Utrecht Science Park, and the city of Utrecht, the Netherlands. Utrecht also holds the title of gaming capital of Europe which is one component of a metaverse that can increase novel types of collaboration via augmented or virtual reality technologies. Such an interconnected metaverse could also increase the number of start-ups that would operate in Utrecht and the Netherlands in all forms of 3D biomanufacturing from health to food, textiles, and biofuels.

The Netherlands ranks third globally when combining world competitiveness rankings, world innovation rankings, human development index, and the world happiness report. Utrecht was once voted the fourth happiest city in the world. It is also one of the most interconnected countries, ranked first in English proficiency and has the highest density of cycle lanes. All of which is important for international entrepreneurs within the 3d bio fabrication and biomanufacturing and deep technology industries that need to build, connect, and grow outside of the metaverse.

The secondary component of this partnership will result in Cart Allum being able to work with Ourobionics and others in the industry to further develop their own sustainable blockchain technology into a platform with the ability to track, trace, and secure all aspects of the supply chain from hardware, biomaterials, reagents, cells, and accessories to final applications in the 3D bio fabrication, organ on a chip, regenerative medicine, *in silico*, medical device, or future human-machine interface industries. Working together the companies can decentralize the 3D bio fabrication supply chain and promote a more circular economy by refining the management of the entire supply chain.

These alternative supply chain systems have the potential to provide solutions to future supply chain disruptions, whilst boosting a more circular and sustainable economy. The start-ups are realistic in what can be done soon, but that it will be a long-term project with many combined efforts, milestones, and deliverables. However, it is important to make a start now that all the technologies are available and in alignment, as it is simply a matter of connecting the dots, releasing and connecting more platforms, whilst strengthening connections with those in the industry.

Overall, a 3D bio fabrication and biomanufacturing metaverse with novel supply chain solutions could potentially increase the level of global interdisciplinary collaborations, global technology sharing, rewarding of researchers and inventors, and enhance future start-up or academic spin-out formation. This is an important step for all sectors of deep technology and demonstrates the utility of metaverse and blockchain technologies outside of the hype.

By 2023 the plan of the start-ups is to expand this roadmap into all sectors that require the use of 3D bio fabrication and biomanufacturing technology in food, textiles, biofuels etc. This is one step on the roadmap originally set out by Ourobionics in early 2021 to take the industry beyond bioprinting and empower all researchers and developers at a global level.

The blockchain platform technologies under development by Cart Allum for the "3D Bio fabrication and Biomanufacturing Metaverse" will be tested and connected with other metaverse technologies such as augmented reality (like what is seen here with the hololens), artificial intelligence, and social network or gamification systems creating a new evolution in 3D bio fabrication and biomanufacturing collaboration and networking rewards. Platform technology solutions like the idea will be used to tag digital files (such as NFTs) that can then be uploaded to any existing database, alongside an artificial intelligence 3D bio fabrication database created to optimize the use of different 3D bio fabrication and biomaterial technologies needed for final applications in regenerative medicine and human-machine interfaces.

The "3D bio fabrication and biomanufacturing metaverse" will be decentralized and open to the public with the potential to strengthen the interconnection amongst the 3D bio fabrication community, enhance the level of collaboration, and utilize a cryptocurrency reward system for researchers, industry professionals, clinicians and other start-ups or stakeholders working with 3D bio fabrication, organ on a chip, tissue engineering, synthetic biology, regenerative medicine, and human-machine interface technologies.

An important step of their partnership will be in the development of an independent and decentralized sustainable "OuroCoin" in a collaboration that will connect and reward 3D bio fabrication and biomanufacturing researchers in cryptocurrency that can work with any online database, hardware or software to tag, trace, and reward the original researchers that created the digital 3D printable designs, 3D *in vitro* models, novel 3D biomaterials, custom 3D bio fabrication or biomanufacturing protocols, open-sourced technology, or publications in open science.

The future blockchain platform technologies that extend from the OuroCoin will be released and be independent decentralized platforms or entirely new start-ups open to the public domain and interconnected with other metaverse platforms and start-ups to enhance the level of new forms of collaboration between academic institutes, start-ups, scale-ups, citizen scientists, clinicians, and industry professionals. The second step is to work with other institutes and companies in alliance to further enhance the global 3D bio fabrication and biomanufacturing metaverse platform. By strengthening the consortia of global partnerships over time they aim to drive the full potential of what would be the future of "3D Bioprinting and Biomanufacturing Metaverse" to further enhance what is now known as the fourth industrial revolution "Industry 4.0".

Since the publication of this chapter the founder of Invictech created a platform known as *Ex Vivo*. *Ex Vivo* is an early-stage DAO that takes the concepts of my editorial and allows scientists and engineers to share and gain revenue from unused data, files, images, and protocols. Over time it will utilize Cart Allum blockchain when it has been fully rolled out.

4. What other industries can blockchain technology start-ups disrupt?

There is a lot of focus on the use of blockchain in the form of a banking system replacement or a new form of currency and digital asset. All these solutions are possible within blockchain technology, but the blockchain has the potential for so much more and I imagine with 5–10 yr there will be an abundance of blockchain companies using the technology for decentralized science, verification of research data and results, remuneration of scientists and engineers, supply chain management, data breach protection and more. These are the main areas that Cart Allum have focused their attention on but over time more can happen. Cart Allum's sustainable blockchain white paper could lead to licensing of technology to make and create the new generations of technology.

When one looks at the banking and finance sector one witnesses the largest organizations take charge from Blackrock to JP Morgan Chase. From a macro perspective blockchains can act as digitized, secure, and tamper proof ledgers to enhance accuracy and data sharing amongst financial powerhouses (cb Insights, 2022). JP Morgan Chase created the JPM Coin for cross-border payment facilitation and the same approach has been replicated by Goldman Sachs and Citigroup (cb Insights, 2022). If positioned correctly, blockchain can disrupt the $5 trillion banking industry by focusing on the creation of new solutions for key services that banks provide such as payments, clearance, and settlement. New start-ups that focus on payment facilitation will do well in this ecosystem as it is highly profitable for banks with B2B cross transactions expected to hit a valuation of $35 trillion alone (cb Insights, 2022).

One has witnessed the world's largest hedge fund Blackrock enter the blockchain world and this is probably due to the huge potential of blockchain in the world of buying, selling, and trading of stocks and hedge funds. Start-ups in this sector can automate and fully secure the process more than traditional methods (cb Insights, 2022). One subsidiary of overstock wants to use blockchain to enable stock transactions online. Their tZERO platform integrates cryptographically secure and distributed ledgers to reduce settlement times and costs (cb Iinsights, 2022). Similarly, the blockchain company chain helped build a live blockchain integration that connected Nasdaq's stock to Citigroup's banking infrastructure connected to Nasdaq's stock exchange. Nasdaq has even partnered with R3 to build Corda, a blockchain software that can be used by financial institutions to create and manage their own digital asset marketplace (cb Iinsights, 2022). Numerai is a start-up taking on the traditional hedge fund model and decentralizing it (cb Insights, 2022). It does so by sending thousands of independent quants encrypted datasets and gets them to build predictive models with those that create the best models to get rewarded in tokens (cb Insights, 2022).

Another industry that will benefit from blockchain software is crowdfunding. The existing industry already disintermediates capital formation by giving individual investors the ability to fund companies and entrepreneurs which fully aligns with blockchain capabilities. One example is the movie BRAID which was the first major feature film to be financed on the Ethereum blockchain via a $1.4 million campaign on Weifund (cb Insights, 2022). A Kickstarter and Indiegogo competitor called Pledgecamp wants to use transparent smart blockchain contracts to decentralize the process so that investors can see where and how the invested money is being spent and can provide input about the direction of the project (cb Insights, 2022).

In the automotive or travel industry there is a need to record and track physical assets for ownership and tamper proof resilient systems (cb Insights, 2022). Paper records are always prone to forgery and physical degradation, and data sets can be hacked or full of human error. Blockchain software technology is immutable and has more than one entity controlling the ledger so it is the solution for many of these issues (cb Insights, 2022). Blockchain software technology implemented into the supply chain system can have a positive impact on the automotive recalling which impacted 32 million vehicles in 2020. One consortium Mobility Open Blockchain Initiative is already working on a blockchain solution for the tracking and tracing of vehicle parts, vehicle birth certificates, and maintenance history. Blockchain software start-ups can also create an unfragmented sales process on all sides of the transaction. One example is car Vertical, a start-up with blockchain technology that can track car history and previous owners alongside insurance history (cb Insights, 2022).

Similar technologies can be plugged into the flight industry based on all the data that goes into booking of flights (cb Insights, 2022). Blockchain software can reconcile data to ensure a safer, more efficient journey. Smart contracts can speed up airlines security systems and create accurate logs of aircraft maintenance, etc. (cb Insights, 2022). The aerospace and defense industry seems to be pushing more into the use of blockchain with over 61% of companies using blockchain or distributed ledger technology according to accenture (cb Insights, 2022). One marketplace Go Direct Trade uses blockchain ledger technology for maintenance and manufacturing histories of its 25,00 parts for resale (cb Insights, 2022).

In the hospitality industry hotel chains lose 30% of their revenue in commissions to third party booking services with small chains losing 18–22% of their revenue to third parties (cb Insights, 2022). Blockchain technology can change this and ensure that those in the hotel industry get a larger portion of the sales. One start-up in this space winding tree is already building a decentralized B2B travel market place (cb Insights, 2022). Similarly, the highly regulated construction industry requires a blockchain system to verify identities of tradespeople, quality of work and dependability. Blockchain software can solve this challenge by making it simpler for general contractors to track progress across teams and sectors (cb Insights, 2022). The Amsterdam-based company Heren Bouw already uses a blockchain to document the transaction system to improve large development projects in the city for more accurate, audible records (cb Insights, 2022).

In the property industry there are many pain points due to the lack of transparency during the transactional stages with endless paperwork, fraud potential and errors in public records (cb Insights, 2022). Blockchain software reduces the paper-work and speeds up the transactions in the real estate industry. It can also record, track/trace, and verify transfer of land titles or wills (cb Insights, 2022). Similarly, when one looks at the energy industry several start-ups will appear and grow here because of the fact that distributed blockchain ledgers can minimize or eliminate the need for intermediaries. One start-up example in this space is LO3 Energy focused on changing the energy exchange process with an open sourced blockchain (cb Insights, 2022). When one looks at the oil and gas industry, blockchain can automate and enhance the ability to validate and enforce contracts between stakeholders in the supply chain (cb Insights, 2022). It is already being done by Abu Dhabi National Oil Company to track production quantities and reduces the time to execute transactions (cb Insights, 2022).

5. Conclusion

Rather than going into great detail all of these same core principles and use cases surrounding blockchain software technologies can be applied by new start-ups to multiple industries including: the insurance industry, inheritance industry, healthcare (Health verity), genomic data (Vulpine Labs Inc, Zenome, Encrypgen), research and clinical trials, mining (DeBeers-Tracr), fishing (ConsenSys), pharmaceutical industry (Chronicled), agricultural (Agridigital), retail (Bleexy, ConsenSys), claims (Change Healthcare), cannabis (MileHighLabs), education (Hyland Credentials), entertainment (MediaChain) logging (Veridium Labs) business sectors (cb Insights, 2022).

Some of the main issues surrounding the use of blockchain technology in start-ups such as decentralized science or open science include scalability. The scalability of blockchain systems is an issue in very large systems and many technologies experience severe congestion, increased latency and costs. Cart Allum Blockchain Solutions attempts to resolve this with a more sustainable blockchain technology detailed below. Over time it is anticipated many more blockchain companies will appear and build across every industry.

6. Cart Allum Blockchain Solutions White Paper (Dawson, 2021); Modified version of original publication March 17, 2021

This white paper proposes a new blockchain ecosystem based on a multi-dimensional Merkle tree and will use consensus models, depending on the function or application defined at the root level. The consensus models used will include Delegated Proof-of-Stake (DPoS), Hybrid Proof-of-Work (HPoW), Proof-by-Mutual-Agreement (PbMA), Proof-by-Settlement (PbS) and Proof-by-Verification (PbV). Using the appropriate consensus model depending on the function or application requirement at the root level, allows for complete parallelism and extremely fast processing times of transactions. Every action will be timestamped using a UTC timestamp that will be relative to the source and then standardized in the blockchain. All participants will be rewarded for their work with a proportional fee. Any false or tampered transactions will cost the participant their transaction fee plus a fine and an administrative fee. Disputes will be handled by the system at a minimal fee and any positive outcomes of a dispute will restore the fee back to the user of the successful dispute. All transactions and actions, true or false, will be added to the blockchain ecosystem, thus giving 100% transparency of the end-to-end process. Verification nodes will be distributed across the ecosystem that will intermittently do audits on assigned layers of the blockchain ecosystem. No single distributed node will ever hold all the information, which will ensure that no one or multiply parties working together will ever be able to manipulate the network with a majority attack. For financial applications in a particular blockchain ecosystem, the ownership of an artifact will stay with the owner, although it will be moved to escrow on the initiation of a transaction. It will only be released once the settlement and verification have been completed. This will ensure that there will be no hold-up in transactions processing and block creation, as this process will be part of the block design. Any tampering or false claims will be visible in the blockchain ecosystem as will disputes and reversals. The ownership of an artifact can be classified into three states: (1) 'owned'; (2) 'in escrow'; and (3) 'in dispute'. The various mutations between these states will be managed by the various fault tolerant nodes within the ecosystem, grouped in an organic pod system.

The Cart Allum Blockchain Ecosystem is an implementation of multi-level fault tolerant replicated state machines grouped together in pods (forests). In a pod (forest), there can be multiple trees, each with its own branches and consensus model configuration. This is a result of the unique block and network design. The best way to visualize the system, is to think of how the human body and the nervous system works.

The network will start with the main state machine and a single functional state machine spawned from the main network that will support the initial digital application. As the network grows, new state machines will be added for any new digital application added and registered on the central state machine and all the other existing state machines. Initial consensus will be handled through a delegated proof of stake consensus model, where guardians will request to be added to a pool of leadership stakeholders. Participants in the relevant state machine will elect new leadership stakeholders from the election ballot. Elected stakeholders will elect a leader for each block from the pool of leadership stakeholders registered at the time. Elections for the leadership role will be independent of the size of the stake and will be started as soon the previous block is added to the chain.

These various nodes will split into functional groups that will manage subscriptions, delegation of leaders and guardians; run elections to elect leaders and guardians; verify and register/deregister pod-leaders (forest guards or guardians) and participants; register and verify new forests, trees, and branches; archive 'ancient' forests and trees.

Some applications added to the ecosystem, might require different consensus models to be efficient, and will be handled at the time of registration. As the blocks are defined with their own 'intelligence' built in, it will be possible to update a consensus as required or as new algorithms are added or discovered.

The longevity of Bitcoin can probably be attributed to the fact that it focuses on a specific solution and all the entries in the blockchain (and distributed ledger), is directly related to the history of Bitcoin transactions. Although a lot of systems are using this to underpin and implement different solutions, the base of Bitcoin is still the ownership and movement of Bitcoin. While the Proof-of-Work algorithm has its drawbacks and there are certain future issues that Bitcoin will still be subjected to, the solution in its purest form, is still one of the best, because of its simplicity.

Taking the lessons learned from Bitcoin and most of the other blockchain networks, the Cart Allum Blockchain Ecosystem is designed from the ground up, take what is good in current systems, start with the simplest of solutions, but have the power to be adaptable as it grows to support different solutions, without compromising the integrity of the existing networks.

Cart Allum's blockchain ecosystem will address the following issues identified and found within current distributed public, private and hybrid blockchains systems:

a) Rework the monolithic application implementations of current blockchain systems. The problem with most, if not all, of the current blockchain systems are that once they are setup and running, it is next to impossible to amend the consensus models, or underlying structures, without invalidating the integrity of what is already secured and written to the blockchain ledger. It also means that different types of applications that use a specific blockchain system to secure its 'ledger of transactions or actions' are stuck with the implementation that it started with, unless everything is 'replayed and saved to another system' which is counterintuitive to what blockchain wants to achieve.
b) Increase the speed of transaction throughput that currently limit the general adoption of blockchain solutions in time-critical systems, where a high-volume of transactions, are processed by customers expecting to have sub-second responses and completions, and with high security and integrity guards. Banks and processors today

process transactions at over 10,000 transactions per second and most blockchain systems cannot support this in its current form.

c) No mutational, end-of-period, or historical archiving possibilities for old, out-of-date data, or data falling under different statute of limitations retention requirements are available on most of the current blockchain solutions. This, while keeping the integrity of the existing blockchain, blockchain branch or shard.

d) Remove the reliance on the fact that all transactions on the blockchain should be true and correct. Cart Allum's blockchain will record the good and bad transactions in its historical blockchain records and bad transactions will be marked as such, once proved. This will be used to identify rogue participants within the system and automate an electronic judicial system. It is believed that using the immutability of the blockchain to give an accurate record of all good, bad, and suspicious actions, can improve the transparency that can be used to identify and sanction, limit, or remove participants and rogue operatives.

e) Remove the reliance or constraint on the timing of transactions that requires the correct ordering for the integrity of the blocks and transactions on a blockchain. There will be multiple metadata time elements saved with each transaction and block, but late transactions and actions should not stop the processing and addition of blocks. Transactions that cannot be proven within a block will be marked as such and added to an open transaction set that will be handled on the next available block.

f) Remove the reliance on bigger third-party miners or stakeholders that creates an ecosystem, where the smaller participants do not have a realistic chance of competing with participants with almost unlimited resources. Cart Allum will implement a system where participation will be equal, but rewards will be proportional. It is important that one does not devalue the contribution of bigger participants, but one needs to balance this against one of the challenges of the trilemma, in decentralization. This is in complete contrast where both participation and rewards are proportional and favors the participants with the most resources and leads to a less than optimal decentralization implementation of the network. It is believed that there will be enough chance for the fortunate to gain a good return on investment, but this should not be to the detriment of the participation of those who are not as fortunate.

g) Remove the dependency on a single or one-dimensional Merkel branched blockchain. This addresses one of the sustainability issues identified in current blockchain systems, where blockchains are just one long chain of records that keeps on getting bigger, without the possibility of adapting to evolving requirements, market forces and new developments. As an example, some of the blockchains systems, like Ethereum, Cardano, Solana and similar solutions that have different decentralized applications (DAPP's) running against them as a ledger, have a lot of unrelated information all grouped together in a single chain.

h) Establish an economy of scale solution to address the difference in equality, between countries and people who have plenty of resources that can dominate the cryptocurrency space against parts of the world who do not have the resources to compete. There is a lot of talent going waste in countries where resources, are scarce or economies of scale price legitimate participants out of the market. This can be basic resources some take for granted, like electricity, running water, good living standards and conditions, safety, and access to the internet, which is seen as a human right or necessity in some countries, but in most of the world it is still seen as a luxury.

Solving the blockchain trilemma has been the holy grail of achievements that has eluded all the implementations of blockchain solutions thus far.

Security

There are still concerns, around the vulnerability and security of the private keys and the reliance on keeping a private key under lock and key and safe from parties that are constantly trying to break into systems and wallets to misuse these. At this point, it is a single point of failure in all the decentralized blockchain systems. The fact that some integrity of the whole blockchain can be compromised, by rogue actors, if they can misuse stolen private keys, are a threat that is not only real, but there are well known instances of this occurring. This has led to countless companies opting for a more centralized system, to keep tighter control on the security of their members and their private credentials. It also means that it is less scalable, as adding new parties to the system is not as easy and more KYC is required than would be possible or advisable under a fully decentralized system, where 'anybody' can join, by installing and running a node. This inevitably leads to one of the legs of the Triangle breaking two of the others.

Decentralization

When processes and artefacts are delegated away from a central authority. For a fully decentralized distributed blockchain network, it means that all nodes in the decentralized network can be run completely autonomous and no one node or small set of nodes can control or determine the outcome of the state of the network.

What else?

There is a fourth part of any technology solution and that is the 'First Mover Advantage'. In the decentralized and cryptocurrency space this is Bitcoin and to a lesser extent Ethereum, but as one can see from history, being the first solution in the technology space, does not always mean that it will be a lasting, only, or final solution. This should be seen as an opportunity, as the first mover lays a trail and brings the technology to a global audience. It is up to the followers to build on the success of the first mover, but bring their own brand with marked improvements, new innovations or improved and new functionality.

First mover advantage examples

Netscape (founded April 4, 1994; 27 yr ago), but now we have **Google** (Launched 1997; 25 yr ago), although it was only in August 2009 that Google invested and improved their services, by moving their backend indexing service into Bigtable, that Google really became the go to search engine as it improved its speed and indexing service. What is still not such a well-known fact, is that Google search and indexes only covers a small percentage of the internet, as most of the internet (estimated at 90%+) are located at DNS inaccessible servers, called the Deep Web.

Block design

CBE will implement a unique block design to enable the following:

- dedicated decentralized applications at Layer-n
- increase speed of transaction processing (TPS)
- configurable consensus algorithm
- easier incorporation, connections, or interoperability with other blockchain systems
- enhanced networking capability
- archival functionality and possibility

The block design is considered the integral part for making the Cart Allum Blockchain Ecosystem as one wants to support the current and the future possibilities of digital applications. To start, l the focus will be on the basic functionality and will add functionality and decentralized application support, as one grows and expands.

When designing the block, I used some experiences from what I have learned and implemented over the years in the real-time transaction processing systems and the autonomy of a transactional message to exist and be processed over time and in parallel across various systems, as it is passed from one to the other.

A transaction block will consist of header records, data records, linked file specific records, and set of footer and signature records. It will not be necessary to have all the elements as some will be optional depending on the configuration, and elements will be enabled/disabled, depending on the digital application implementation.

The header record will hold the number of records, the length of all the records contained and the offsets an array with the offsets where each transaction record start. It will also hold the pre-defined or agreed conditions for the transactions to be added in the block. This will depend on the DAPP application using the block.

The transaction or data record will hold the transactions and any new transaction will be added to the end of the data record, while the block is still open, and the transactions satisfy the entry requirements to be entered into the block. If not, the transactions will be added to the next open block where it satisfies the entry requirements. If it does not satisfy any of the entry requirements for any current open block, it will trigger a process to create a new block and start an election process of the leader of that block. The actual process will depend on the defined block configuration and current agreed consensus model of the block. This can be changed if the choice exists for the type of digital application defined in the specific blockchain.

The data record is not limited by the number transactions or size of the block, as it is done in most of the blockchain systems that currently exist. How the block will be defined, depends on the application linked to the blockchain implementation, the entry requirements to be placed in an open block.

The block design gives the flexibility for different types of digital applications to implement different requirements on block level, depending on the type of the digital application, the available consensus models for the type of application, the scalability requirements, as well as the speed requirement of the block and underlying transactions.

Network design

As described earlier, our network can be visualized as the human body and its nervous system, but the autonomy will not be controlled by the brain alone, but by each individual functional branch of the system. The brain or central foundation will only be there to ensure the development, maintenance, and integrity of the programmatic building blocks of the system, but even there, participants in the network will be elected on a rotational basic to oversee the integrity and transparency of the inner workings of this body.

Throughout the network, our mantra will be implemented of *"**participation will be equal, and reward will be proportional**"*.

The networkers

To be able to implement our network, the following initial node types, roles, and groups/pools within the system will be defined (*this is the current design, but does not limit the system to be expanded with new types*):

NODE TYPE

- Management node
- System node
- Participant node
- Leader node
- Guardian, validator, or replication node
- Overflow node
- Verification node
- Settlement node
- Reconciliation node
- Smart contract node
- Archive node

ROLES

- Digital applications (DAPP) users
- DAPP election administrator
- DAPP leader
- DAPP guardians
- DAPP verifier
- DAPP dispute officer
- DAPP judicial officer
- Board member

GROUPS/POOLS

- Participant pool per DAPP
- DAPP leadership
- Election pool
- Leadership pool

- Verification pool
- Functional pool
- Board leadership
- Sanctioned
- Probation
- Excluded

There are certain exclusions, that will apply to the membership(s) across groups/pools.

- Participant in a DAPP cannot have any leadership role on the DAPP
- Participant or leadership member in a DAPP cannot have any membership in a functional pool on the DAPP
- The participant cannot be in more than 50% of the leadership pools of the total number of registered DAPP's and will not be allowed into the election pool as a candidate, until this ratio is smaller than 50% again.

The general inner workings from within a network

At any given time, a leadership node will be assigned to be the designated elected leader in charge of a specific block or set of blocks within a designated pod and will generate a 'Proof of Traceability' or 'Proof of History' sequence of the transactions within the block, providing the network global read consistency and a verifiable passage of trace-transparency and time. The leader assigns transactions to a designated block, sequences the transactions or user messages within the block and orders them such that they can be efficiently processed by the other nodes in the system, maximizing throughput. It executes the transactions on the current state that is stored and publishes the transactions with a signature of the final state to the replication nodes within the designated pod, that is monitored by the guardians.

If a transaction falls outside the designated entry requirements of any open block, the leader will pass the transaction to the overflow node, where the current assigned distribution officer will verify this against all open blocks. If it finds an open block that satisfies the entry requirement of transaction, it will pass the transaction to that leader for processing. If no open block satisfies the transaction's entry requirements, it will be passed to the election administrator node that will start a process of setting up a new block with specific entry requirements and start the leadership election to elect the leader to take ownership of the new block.

For blocks placed on the replication nodes, the guardians will then execute or verify the assigned transactions on their copies of the state and publish their computed signatures of the state as confirmations or votes. The published confirmations serve as votes for the consensus algorithm.

In a non-partitioned network, at any given time, there is one primary leader. Each guardian node can become a leader node through a subscription-based or candidate staking election process and a delegated Proof-of-Stake algorithm. The election configuration is defined per designated pod. The Delegated PoS algorithm is covered in depth next.

If other consensus models are defined on the designated pod, then the steps will be followed to reach consensus on the block using the defined algorithm.

The addressable network

The normal network implementation of current decentralized solutions, use IPv4, as their choice of adding nodes into the network. The problem with this is that there is already an issue due to the public addressable and available IPv4 addresses left. It means that most of the systems, will have to either piggy-back onto an existing public addressable IPv4 address, or will have to somehow find a way to acquire more IPv4 addresses, to ensure that the network is scalable to the nth degree. A lot of the blockchain systems have claimed that they are aiming to be decentralized to 5 billion people (where every person will have to own their own node and be publicly addressable over the internet). The current available publicly addressable IPv4 addresses is 2^{32}, which is equal to 4,294,967,296 addresses. So, even, if all the IPv4 addresses were available, which they are not, it is less than 5 billion (5,000,000,000) that a lot of these systems claim to be aiming for.

A better solution would be to build the network natively on IPv6, which will give one a possible 2^{128} (3.4×10^{38}, or 340 trillion) unique IP addresses.

Using this as the basis for our nodes and having that combined into the direct address of each node, with the hash of the respected user, and some other user specific information, gives one direct addressability and an identity specific security that will make sure the network is more transparent, including the address of the node into the calculation and signature of the block on the chain will add the traceability used within one of our consensus models and it means that ownership of a proven artifact can be traced directly to the owner of a node.

Participation

To participate in the network, a user can become a DAPP user, an authoritative stakeholder, a non-functional stakeholder, or a node implementer. This is the current type of participant. New participants and roles might be added as the systems and requirements grow.

A DAPP user

A DAPP user without being a stakeholder, means you are using a digital application that interacts with the Cart Allum Blockchain Ecosystem. This type of participant does not have to maintain a state machine of the blockchain but interacts with a specific blockchain and have voting rights to participate in the election guardians and leaders.

An Authoritative Stakeholder

An Authoritative Stakeholder, installs and runs a guardian, validator, or replication node. They then have the choice to participate in the network in the following ways (these are mutually):

- stake a percentage of their cryptocurrency to be entered into the leadership election pool
- stake a percentage of their cryptocurrency to be entered into the board level election pool
- stake a percentage of their cryptocurrency to be added to the judiciary pool
- stake a percentage of their cryptocurrency to be added to the functional pool
- they can also just choose to become a normal voting member for a greatly reduced stake, but cannot join more than 50% of the total number of DAPP pools available

There are certain exclusions for membership to pools, to ensure that a stakeholder cannot be in the leadership pool and functional pool of the same DAPP. A stakeholder can only join a pool, if they have a sufficient percentage of cryptocurrency left, as required by the pool they enter.

All the rewards will be compensated at the current going rate of the cryptocurrency reward scheme when they are elected to the position. The rewards will be proportional to the stake or a fixed fee, depending on the agreement contract when they joined the specific DAPP as stakeholder.

A Non-functional Stakeholder

A Non-Authoritative Stakeholder, installs and runs a functional node for a DAPP or a set of DAPP's. They do not participate in elections or can put their names forward for elections to become leaders or guardians of a validator node to create or validate a block.

They can put their name forward to become board members or judiciary members through the relevant election process, and this will require them to stake a percentage of their cryptocurrency to participate.

Their reward is a fixed fee depending on the function. The functional nodes cannot alter or confirm the state of the designated DAPP and blockchain, instead they run utility functions to verify and do other non-intrusive maintenance and checks on the assigned blockchain.

A Node Implementor

A Node Implementor runs a node to maintain the main chain, application chain, a DAPP or multiple DAPP's, they do not participate in any other activity, except adding to the expansion of the decentralized network.

They can upgrade to become an Authoritative or Non-Authoritative Stakeholder.

They earn rewards for uptime and replication speed.

Consensus Models/Algorithms

The following Consensus Models/Algorithms will be used, depending on the function, chain, or pod within the Cart Allum Blockchain Ecosystem:

- Consensus model description mentioned earlier Delegated Proof-of-Stake (DPoS) mentioned earlier
- Hybrid Proof-of-Work (HPoW) mentioned earlier
- Proof-by-Mutual-Agreement (PbMA) mentioned earlier
- Proof-by-Settlement-Process (PbSP) mentioned earlier
- Proof-by-Verification (PbV) mentioned earlier
- Proof-of-History (PoH) mentioned earlier
- Proof-of-Traceability (PoT) mentioned earlier

In the current blockchain marketplace there are various consensus algorithms defined and used in the following blockchain systems:

- Proof of Work (PoW) Bitcoin, Ethereum Classic, Litecoin, Doge, etc.
- Proof of Stake (PoS) Cardano, Ethereum 2.0, Nextcoin, Purecoin, etc.
- Delegated Proof of Stake (DPoS) Lisk, EOS, Bitshare, Ark
- Proof of Authority (PoAut) Vechain THOR, POA
- Proof of Capacity (PoCap) Chia, Burstcoin, SpaceMint
- Proof of Weight (PoW) Algorand, Filecoin, Chia
- Proof of Importance (PoI) nem
- Proof of Burn (PoB) Slimcoin, TGcoin
- Proof of Activity (PoAct) decred
- Practical Byzantine Fault Tolerance (PBFT) Hyperledger, Zilliqa
- Federated Byzantine Agreement (FBA) Ripple, Stellar
- Delegated Byzantine Fault Tolerance (DBFT) Neo
- Directed Acyclic Graphs (DAG) IOTA, Nano, Byteball

- Proof of Existence (PoE)
- Proof of Elapsed Time (PoET)
- Proof of Believability (PoB)
- Proof of Service (PoSrvc)
- Proof of Contribution (PoContrib)
- Proof of History (PoH) Solana

For our implementation, which would focus on the use of consensus for purpose, the consensus algorithms can and should be categorized. From various sources these categories are currently proposed as:

- Proof of Work
- Chain-based Proof-of-Stake
- Hybrid consensus models, e.g., Proof-of-Activity, Hybrid PoW, Hybrid PoS
- Proof-of-Burn
- Proof-of-Capacity/Space
- Byzantine methods, including Practical Byzantine Fault Tolerant (PBFT)
- Directed Acyclic Graphs (DAG)
- Trusted Computing Algorithms

**** for more information on all the above algorithms and details on how each of them works, and the implementations, please contact me for an addendum to explain them all*

- **Proof-of-Work (PoW):** The legacy Proof of Work mechanism of Bitcoin is considered a secure and efficient algorithm to reach a consensus within a blockchain network. However, the Ethereum Classic hack in 2020 revealed that PoW is penetrable and that nefarious actors can exploit networks using the PoW mechanism. Though Bitcoin's PoW has never been hacked, it is open to 51% attacks, if any one verifier/miner amasses enough processing power or can pool together to get close to the 51% processing power. This method has also received a lot of criticism for being energy expensive. The larger the energy requirement gets to confirm a block, the more the chance will exist that the threshold of 51% can be reached and the value within the Bitcoin blockchain can be manipulated. Now there are still enough miners to be able to secure and verify a block and keep the integrity of the blockchain. This, however, is not a hypothesis that was foreseen by the creator of Bitcoin, as it means the closer, one gets to the ceiling of the 21 million Bitcoins the more energy would have to be spent to mine a single block and work out the mathematical problem to secure the block on the blockchain. At this late stage with estimations of the worth of the chain and the value of Bitcoin done by pro-Bitcoin analysts and even under worst case scenarios, the number of miners left to spend this amount of energy will be down to a small number of parties being able to afford this. This will be the time, when the Bitcoin network, will be at its most vulnerable and if one assumes the worst case, the value and impact can be catastrophic on all the trust and value built up over the years. Therefore the 'cheap' energy being turned into a Bitcoin currency, is a very good idea now, if one extrapolates the amount of energy required to mine the final Bitcoin blocks (expected by 2140), it would be inconceivable that there would be enough energy, even considering using cheap and energy on the outer rims of existence.

- **Proof-of-Stake (PoS)**: For the reason mentioned above, Proof of Stake has started to gain in popularity. It is more energy efficient and does not require heavy machinery for creating and validating new blocks. It also has an increased throughput speed, however, like its predecessor, PoS is also vulnerable to 51% attacks as well as manipulation of stakeholders.

This chapter discusses PoW and PoS, as well as their security vulnerabilities. Along with that, let us discuss Proof of Authority (PoA) and try to scrutinize if it is the most secure consensus mechanism out in the market:

Description

Each of the mentioned consensus models can be used independently or as a synchronous system of models where more complex consensus steps to reach consensus are required. The system is designed to use these consensus models/algorithms, depending on the block, function and/or pod configuration.

The models required and work to be completed for each will be detailed next.

The system will use cryptographic hash functions and algorithms to automate the calculations and as this is not a one-dimensional system, these calculations will be done in parallel, in various nodes, increasing the speed of the system as it grows, opposed to slowing down, as most of the current blockchain ecosystems using a single monolithic chain that keeps on growing and use a fixed consensus model for all functions and consensus.

One aims to show that using a decentralized multi-dimensional fit-for-purpose system, can speed up the system as it grows.

Delegated-Proof-of-Stake (DPoS)

The Cart Allum implementation of the DPoS algorithm use the following steps:

- Users within the ecosystem subscribe/register to the pod where they want to become a guardian/validator.
- Users cannot subscribe or apply to the pod if they are a participant.
- Participants and non-Authoritative stakeholders registered as voters only within the pod, vote and approve delegates from the subscription list to become a guardian/validator.
- Once approved each guardian/validator goes into an elected official list where a round robin process will assign a leader per block of transactions.
- The election leader will determine if new members are allowed and will arrange voting rolls with enrolled candidates as well as run the elections, once this is required
    - the requirement to have new elections for guardians/validators in a specific pod, would be when (1) an elected official retires; (2) an elected official is sanctioned; (3) there is an increase in the required percentage of required elected officials; (4) an elected official is removed, due to exceeding the non-participation rules defined by the pod
- If the total number of guardians/validators will be 'n,' then:

  'n–1' where '1' is the leader will act as guards on a first come first validate rule, until 66% of the total number of guardian/validators have agreed consensus, as calculated by the leader. The algorithm will use a proof-of-traceability calculation from the current block of transactions and a random pre-configured number of transactions will be used in the calculation by each guardian.
- Delegates are called witnesses or block producers.
- Using DPoS, you can vote on delegates by pooling your tokens into a staking pool and linking those to a particular delegate. You do not physically transfer your tokens to another wallet, but instead utilize a staking service provider to stake your tokens in a staking pool.
- A limited number of delegates (most protocols choose between 20 and 100) are chosen for each new block, so delegates of one block might not be delegates of the next.
- Elected delegates receive the transaction fees from the validated block, and that reward is then shared with users who pooled their tokens in the successful delegate's pool.

- The more one stakes, the higher a share of the block reward one receives. The rewards are shared based on each user's stake; so, if one's stake represents 5% of the total staking balance, one will receive 5% of the block reward.

The first iteration of DPoS was developed in 2014 by the former EOS Chief Technology Officer (CTO), Dan Larimer. Larimer first implemented the consensus algorithm on decentralized crypto exchange platform BitShares in 2015. Today, several blockchains, including Cardano, Solana, EOS, Steemit, BitShares and TRON use DPoS.

Pro's:

- Cheaper transactions
- Scalable
- Energy efficient
- Coin age does not matter and moving coins is less costly
- All mature coins have the same stake weight/value
- Downtime and large inputs will significantly impact the stakeholders interest under DPoS, which would force stakeholders to be online and available

Con's:

- Partially centralized—the election of Delegated Stake Holders
- Stakeholders not being available, impacts the security and integrity of the network

Hybrid-Proof-of-Work (HPoW)

The Hybrid-Proof-of-Work consensus model/algorithm is designed to be much more energy efficient and incentivizes smaller miners and participants to join and contribute to the network. It removes the reliance on a huge mining reward but incentivizes solo miners who contribute directly to the network.

It does rely on a larger number of nodes to guarantee fault tolerance and the network becomes more decentralized and more secure, with every new node that is added to the network.

It still uses the standard PoW algorithm, but incentivizes the miners who do not only mine, but who use the network as well.

This contrasts with how standard PoW with huge mining farms that work only to gain the huge mining rewards and do not contribute to the network or grow the network with new participants and nodes. Current participants will just increase its mining operation and it gets harder to enter the network once the difficulty expects a major investment and expenditure of energy to mine the next block.

Pro's:

- Unprofitable mining
- Allows a greater diversity of miners and participants
- The bigger the network, the more secure and decentralized it gets

Con's:

- Need a large diversity of nodes and participants to get to a point of fault tolerance, so is not suitable for only a small number of participants
- Ability to attract large investment of resources and funds, might be compromised, if this is used as the only model

Proof-by-Mutual-Agreement (PbMA)

The Proof-by-Mutual-Agreement consensus model/algorithm is designed to be used with contractual applications on the network. It will allow a contract to go through several iterations or mutations until a final agreement can be reached between all parties involved and will then be checked and signed by a random validator on the relevant network and added to the network as an independent block related to a specific contract.

The conceptual working of this consensus algorithm is still in beta state, and more detail will be added to new versions of the White Paper, once it has been completed.

The design and implementation of the network, enables the function specific digital and decentralized applications to be added once they become available.

As this is work in progress, setting up pro's.

Proof-by-Settlement-Process (PbSP)

The Proof-by-Settlement-Process consensus model/algorithm is designed to group together a set of blocks on a blockchain and write a new settlement block, to confirm the integrity of the current chain, from when the previous settlement block was added. This is a randomized periodic function using a DPoS and PoT underlying a set of functions to ensure the validity of the relevant network.

It also means that the integrity of the network is guaranteed using a four-eyed-principle and shortens the length of having to verify the network from the genesis record.

It is the system required by the network to be able to have the archival ability.

This process will also verify the current state of the currency if this is the only function of the network. The blocks dropped into the network by this process/algorithm, will link the network to the other networks in the multi-dimensional Merkle-tree.

Proof-by-Verification (PbV)

The Proof-by-Verification consensus model/algorithm works similarly to PbSP algorithm as was described earlier, but this was designed specifically to enable governance from authorities and central banks, if required.

The conceptual working of this consensus algorithm is still in beta state, and more detail will be added to new versions of the White Paper, once it has been completed.

The design and implementation of the network, enables the function specific digital and decentralized applications to be added once they become available.

*** *The following algorithms are not consensus models to the letter of the definition, but instead is used as a consensus algorithm or method within each block of transactions or set of records within a block. Thus, it will form the basis where the set of transactions within a block will be guaranteed to be added in a specific sequence and that no injection of transactions can occur within the block layer. It gives and assures that the block, the leader, primary or counterparty receives cannot be tampered with by other validators working on the same thread.*

Proof-of-History (PoH)

The Proof of History (PoH) algorithm to reach consensus in a transaction block relies on cryptographic methods and hash algorithms to create a reliable ordering of transactions/events recorded to the 'ledger'. This is achieved by including a timestamp into metadata of each transaction. This will solve the issue of agreement on ordering and time, and it allows for almost instant finality of hundreds of thousands of transactions per second.

The system is designed to work as follows:

- With a keyed or unkeyed cryptographic hash function, whose output cannot be predicted without running the function (examples of hash functions: MD5, MD6 (keyed or unkeyed), sha128, sha256, sha512, ripemd, etc.), run the function from some random starting value and take its output and pass it as the input into the same function again.
- Record the number of times the function has been called and the output at each call.
- The starting random value chosen could be any string, like the abstract of this White Paper.

For example:

PoH Sequence Index Operation Output

1) HASH1: sha256 ("starting value") = hash1
2) HASH2: sha256 (hash1) = hash2
3) HASH3: sha256 (hash2) = hash3

Where hash N represents the actual hash output. It is only necessary to publish a subset of the hashes and indices at an interval.

Index Operation Output

1) HASH1: sha256 ("starting value") = hash1
2) HASH200: sha256 (hash199) = hash200
3) HASH300: sha256 (hash299) = hash300

If the hash function chosen is collision resistant, this set of hashes can only be computed in sequence by a single computer thread. This follows from the fact that there is no way to predict what the hash value at index 300 is going to be without running the algorithm from the starting value 300 times. Thus, one can infer from the data structure that real time has passed between index 0 and index 300.

In the example to the left, hash 62f51643c1 was produced on count 510144806912 and hash c43d862d88 was produced on count 510146904064. Following the previously discussed properties of the PoH algorithm, one can trust that real time passed between count 510144806912 and count 510146904064.

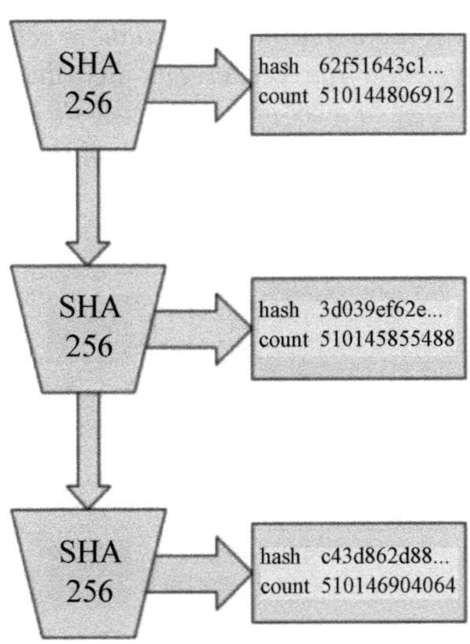

Then with some event or data:

The sequence of hash calculations can also account for some event, metadata or data being added, before the next hash was calculated, as follows:

1) HASH1: sha256 ("starting value") = hash1
2) HASH300: sha256 (hash299) = hash300
3) HASH333: sha256 (append (hash332, event/data hash)) = hash333
4) HASH334: sha256 (hash333) = hash334

It means hash333 is calculated from the previous hash, hash332 and the hash of the event or data appended into a binary datagram, so that the previous hash and the event/data is now part of the historical sequence output.

In the example to the left, the input cfd40df8... was inserted into the Proof of History sequence. The count at which it was inserted is 510145855488 and the state at which it was inserted it is 3d039eef3. All the future generated hashes are modified by this change to the sequence, this change is indicated by the color change in the figure.

Every node observing or validating this sequence of events can determine and validate the order that events or data was added to the sequence, by verifying the real time between the insertions.

Verification can occur in parallel, by all the assigned Guardians or Validators. The verification process can happen in significantly less time by each validator, using a multicore computer, by splitting up the given data into the same number of slices as available cores and then verifying in parallel each of the hash calculations of the slice per core.

*** *It is important to note that not one validator will receive all the hashed transactions to validate, and the Leader will distribute the total number of transactions to be validated in a set of randomized slices of the whole, in such a manner that 100% coverage will be attained over all the validators.*

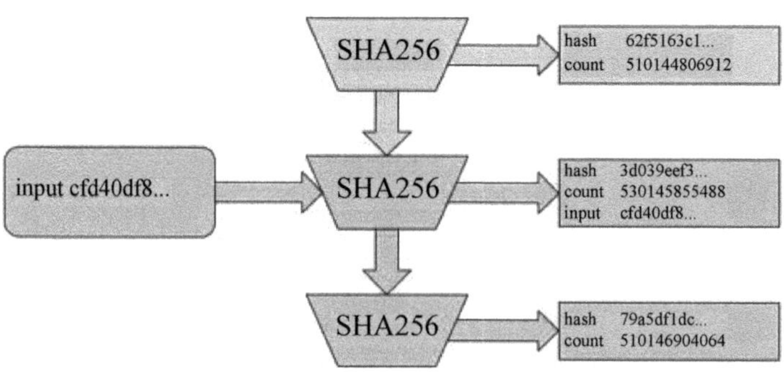

Proof-of-Traceability (PoT)

The Proof of Traceability is based on the Proof of History algorithm, but also includes unique identifiers per transaction linked to the data within the transaction and/or the origin of the transaction. This enables the direct traceability of the transactions and blocks on the chain and further strengthens the trust and ordering within a block.

This can be done with any pre-defined field that can be used to group and order transactions within a block.

The conceptual working of this consensus algorithm is still in beta state, and more detail will be added to new versions of the White Paper, once it has been completed.

The design and implementation of the network, enables the function specific digital and decentralized applications to be added once they become available.

An example with User Traceability:

PoT Sequence Index Operation Output with User Traceability

1) HASH1: sha256 (user-UUID, "starting value") = hash1
2) HASH2: sha256 (user-UUID, Calculated-Trace, hash1) = hash2
3) HASH3: sha256 (user-UUID, Calculated-Trace, hash2) = hash3

Where hash N represents the actual hash output. It is only necessary to publish a subset of the hashes and indices at an interval.

Index Operation Output

1) HASH1: sha256 (user-UUID, "starting value") = hash1
2) HASH200: sha256 (user-UUID, Calculated-Trace, hash199) = hash200
3) HASH300: sha256 (user-UUID, Calculated-Trace, hash299) = hash300

An example with Location Traceability:

PoT Sequence Index Operation Output

1) HASH1: sha256 (location-UUID, "starting value") = hash1
2) HASH2: sha256 (location-UUID, Calculated-Trace, hash1) = hash2
3) HASH3: sha256 (location-UUID, Calculated-Trace, hash2) = hash3

Where hash N represents the actual hash output. It is only necessary to publish a subset of the hashes and indices at an interval.

Index Operation Output

1) HASH1: sha256 (location-UUID, "starting value") = hash1
2) HASH200: sha256 (location-UUID, Calculated-Trace, hash199) = hash200
3) HASH300: sha256 (location-UUID, Calculated-Trace, hash299) = hash300

System Architecture

System architecture for distributed blockchain networks, cannot be mandated or forced. Our blockchain ecosystem, will have to make certain assumptions to get maximum participation and ensure the best integrity and performance for the hosted nodes that hold the state machine(s). State machine replication for a fault-tolerant and distributed network is one of the most challenging parts to get right, but by our block and network design, we aim to eliminate some of the common pitfalls that normally plague such distributed systems.

From our point of view, we do not want to exclude participants, just based on what they can spend on hardware, so we have built in a tiered system that will group a participant into a specific hardware group, depending on the machines capabilities, where the node has been installed.

One should consider the value chain that will enable smaller players to participate in the ecosystem. If this cannot be done, then one of the base principles of distributed blockchain systems are already out of the door, i.e., decentralization.

Components and inner working of the State Machine

Leader, 'Proof-of-Traceability' (PoT) or 'Proof-of-History' (PoH) generator

The Leader is an elected PoT or PoH generator. It consumes arbitrary user transactions and outputs a PoT or PoH sequence of all the transactions that guarantees a unique global order in the system. Under PoT, the transactions can also be directly traced to the pier nodes that added a transaction. After each batch of transactions, the Leader outputs a signature of the state that is the result of running the transactions in that order. This signature is signed with the identity of the Leader.

This is then sent to the validators to verify, by sending the state machine to the replication node(s).

Validators/Guardians, e.g., 'Delegated Proof-of-Stake' (DPoS)

The Guardian or Validator nodes replicate the blockchain state and provide high availability of the blockchain state. The replication target is selected by the consensus algorithm, and the validators in the consensus algorithm select and vote the 'Proof of Replication' (**PoR**) nodes they approve of based on off-chain defined criteria.

The network could be configured with a minimum 'Delegated Proof of Stake' (**DPoS**) bond size, and a requirement for a single replicator identity per bond.

These nodes are consuming bandwidth from validators. They are virtual nodes and can run on the same machines as the Validators or the Leader, or on separate machines that are specific to the consensus algorithm configured for this network.

Network Limits

The leader is expected to take incoming user packets, order them in the most efficient way possible, and sequences them into a 'Proof of Traceability' (**PoT**) or 'Proof of History' (**PoH**) sequence that is then published to downstream Guardians or Validators. Efficiency is based on memory access patterns of the transactions, so the transactions are ordered to minimize faults and to maximize prefetching or caching hits.

On a 1 gbps network connection the maximum number of transactions possible is 1 gigabit per second/176 bytes = 710 k TPS max. Some loss, 4% is expected, due to Ethernet framing. The spare capacity over the target amount for the network can be used to increase availability by coding the output with Reed-Solomon codes and stripping it to the available downstream Validators.

Computational Limits

Each transaction requires a digest verification. This operation does not use any memory outside of the transaction message itself and can be parallelized independently. Thus, throughput is expected to be limited by the number of cores available on the system's CPU or GPU.

GPU based ECDSA verification servers have had experimental results of 900 k operations per second.

Memory Limits

A native implementation of the state machine with a 50% full hashtable of 32-BYTE entries for each account, would theoretically fit 10-billion accounts into 640 GB. A steady state random access to this table measured at 1.1 × 107 writes or reads per second. Based on two reads and two writes per transaction, memory throughput handles 2.75 m transactions per second. This measured on an Amazon Web Services 1TB × 1.16 × large instance.

Smart Contracts

Smart Contracts - General

As with the current unique block design, it means we are more flexible on how to implement Smart Contract and what scripting language can be used. The program once written to the block, will be immutable, but the user will have the option of using the best fit depending on their needs and what is available, depending on the underlying digital application on the specific blockchain.

This means that new smart contract scripting languages can be added as they are developed, tested, and made available to the digital applications that subscribe to them.

The Smart contracts are managed in the core of the network, as each DAPP network will have its own smart contract node pool running.

The main reason for this specific implementation paradigm is the realization that not all DAPP's have the same underlying functionality or will require the same properties for the commodity, or artefact that is secured in the DAPP and onto the relevant blockchain.

High Performance Smart Contracts

Smart contracts are a generalized form of transactions added to an implementation with predefined steps related to properties of an artefact or object and processes under predefined conditions. These programs run on each node or specified set of nodes, depending on the configuration of the blockchain system and can modify the state of the relevant blockchain as determined under the contract.

Our design will initially implement and leverage the extended Berkeley Packet Filter (eBPF) bytecode as fast and easy to analyze and execute Just-in-Time (JIT) bytecode as the smart contract language. This is very similar to what Solana is doing, but we have tried to simplify the implementation and language and build in more rails to ensure that there is a one-to-one relationship between the input rules and resultant execution of the rules. One of the major problems with smart contracts in the past, is the fact that the same input, end up in several different outputs or results. This is not the way we like our code to act.

One of its main advantages of this implementation is the zero cost Foreign Function Interface (FFI) or Java Native Interface (JNI).

Intrinsic or functions that are implemented on this platform, will be directly callable by programs outside the node where it is implemented. Calling the intrinsic code, suspends that program and schedules the intrinsic code on a high-performance server. The intrinsic code are batched together to execute in parallel on the CPU or GPU, if available, or whatever core processor is available at the time.

Care must be taken on ensure that some of the features of the use of FFI may also cause issues depending on the underlying language used.

The eBPF backend has been included in LLVM since 2015, so any LLVM front end language can be used to write smart contracts. It has been in the Linux kernel since 2015, and the first iterations of the bytecode have been around since 1992. A single pass can check eBPF for correctness, ascertain its runtime and memory requirements and convert it to ×86 instructions.

The Future of our Smart Contracts

As the system and the team expands and develops, one should look at implementing other Smart Contract functionality. It must start somewhere.

Over the years I have worked with various JIT scripting languages and not all of them are as easy to learn or as powerful as others. Our approach will be to look at the applications that we have and see if we can improve the Smart Contract experience for our user.

References

Anderson, Mally. 2019. Exploring Decentralization: Blockchain Technology and Complex Coordination https://jods.mitpress.mit.edu/pub/7vxemtm3/release/2.

Buranyi, Stephen. 2017. https://www.theguardian.com/science/2017/jun/27/profitable-business-scientific-publishing-bad-for-science.

cb Insights. 2022. https://www.cbinsights.com/research/industries-disrupted-blockchain/

Daley, Sam. 2021. https://builtin.com/blockchain/blockchain-companies-roundup.

Dawson, Philip J. 2021. Cartallum Blockchain Solutions White Paper: A sustainable blockchain infrastructure for a sustainable future. https://www.cartallum.com/whitepaper.

Fortune Magazine. 2022. This is fraud coinbase CFO says of FTX as more crypto fintechs get caught in contagion. https://fortune.com/2022/11/17/this-is-fraud-coinbase-cfo-says-of-ftx-as-more-crypto-fintechs-get-caught-in-contagion/.

Gray, Stephen G. 2023. Published editorial on 3D Printing Media: https://www.3dprintingmedia.network/the-dawn-of-a-3d-biofabrication-biomanufacturing-metaverse/.

Härdle, Wolfgang Karl, Harvey, Campbell R. Reule, C.G. Raphael. 2020. Understanding cryptocurrencies. Journal of Financial Econometrics 18(2): 181–208.

Sicard, Francois. 2022. Can decentralized science help tackle the deterioration in working conditions in academia; https://www.frontiersin.org/articles/10.3389/fbloc.2022.1066294/full.

Tenorio-Fornes, Ambar et al. 2021. Decentralizing science: towards an interoperable open peeer review ecosystem using blockchain; Information and Processing Management Volume 28, Issue 6. https://www.sciencedirect.com/science/article/pii/S0306457321002089.

Tsekou, Dora. 2021. Asymmetric volatility; Effect of Covid-19 shock on cryptocurrency and S&P 500, University of Amsterdam.

Chapter 6
Smart Main Contracting

*Wilfred van der Plas BBA BEng** and *Dion Franken BBA*

1. Introduction

Smart main contracting focuses on the application of emerging technologies in real estate exploitation in order to achieve a sustainable and future-proof physical living environment.

During a workshop, the participants were asked a few questions about smart contracts and maintenance. Eighty-five percent of the participants face challenges in performing maintenance on their buildings or the maintenance they perform. Shocking! Two important points they mentioned are trust and the ongoing discussion about what has been done versus what is being invoiced.

Is a smart contract a possible solution? Seventy percent of the participants are not familiar with the term. Thirty percent who do know the term have done little or nothing with it. However, after some introduction to the topic, 75% do think that a smart contract could be one of the solutions for daily maintenance tasks. Fear of the unfamiliar?

In the first part of this chapter, the emerging technologies will be discussed in more detail. Then exploitation of real estate will be examined. Following this, the application can be created. The chapter concludes with an integrated application of emerging technologies in real estate exploitation.

Business develop manager DWA.
* Corresponding author: Wilfred.vander.plas@dwa.nc

2. Emerging technologies

2.1 Blockchain

General

With the term blockchain, many people think of Bitcoins. However, Bitcoin is only an application of a blockchain. The theory of the blockchain and the mathematics behind it were conceived by Stuart Haber and W. Scott Stornetta (Beyer, 2019). They introduced the article entitled "How to Timestamp a Digital Document". In this article, they described time stamp documents, a popular use case for blockchain technology (Haber, 1991). These time stamp documents are encrypted and recorded with a cryptographic encryption. Cryptography has been around much longer than the blockchain theory and goes back, with many variants, to ancient Egypt. The purpose of cryptography is to hide texts so that they cannot be read by unintended people (Stallings, 2000). The timestamp method is an encryption based on time. This time encryption is called a hash. Here the fingerprint is unique to each block on the blockchain (Beyer, 2019).

To explain a blockchain in broad terms, it can be compared to a group in WhatsApp. In a WhatsApp group, every ones b mobile has the full version of the conversation. This works via a decentralized network. Decentralized means that it is not stored centrally on only one (in this case) a mobile, but on all mobiles within this group. This allows all users to send and read messages within the group at any time. Once a message has been sent to the group, it can no longer be modified or (when these group functions were new) deleted. Each message also indicates the phone from which the message originated. This is distinguished by the identification number and, in this case, the telephone number. Suppose that user X has switched off the phone and therefore no longer receives the messages sent by the other person. This is not a problem, because when user X turns the phone back on, they receive the sent messages in chronological order. It is like a time stamp. In addition to this comparison with the time stamp, a sent message can be compared with a block of the blockchain. The text of a message is therefore the content of the block. In this case, the chain is the time sequence in which the messages are connected to each other. The phone number used to identify the sender is also applied in the blocks of the blockchain.

Figure 6.1. Example of blockchain.

Open, closed, hybrid blockchain

In the WhatsApp group example, people can only read and write messages if they are part of this group. Assuming there was a way in which anyone who logged in on WhatsApp would have a group with each user, and anyone who uses the app could read and type in it. In the blockchain world, this is called a permissionless/public or a permissioned/private blockchain (Lui, 2019). However, it does not end there. If there was a possibility to send certain messages to a select group within a public group, then these messages could only be seen by those people and not by everyone who logs in. This is called a hybrid blockchain (Suiker, Hoe kan ik blockchain integreren in mijn bedrijf?, 2018). The differences are as follows.

If a company wants to work via a blockchain, the company first needs to determine what data they want to put in it. For example, if these are personal data, the company may not simply disclose these data to everyone because this is prohibited by law? (Bart W. Schermer, 2018). With a private or a hybrid blockchain, these data can be kept hidden from the public.

Table 6.1. Open, closed and hybrid blockchain.

	Permissionless/public	**Permissioned/private**	**Hybrid**
Users	Users are anonymous	All users are known	Some of the users are unknown for a selected part of the blockchain
Reliability	Users can be unreliable	All users are trusted throughout the network	Both unreliable and reliable users
Accessibility	Anyone can read the data on the blockchain	Only people with permission can read data from the blockchain	A choice can be made with which users see any part of the blockchain
Editing right	Anyone can add data to the blockchain	Only people with permission can add data to the blockchain	A choice can be made of who may add to the blockchain.

2.2 *Ethereum explanation*

General

Ethereum was one of the first alternatives to Bitcoin and is the second most popular cryptocurrency (Semrush.com, 2018). Ethereum and Bitcoin have many similarities, and also some differences. Before going further into the similarities and differences, the origin of Ethereum and what Ethereum entails will be described. With this knowledge, it will be easier to understand what is meant by the similarities and differences.

Ethereum, like Bitcoin, works through a blockchain. When a transaction with ETH (the currency of Ethereum) is done, this transaction must be recorded in a block on the blockchain. The "chain" is a cryptographic reference to the previous block, called the "Parent". The data of a block cannot be changed without changing all subsequent blocks, which would require the consensus of the entire network (Hirsh, 2020).

The difference between Ethereum and Bitcoin begins with the underlying ideas on which Ethereum developed. While the developer of Bitcoin is concealed, the creator of Ethereum is known from the very beginning, namely Vitalik Buterin. The advantage of this is that it is known why he developed Ethereum and what he wanted to achieve with it. First, it is good to know that Buterin joined the Bitcoin community early, in around 2011. With his great admiration for this development, he started the Bitcoin Magazine. Through his research and his passion for the possibilities, Buterin began to think that much more can be done with the idea underlying Bitcoin. The current Bitcoin network is particularly good at what it does, but is limited in additional capabilities. During his interview with Business Insider, Buterin indicated that there were other people who shared this idea with him ? (Jacqui Frank, 2019). This was then the idea behind creating Ethereum, a blockchain network on which decentralized apps can run and on which smart contracts can be encrypted. Ethereum went live for the first time on July 30, 2015 (Cryptonews, 2021).

The table below shows the biggest differences between Bitcoin and Ethereum. Technically speaking, there are additional differences, but for this research, the following differences are sufficient to understand what Ethereum can do.

In addition to the differences mentioned in the table, there are also several technical differences. For example, Ethereum has an EVM, an Ethereum Virtual Machine. An EVM is a computer that works like a legal code. Every user of the network has sworn to abide by this. Each node (user) has stored a copy of this legal code on their own computer. In

Table 6.2. Differences between Bitcoin and Ethereum.

	Bitcoin	**Ethereum**
Created	March 1, 2009	July 30, 2015
Number of coins	21 million	No Limit
Function	Payments and trading with Bitcoins	Payments and trading with ETH, smart contracts, decentralized apps
Developer	Unknown	Vitalik Buterin
PoW and PoS	Bitcoin only works via the Proof of work	Ethereum works with PoW and for Eth2.0 with Proof of stake

addition, any user can send a request to this computer to perform random calculations. When such a request is made, it is verified, validated, and executed by other users (Richards, 2021). The status of the EVM is then updated and sent to other users.

A request for a calculation is called a transaction request. The record of all transactions and the current status of the EVM are stored in the blockchain, which is then stored and approved by all nodes. Once stored in the blockchain, it cannot be modified. Each request can be traced back to the original sender by a kind of signature (Hollander, 2019). Ethereum itself is free to use. However, for transaction requests, "gas" must be paid for the miners (Rosic, 2021). This is a premium that must be granted to the person who ultimately does the work of verifying the transaction, executing it, recording it on the blockchain and sending it to the network.

Ethereum 2.0

Ethereum was launched in 2015 and is to date is very popular (Ethereum.org, 2021). The developers had a certain vision in mind with Ethereum, and to achieve this they knew from the beginning that an update of the original Ethereum network would be needed to make this vision a reality and to develop the real potential of Ethereum (Marcus, 2020). The upgrade of Ethereum is called ETH2.0/Ethereum 2.0 and should improve the current network in terms of speed, efficiency, and scalability, without sacrificing security and decentralization. This is made possible by the Beacon chain, a new structure that converts the proof of work consensus into a proof of stake consensus (Beck, 2020). However, despite this change, nothing has changed for the users, and they can simply continue with the things they were previously doing.

Proof of work

With the proof of work consensus, it takes about 12 sec for a new block to be mined by a miner and then added to the blockchain. As more and more users of the network are added, there is a risk of a long waiting time before a transaction is added to the blockchain, depending on the amount of gas that is attached to the transaction (Morabito, 2017). The more the gas, the higher the reward for the miner, so the better a miner wants to mine the transaction in a block (Bahga, 2016). If the transaction has a low gas value, it is less interesting for the miner to add it in the next block, which can result in a longer waiting time before the transaction is on the blockchain. This hinders the network in scaling up in use and size. This creates the need to accelerate this process and to adapt it in a certain way so that new blocks can be added to the network more quickly.

Proof of stake

Like proof of work, proof of stake works with a consensus to achieve unanimity in a decentralized manner. The way in which this unanimity is achieved is different. It requires users to deploy 32 ETH in order to become a validator in the network (Staking, 2021). A validator has the same responsibility as the miners of the proof of work, namely processing transactions and creating new blocks so that all nodes (users) can give their approval to the status of the network (Wackerow, 2020).

In contrast to proof of work, validators do not have to use large amounts of computing power because they are randomly selected and do not have to compete with each other's computing power. They do not need to mine blocks, they only need to create blocks when they are chosen or validate blocks if they do not need to create blocks (Wackerow, 2020). This validation is known as certificates. Certificates can be described as saying "this block looks good to me". Validators will receive rewards for introducing new blocks and for confirming the ones they have seen.

In this way, miners no longer need energy-sapping computer power stations for computing power but can simply do so via a simple laptop or even a mobile phone (Staking, 2021). This not only saves a miner a lot of investment costs to assemble a computer centre, it also saves a lot of energy. This should save the entire Ethereum network 99% in energy (Fairley, 2019).

Ethereum DAPPs

With the differences between them, it is easy to see that Buterin had big plans for Ethereum. For example, he has created the opportunity to create decentralized apps and smart contracts via a blockchain. The DAPPs application is discussed below: what it contains, how it works and what it can be used for.

A DAPP (fully decentralized application) works via a Peer-to-Peer network (P2P) and can be viewed and edited by everyone (open-source) (Suiker, Dapps - wat zijn het en hoe gebruik je ze?, 2018). This is different from normal applications (centralized applications). A normal application is managed by the company or developer whose owns the app. What this app does with the data is often not clear to the users. In addition to this difference, there are other differences (Frankenfield, 2021).

- The codes of standard apps are usually not public; with a DAPP, they are always public.
- The data on a standard app is the property of the company or developer; no one is the owner of a DAPP.
- Data on a standard app can be altered; data on a DAPP cannot be altered.

- In the case of a standard app, the company or developer is responsible for the encryption; in the case of a DAPP, all users are responsible for this.
- Normal apps can go offline for a number of reasons; once they run on smart contracts, Dapps will not go offline.

In addition to the differences, Dapps also have more capabilities than standard apps. A good example of this is Golem (Mearian, 2019). Golem is a DAPP on Ethereum that makes it possible to use the computing power of other computers if someone comes up short. This also works the other way around, so that someone can lend their computing power to anyone who needs it urgently at that moment. In this way, it is no longer necessary to join an expensive company to buy this computing power (Golem network, 2021).

Table 6.3. Difference between app and Dapp.

	Standard APP	DAPP
Transparent	The codes of standard apps are usually not public	The codes of a DAPP are in the blockchain and are accessible to everyone
User data	The data on a standard app are owned by the company or the developer	No one owns the data
Alteration	The app owner can edit and delete data themselves	No one can edit and delete data
Encoding	The app owner is responsible for encoding the app	All users are responsible for encoding
Run-time	May be offline due to a malfunction, maintenance, or other issues	Once live, a Dapp cannot go offline

2.3 *Smart contract*

General

Like the blockchain and cryptocurrency, there was a theory about the concept of smart contracts long before it was put to in practice. Smart contracts have been made operationally largely by Ethereum, but came up long before the idea of blockchain and Ethereum. Smart contracts are not by definition "smart". It is a pre-programmed code, and all the smart contract does is follow this code, so there is no proactivity. In addition, a smart contract is not always a contract (Rikken, 2016). According to the Van Dale, a contract is a written agreement, and smart contracts are not always used for agreements.

The history of smart contracts

Nick Szabo published the document "Smart Contracts: Building Blocks for Digital Markets" in 1994, which contained the theory of smart contracts. In this document, he gives the following description of a smart contract: "*A smart contract is a set of promises, specified in digital form, including protocols within which the parties perform on these promises* (Szabo, Smart Contracts: Building Blocks for Digital Markets, 1994)."

The description is thus broad, without a clear idea of what it means. In the same document, Szabo gave (Szabo, Smart Contracts: Building Blocks for Digital Markets, 1994) a practical example of a vending machine. In a candy vending machine, a set of promises are programmed in advance in the candy vending machine (how much does each product cost, how many products are there, etc.), with the protocol that now a user deposits the requested amount of money (fulfils the promises of costs), the machine ejects the requested product with the change if necessary (fulfils the promise of delivery). This indicates that when the machine has established that an encoded value has been met, an action is initiated.

This development of Szabo has been made operational by various platforms. For example, smart contracts work via the Bitcoin blockchain to trade Bitcoins (Rotkiewicz, 2020). The largest and most stable platforms today are:

- Ethereum;
- EOS;
- Algorand;
- Tezos;
- Stellar.

Ethereum smart contract

Although Ethereum is not the first platform that works with smart contracts, it is the first platform where smart contracts can be used for multiple functions, compared to the Bitcoin where the platform can only trade Bitcoins (Coingeek.com, 2021). This makes Ethereum the first network where smart contracts can be encrypted on a blockchain to initiate automated actions (Entriken, 2020).

Smart contracts from the Ethereum network work as a kind of user account. This means that, like a user account, they have a balance, can send transactions over the network and these transactions can be added to the balance of the smart contract (Richards, 2021). However, the difference is that a smart contract account is not managed by a user and therefore no human actions are involved. Smart contracts are implemented on the network and work as they are programmed. A user account can be used to communicate with the smart contract by sending information such as a transaction (Entriken, 2020). The idea is that, based on this information, the smart contract will perform a function as defined in the code of the smart contract. This makes a smart contract deterministic because it always gives the same output with the same input, which makes a smart contract predictable (Christidis, 2016).

The encoding of a smart contract is done via a programming language. A programming language is like a language that is written. With many different languages in the world, there are also many different coding languages. There are thousands of different coding languages, 50 of which are the most widely used today (Flower, 2020). A smart contract can be programmed on Ethereum in different languages. Solidity is the most widely used encoding language for smart contracts on Ethereum. Solidity can communicate with other networks and platforms, which is the reason that many developers to encode the smart contracts via this language (Moulakhnif, 2019). A smart contract encoded in solidity as a vending machine looks like the one in Figure 6.2.

In order to get a better idea of how a smart contract works in practice, the following fictitious example has been created (Rikken, 2016): Suppose there is a blockchain network with which Alice, Bob and Carol work and

```
pragma solidity 0.6.11;

contract VendingMachine {

    // Declare state variables of the contract
    address public owner;
    mapping (address => uint) public cupcakeBalances;

    // When 'VendingMachine' contract is deployed:
    // 1. set the deploying address as the owner of the contract
    // 2. set the deployed smart contract's cupcake balance to 100
    constructor() public {
        owner = msg.sender;
        cupcakeBalances[address(this)] = 100;
    }

    // Allow the owner to increase the smart contract's cupcake
balance
    function refill(uint amount) public {
        require(msg.sender == owner, "Only the owner can refill.");
        cupcakeBalances[address(this)] += amount;
    }

    // Allow anyone to purchase cupcakes
    function purchase(uint amount) public payable {
        require(msg.value >= amount * 1 ether, "You must pay at lea
1 ETH per cupcake");
        require(cupcakeBalances[address(this)] >= amount, "Not enou
cupcakes in stock to complete this purchase");
        cupcakeBalances[address(this)] -= amount;
        cupcakeBalances[msg.sender] += amount;
    }
}
```

Figure 6.2. Example of smart contract (Entriken, 2020).

where digital assets (cryptocurrencies, for example) of type X (for example, ETH) and Y (for example, BTC) are traded. Bob creates a smart contract on the network that defines: a "Deposit" function that allows units of X to be added to the contract, a "Trade" function that returns one unit of X (from the balance of the contract) for every five units of Y it receives, and a "Withdraw" function that allows Bob to pay out the balance of the contract.

Bob sends a transaction to the address of the smart contract, activates his "Deposit" function, and three units of X are moved to the contract. This transaction is registered on the blockchain. Alice, who owns 12 units of Y, then sends a transaction that moves 10 units of Y to the "Trade" function of the contract and gets two units of X back (5 yr = 1 x so 10 yr = 2 x). This transaction is also recorded on the blockchain. Bob then sends a signed transaction to the "Withdraw" function of the contract. The contract checks the signature to ensure that the withdrawal is initiated by the contract owner and returns the balance (1 unit X and 10-units Y) to Bob.

Deterministic and non-deterministic

The example above is a good model of a deterministic smart contract. Deterministic smart contracts are smart contracts that only work based on the data that come from the blockchain to which it is linked. In such a case, a smart contract can work because all the information that the smart contract needs is stored in the blockchain (Morabito, 2017). But if this is not the case and more information is needed that does not come from the blockchain, a non-deterministic smart contract will be drawn up.

A non-deterministic smart contract works via an external database, also known as an Oracle ? (Maher Alharby, 2017). This is especially applicable if a smart contract is supposed to work with real-time data such as weather. An Oracle can be seen as a third party that provides the necessary data. This may seem strange because the idea behind a smart contract is to eliminate the third party (Li, 2020). The real-time data and the necessary data could also be sensors that work via the Internet of Things (IoT) ? (Arshdeep Bahga, 2016).

DAO

Smart contracts can be connected to not only an Oracle, they can also be connected to each other. A set of smart contracts linked together is called a DAO. A DAO is a decentralized autonomous organization. This means that as soon as the set of smart contracts is connected to IoT sensors, big data analyses or artificial intelligence, for example, it can take decisions and be operational without the actions of people (Rijmenam, 2018). Like a smart contract, a DAO can no longer be modified once it has been executed and will always follow the code that is encrypted in it ? (Jennifer Li, 2020). It is therefore essential to ensure that the smart contracts that make up the DAO comply with the regulations and function as intended, as they cannot be "disabled" after they have been executed.

Over time, several DAO's have been installed on the Ethereum network. Such a DAO was programmed on Ethereum in 2016 and acted as a kind of venture capital company (Morabito, 2017). When the DAO owned more than US$150 million in ETH, it was hacked because hackers had discovered weaknesses in the codes of smart contracts on which the DAO was running ? (Arshdeep Bahga, 2016). In the end, the hackers were able to steal $40 million before the hack was discovered and the blockchain was redirected to a new status via a planned hard fork (Cryptopedia, 2021).

Smart contract applications

In the example in question, a smart contract is used for exchanging cryptocurrencies. In practice, smart contracts have been applied in various sectors. Several use cases for applications of smart contracts in various industries are described below.

Digital identity

Smart contracts can enable individuals to manage and control their digital identity with reputation, data, and digital assets (Szabo, Smart Contracts: 12 Use Cases for Business & Beyond, 2016). This allows them to decide for themselves which data they share and disclose to others. For example, someone no longer needs to share their data with a company and trust that the company will then store the data and will not share these data with others. Instead, someone can give a company access to read their data (Geronion, 2020).

Trade financing

Smart contracts can streamline and speed up international transfers of goods (Szabo, Smart Contracts: 12 Use Cases for Business & Beyond, 2016). For example, smart contracts can be used to manage the workflow of approvals and automatically transfer the payment after all signatures and approvals have been collected (Andersen, 2016). Automated payments through smart contracts reduce risks and improve financing and process efficiency for buyers, suppliers, and financial institutions (Sharma, 2021).

Mortgages

In the mortgage sector, smart contracts could automate the exchange of information on payments, purchases, and adjustments (Businessinsider, 2018). In addition, a smart contract can specify how much mortgage is to be paid and an action can be initiated if this action is not or not fully met (Funda, 2020).

Operation of buildings

The earlier business cases described how smart contracts can be used for the identification, payment, and exchange of assets. If these are combined, the following situation may arise (Li, 2020). A smart contract via a blockchain in which

- devices are identified;
- states the status of these devices;
- that if there is a lack of functioning, this is clearly communicated to the parties involved;
- the exchange of components is added as an adjustment to the blockchain;
- the payment is automatically paid to the maintenance party.

In addition, the sensors of a device in a building can serve as an Oracle for the smart contract to pass on data about the status of the device and whether it is ready for maintenance (Liftinsight, 2021).

Due to the diversity of implementation options for smart contracts, their popularity and use has increased considerably in the past few years (Ante, 2020). In Figures 6.3 and 6.4, the number of smart contracts created can be seen. Under this, it is clearly visible that interest in the topic of smart contracts increased in 2018, in the same year in which the number of smart contracts created began to increase more rapidly. Interest in the subject then remained stable, with no notable outliers.

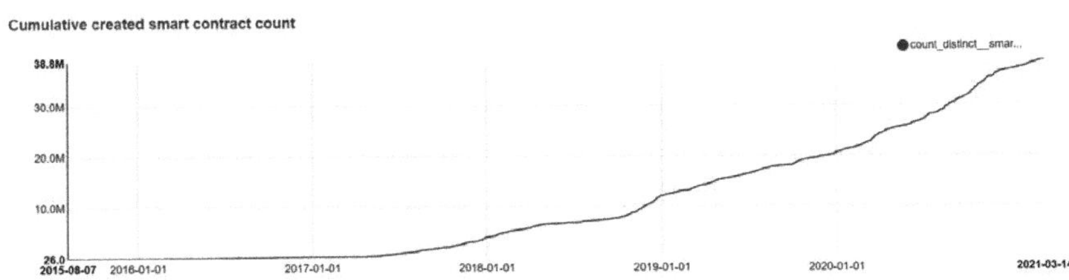

Figure 6.3. Number of smart contracts (bloxy.info, 2021).

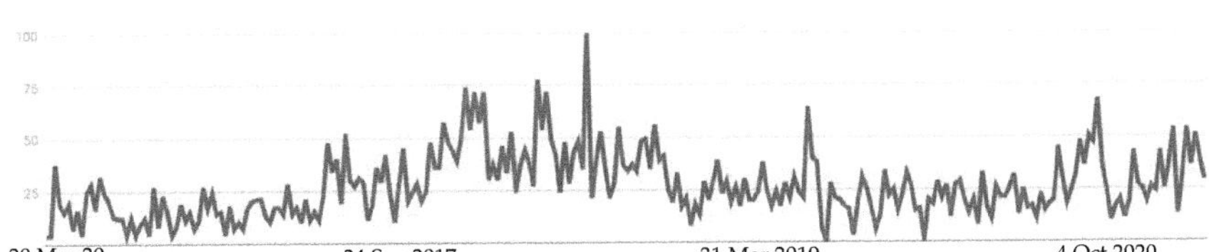

Figure 6.4. Interest in smart contracts.

Pros and cons of smart contracts

Even though smart contracts are already being used in many sizes and are increasing in numbers, smart contracts are still in the discovery and development phase ? (Ir. Olivier Rikken, 2016). In addition, almost all smart contracts work via a blockchain, which also brings with it the advantages and disadvantages of a blockchain (Szabo, Smart Contracts: 12 Use Cases for Business & Beyond, 2016). Below is an overview of a few of the advantages and disadvantages of smart contracts via a blockchain.

Advantages

Reliability – Smart contracts that work via a blockchain have the advantage that there is a high level of reliability in the field of data, which the smart contract uses for the automated actions (Bhardwaj, 2018). In a blockchain, nothing that has been approved can be modified. As a result, the code and status of the smart contract cannot be changed once they have been implemented on the blockchain (Westra, 2018). This makes it virtually impossible to hack into a smart contract (Hamers, 2019).

Decentralized – Due to the decentralized nature of a blockchain, smart contracts work without the need for a third-party intermediary (Manning, 2021). In addition, it is impossible to take a decentralized network offline (Westra, 2018).

Transparent – Due to the decentralized blockchain, everything on the blockchain can be read by the users of the network (Entriken, 2020). This means that all smart contracts on the blockchain are transparent to all users and all their actions can be checked (Morabito, 2017).

Savings – Decentralization and transparency lead to cost savings in different areas (Westra, 2018), for example on the costs for the third party that would normally be required for a transaction (Sheikh, 2019). In addition, the manual operations for providing information are automated, thereby reducing the costs of the processing (Bhardwaj, 2018).

Consistent – smart contracts are programmed with code to give the outcome of every value x (Entriken, 2020). This makes smart contracts predictable and consistent (Westra, 2018).

Disadvantages

Modifying – Perhaps the biggest disadvantage of smart contracts is that once they have been deployed on a blockchain, the smart contract can no longer be modified (Li, 2020). In order to make an adjustment in the smart contract, the original must be completely removed and recreated? (Erik Weitenberg, 2020).

Bugs – This does not mean insects, but unintentional errors in the code of the smart contract (Techopedia, 2021). A well-known example of this is the hack on a 2016 DAO in which US$40 million were lost. If a smart contract is incorrectly encrypted or contains bugs and is decisive for a costly process, this can cost a lot of money (Morabito, 2017).

Energy – The entire Bitcoin network consumes 80 terawatt hours per year. This is as much as the country of Chile consumes. Ethereum is doing considerably better at around 26 terawatt hours per year, equivalent to 2.5 million households (Digiconomist, 2021). With the advent of Ethereum 2.0, this energy consumption will be reduced by 99%, according to Buterin (Fairley, 2019).

Understandable – Smart contracts are encoded in Solidity (Entriken, 2020). If a smart contract is supposed to serve as a replacement for a normal contract (Pal, 2018), the parties may not be able to correctly understand what is stated in the contract (CFI, 2021).

Duration – A smart contract requires gas (ETH) to receive and send transactions. The gas is paid to the miner who records the transactions and adds them to the blockchain (Entriken, 2020). Deploying a smart contract on the Ethereum network costs $4,000 for a simple contract (little code in the contract), and for a complicated contract (many codes in the contract) already around $45,000 (iOlite, 2021). Thus if a smart contract is used that performs a lot of actions in a day, this can get expensive. With the arrival of Ethereum 2.0, these costs will also be reduced, because miners will no longer be paid for transactions.

2.4 *Summary*

Many smart contracts operate via a blockchain. A blockchain is a decentralized network containing data that are connected to one another by means of cryptographic encryption. The decentralized network can be private, public and a hybrid variant, depending on the data that are placed on a blockchain. This data has been accepted and validated by most of the users. Once processed in the blockchain, these data can no longer be modified or deleted and are, due to the decentralized nature, accessible to every user.

The blockchain theory existed for years before the first operational blockchain was set up. The first blockchain was Bitcoin to trade in currencies without a third party, which in this case were banks. Bitcoin has grown in value and popularity since its inception, but its applications are limited to exchanging cryptocurrencies. As a result, various applications have emerged such as the Ethereum network created by Buterin. His vision of this new network is to make the most of blockchain technology. New capabilities have been added in addition to trading cryptocurrencies, such as DAPPs and smart contracts. At the end of 2021, the Ethereum network, on which most smart contracts are based, will be introducing a new version that will enable the full potential of blockchain technology and smart contracts to be realized. The current network consumes a particularly large amount of energy, which is equivalent to millions of households per year. The new version not only ensures that this energy consumption will be drastically reduced by as much as 99%, but also that the smart contract will become financially more attractive for automating processes.

In addition, it has been determined that smart contracts are applications based on codes that can be programmed on a blockchain. The code works via the "if this then that" method. The most used programming language for this is solidity. These smart contracts can transfer values based on promises and conditions encoded in the contract. These values can be cryptocurrencies but also digital assets such as a purchase agreement or information about a machine. All these values combined can make it possible to run a process automatically, provided that the smart contract is coded correctly. An error in the code can cause financial damage. A smart contract cannot be modified, and once a process has been started, it cannot be interrupted.

Finally, the conclusion can be drawn that smart contracts can be used to automate information sharing in maintenance processes. Smart contracts are used in different industries, each with a different application. The implementation of smart contracts in the business sector is still limited and is in the development and discovery phase. Even though the use of smart contracts in the business sector has not yet been fully accepted, the number of smart contracts and their popularity are increasing. Therefore, the maintenance process and how smart contracts can be used for these maintenance processes will be discussed in more detail in the following section.

3. Exploitation of real estate

Maintenance in real estate is a contract- and information-intensive part of real estate exploitation. This chapter describes events surrounding the maintenance process. This covers the maintenance process in a general sense, not regarding specific clients or installations. The first thing that emerges is the creation of the maintenance contract. Then an explanation of the maintenance in general. Next the maintenance contract. Finally, the data for the maintenance process and the quality of those data.

3.1 The maintenance contract

The maintenance process only starts after a maintenance contract has been signed. A maintenance contract contains agreements to which the parties involved must adhere. For example, which sanctions apply if agreements are not kept and which party is liable for which matters. Not every company has the knowledge or capacity to secure a good maintenance party for the maintenance and to draw up a suitable contract with it. Companies sometimes engage third parties to arrange the maintenance tendering, to conduct the contract management (the so-called contract management) and to do the monitoring.

The selection of a maintenance party, the conclusion of a maintenance contract and the drafting of a maintenance contract begin with the inventory of the client's wishes and needs in the area of the assets. For example, the NEN 2767 condition scales can be used for this purpose (Table 6.4 - Condition scale (Franken)). This is a scale from 1 to 6, where 1 is a brand-new building or asset without traces of use and 6 is a building or asset that must be replaced immediately (NEN2767, 2019). Based on this scale, a client can indicate how they would like to see the status of their building and assets. Most clients strive for levels between 2 and 3 (Drissen, 2021). This is the level at which traces of use, things such as rust, traces of a slight leakage and the like are tolerated. This level generally costs a client the least in maintenance (Qualm, 2021). Assuming a client agrees to level 3 and turns out to be in level 4; then the maintenance party will first have to raise the building to level 3. Increasing a condition level can be very costly, depending on what needs to be done to achieve this (Drissen, 2021).

Inspecting the current situation and determining the desired objectives is the first step in the policy plans of a maintenance process and serves as a start for drawing up the contract (Figure 6.2). A gap analysis determines what is needed to close the gap between the current situation and the desired condition. This examines at what kind of package of measures can be offered to fill the gaps between the current situation and the objectives.

Step 2 in the decision-making process is to study possible scenarios. These are risks that are identified and depend on direct and indirect factors. Incidentally, this step is often left out in practice because it is highly speculative (Drissen, 2021).

Table 6.4. Condition scale (Franken).

Condition score	Description	Explanation
1	Excellent	Occasional minor defects
2	Good	Incidental onset of aging
3	Reasonable	Locally visible aging. Functional fulfilment of structural and installation components not occasionally at risk
4	Moderate	Functional fulfilment of structural and installation components occasionally at risk
5	Poor	Ageing is irreversible
6	Very poor	Technically ready for demolition

Based on the earlier two steps, the next stage of the process is then initiated. This includes establishing the basic principles and drawing up the maintenance plan. The plan includes the following points.

- What kind of work is going to be done?
- How should this work be done?
- How is the quality of maintenance and assets demonstrated?
- Who are the stakeholders?
- What is the framework within which the work is done?
- What is the scope of the project?
- The size of the building, for example the number of the client's complexes to be serviced, the number of assets, etc.

With the plan and a selected party, the next phase can begin. This phase is called the operational phase. The operational phase begins with a task-setting annual plan. This annual plan includes the multi-year maintenance budget. This plan is made prior to the maintenance year. This gives these parties the opportunity to adjust and to develop the plan. The parties complete this improved annual task-setting plan in September. Based on this plan, the maintenance contract is drawn up with maintenance divided into three groups: preventive, corrective and project/replacement.

Depending on what the client wishes, monitoring meetings are held every month, quarterly, or half-yearly to review the status, function, and condition. At the end of a contract year, an evaluation is held to discuss how the past year went and what can be improved in this regard. Figure 6.5 shows the entire process, starting with light blue flowing over to the gap analysis.

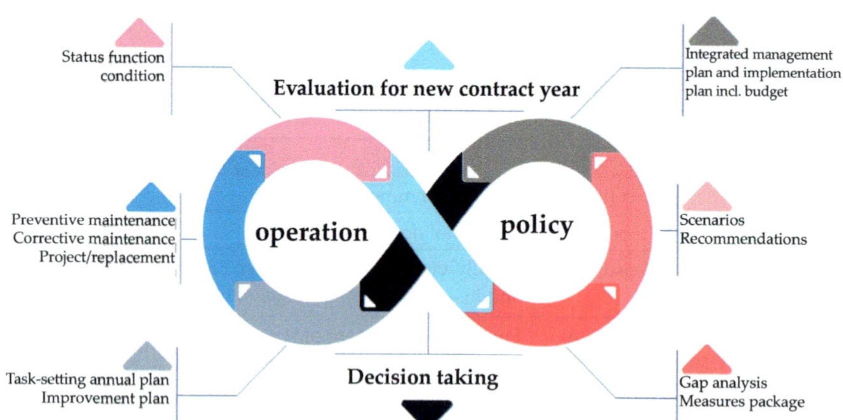

Figure 6.5. Maintenance process (Franken, Onderhoudsproces DWA).

Maintenance categories

The maintenance in the contract is divided into three categories: preventive, corrective and projects/replacement. Maintenance is divided into these categories because different agreements are made for each component and the type of maintenance differs (Drissen, 2021).

Preventive – For most machines, maintenance is required by law (Qualm, 2021). All mandatory maintenance of assets is preventive maintenance and is also called contractual maintenance. This form of maintenance is repetitive. The period between the maintenance is recorded in a contract. This can be twice a year, for example. Preventive maintenance is intended to keep the assets operational and prevent ailments or malfunctions. Assets have a technical service life, and this service life is also based on preventive maintenance (Blygold, 2021). By not performing preventive maintenance, the technical service life of the asset decreases more rapidly.

Corrective – It occurs regularly, even though preventive maintenance has been done, that assets malfunction or fail (Drissen, 2021). Unforeseen repairs to the asset are subject to corrective maintenance. As malfunctions and failures can be caused by various factors, it is very difficult to include the corrective maintenance in the budget or to record it in the contract. In most contracts, there is a limit to the costs that do or do not have to be invoiced. For example, if maintenance of less than 100 euros has been required, it often costs the client more to process these invoices than the maintenance actually cost (Erkelens, 2021). This cost limit is usually around 350 euros. All maintenance that falls under this limit does not have to be checked by the client and is covered by the contractual agreements of the preventive maintenance (Drissen, 2021).

Projects/Replacement – Each electronic device has a technical service life. The technical service life varies per asset and may also differ from the supplier. When the end of the technical service life approaches, the asset must be replaced. If this is done within the contract period, this replacement will be included as a project in the project maintenance. The costs for this are included in the budget when drawing up the contract. For assets with a long technical service life, this is often not well documented, so that an overview of the technical service life of assets cannot be used to complete the project-based maintenance (Opschoor, Data kwaliteit, 2021).

3.2 *Managing the maintenance contract*

A maintenance contract is concluded after the maintenance has been outsourced. The actual maintenance is done by the contractor, whether outsourced to specialized companies. In the contract, the responsibility for maintenance therefore lies with the maintenance party or parties. Legal advisers are involved in drawing up the contract (Steerneman, 2021).

Sometimes, clients need a single point of contact and only need to sign and maintain one contract. The maintenance party or parties then enter a cooperation with subcontractors. From a legal point of view, it is not the case that the party drawing up the contract is also responsible for performing the tasks.

After 1 yr of the maintenance contract being expired, a summary statement is prepared that describes what maintenance has been, what the effects are, the state of reliability, customer satisfaction, etc. All the KPIs that are specified in a contract are discussed and/or checked for compliance in a summary statement. After the year, the cycle comes back (Figure 6.5 – Maintenance process) to the gap analysis, not to see what is still missing but what could be better based on the previous year. The circle of the maintenance process then runs repeatedly until the contract expires.

At the end of the contract, there is the possibility to extend the contract (Drissen, 2021). A contract extension usually takes place if both parties are satisfied with the cooperation during the contract period. A contract period is usually 3 to 5 yr. Satisfaction is high, for example, when a maintenance party has always adhered to the agreements and may have delivered more quality than expected (Qualm, 2021). During the evaluation after each year, a meeting is scheduled with the maintenance contractor and the client. In addition, a maintenance party can, for example, brainstorm with the client to make maintenance even more efficient or to get the quality even better than in the past year. For a client, reliability is an important factor when it comes to contract renewal. Often, the client has no insight into the maintenance party's activities, which creates room for the maintenance party to misuse this situation. If there is an abuse of trust, non-compliance with the agreements or other serious facts, the contract can be terminated prematurely in the extreme case. Before this happens, the client may, for example, impose a fine on the maintenance party.

3.3 *IoT sensors and data*

Data from sensors (IoT) can help with the desired different reports, such as the annual evaluation and quarterly monitoring reports. The client decides how detailed these reports should be. These reports provide a visual picture of how a client's building and assets perform. The data used for this comes from IoT sensors that are mounted in the building and on the assets. It is important that the data used reflect the actual situation (Hajee, 2021). When a report is drawn up based on incorrect, incomplete, and unreliable data, the report no longer reflects reality.

There are several factors that can cause an anomaly in the data: when things fall outside the usual circumstances. These factors are set out in Table 6.5.

Table 6.5. Causes of unreliability (Hajee, 2021).

Factor	Example
Installation	The sensor is not mounted far enough from the wall
Positioning	The sensor is placed in the air flow of another installation
Connection	There is no WIFI signal
Blockage	The sensor is covered with tape
People	Someone blows into the sensor
Processing	The data average is based on incorrect values
Calibration	The calibrated values are incorrect
Wear and tear	A sensor can wear out over time

After all external causes have been ruled out, the sensor itself will be checked for proper functioning. Sensors have their own technical service life. The length of the technical service life depends on the brand and type of the sensor. There are sensors that can last on average around 10 yr, but there are also sensors that can only last 3 yr. When a sensor approaches the end of its technical service life, it may no longer perform properly and may generate incorrect, incomplete, or even no data at all. If this is the case, a message is sent to the client to replace the sensor (Opschoor, Data kwaliteit, 2021).

If it is found that a sensor no longer performs properly, it is often the case that several sensors of the same type will also show technical defects in the short term (Opschoor, Data kwaliteit, 2021). Therefore, in these cases, the client is advised to schedule a project-based maintenance and to replace all sensors with the same brand and type. By replacing the sensors on a project basis, a technician does not have to come back several times to replace a sensor if it has defects. Subsequently, these new sensors only need to be calibrated and checked once.

The responsibility for performance and function lies with the maintenance party or supplier, depending on what is agreed in the contract (Steerneman, 2021). At present, little or no documentation is kept on the technical service life of sensors (Qualm, 2021). Although this is important for the quality of the data generated by the sensors, project-based maintenance is not linked to the technical service life. At present, a decision to replace a sensor is made purely based on human judgement, without considering the technical service life of the sensor.

Data quality

The correct functioning of an IoT sensor is important for data quality (Hajee, 2021). The data coming directly from the sensors must be checked by data analysts. Practice shows that the data generated by sensors is not reliable, correct, and complete. By sampling with a corrected sensor, it is possible to discover which installed sensors do not generate the desired data quality (Opschoor, Data kwaliteit, 2021). According to data analysts, it cannot be assumed after a sample that the raw data directly from the sensors are of the correct quality over an extended period.

In addition to the quality of data generated by sensors, the connection to the database may also be lost (Hajee, 2021). Incomplete data are easier to rectify and discover than data that are available but not correct. When data no longer enter the database from the sensor, this is generally due to the connection to the database and not the sensor itself.

Complaints and malfunctions

In addition to preventive maintenance, there may be complaints or malfunctions. When this occurs, there must be a response (see Figure 6.6). To this end, it must be clear where the complaints can be reported and in what way. These complaints should also be handled within a period agreed in advance. The work to handle the complaint must then be reported back to the person who submitted the complaint.

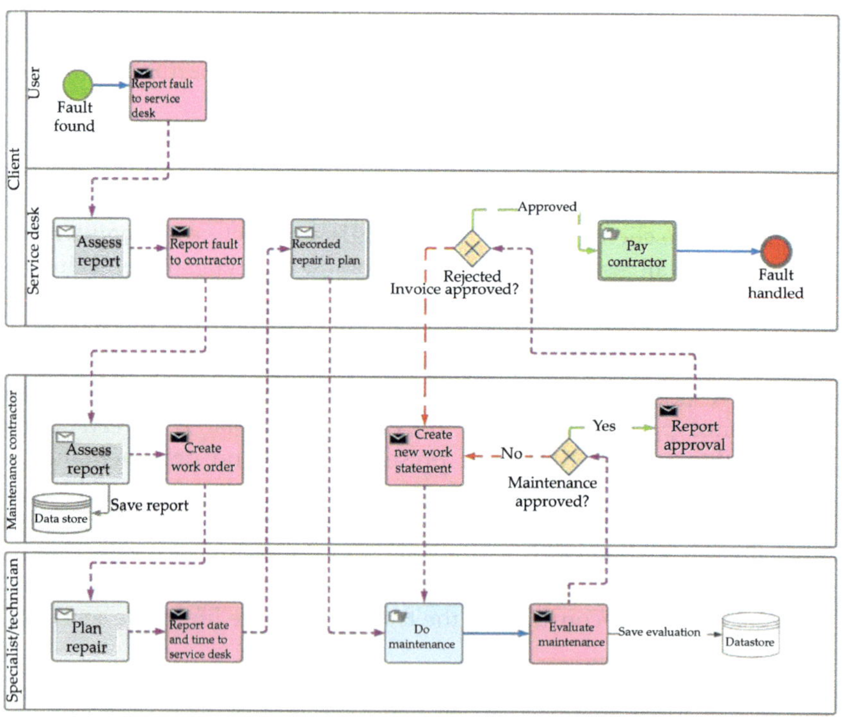

Figure 6.6. Sharing process information (Franken).

Repairs to resolve complaints and malfunctions are coordinated by the maintenance party. Before the repair can be done, it must first be reported to the management. If the management agrees to this, the maintenance party shall engage expert personnel who will perform the repairs under its responsibility. The repair work done is recorded on an invoice.

3.4 Possibilities for improvement

The practice of maintenance shows that the parties are not satisfied with various aspects of the process. Not only the client, but also the maintenance parties benefit from an improvement in the maintenance process, in particular regarding the exchange and handling of information.

The MJOP stipulates when the preventive maintenance of the UTES system will be done. The preventive maintenance is handled by the maintenance technician based on a checklist. After the maintenance, the technician draws up an evaluation report containing the checklist. The report is then sent to the client. This report also contains points for attention and recommendations drawn up by the technician. These recommendations and points for attention are often not adequately addressed. This results in a long list of points for attention and recommendations, which can lead to excessive problems.

When performing corrective maintenance, the evaluations, work orders and logbooks are checked for completeness, but not for accuracy. As a result, the client does not know whether what is described in the logbook has occurred. The insight into the work of the maintenance parties is very limited, as a result of which the client sometimes suspects that the maintenance parties are taking advantage of this. However, they cannot prove this, again because it is not transparent. In addition, maintenance parties face distrust, which they consider to be unjustified. They currently do not have the means to provide this transparency to the client.

For the maintenance parties, it is an obstacle that so many reports need to be drawn up, archived, checked, and sent. It is a complication due to the many hours they must spend on administrative work and not on their primary work such as maintenance. In addition, payment is subject to strict and often many different KPIs. This makes it less interesting for maintenance parties to enter certain contracts. Performance contracts in particular pose a major administrative challenge in constantly proving that the KPIs have been met.

3.5 Summary

Well-maintained and managed real estate is a challenge. To this end, it is important that the maintenance process is transparent to the stakeholders.

At present, the client has no insight into the activities of the technicians. They then pay the invoices that the maintenance party sends, without the client being able to correctly check whether what has been invoiced has been done.

The maintenance contractor encounters hindrances in the primary work process due to the administrative matters they must take care of in order to prove that the KPI values have been met. In addition, they spend a lot of time performing inventories for a new tender in order to be able to draw up a good assessment and overview of the assets. Earlier contractors do not disclose their maintenance history to new contractors. This means that in some cases the contractor has made an incorrect estimate and has very little budget to provide all the maintenance at the client's desired level.

4. Smart main contracting

4.1 How can this be handled?

The following example elaborates how a smart maintenance contract for a building could work.

"The installation is given a QR code with a unique identification number for the installation. When a technician arrives at the site, he scans this code and is redirected to an app. This app contains a digital version of the current checklist. This checklist could also be viewed by the technician prior to maintenance and supplemented after maintenance. During the maintenance, the technician fills in the checklist that he would normally fill in on paper, then fills in the recommendations and points for attention. Once everything is filled in, he logs off. All these data are sent to the smart contract, which then records them on the blockchain. Finally, the mechanic is paid with tokens that are settled with real money at the end of the month."

In combination with IoT sensors, the installation could also link the function to this process. When the sensors indicate that a part of the building installation is not working properly, this information can be sent to a smart contract which then sends the maintenance technician a message with the error code. This facilitates checking how much time elapses between the notification and the registration of the technician at the installation (Erkelens, 2021). The response time can be a KPI defined in the contract. If these values are exceeded, a fine can be imposed on the maintenance party for non-compliance with the KPI agreements.

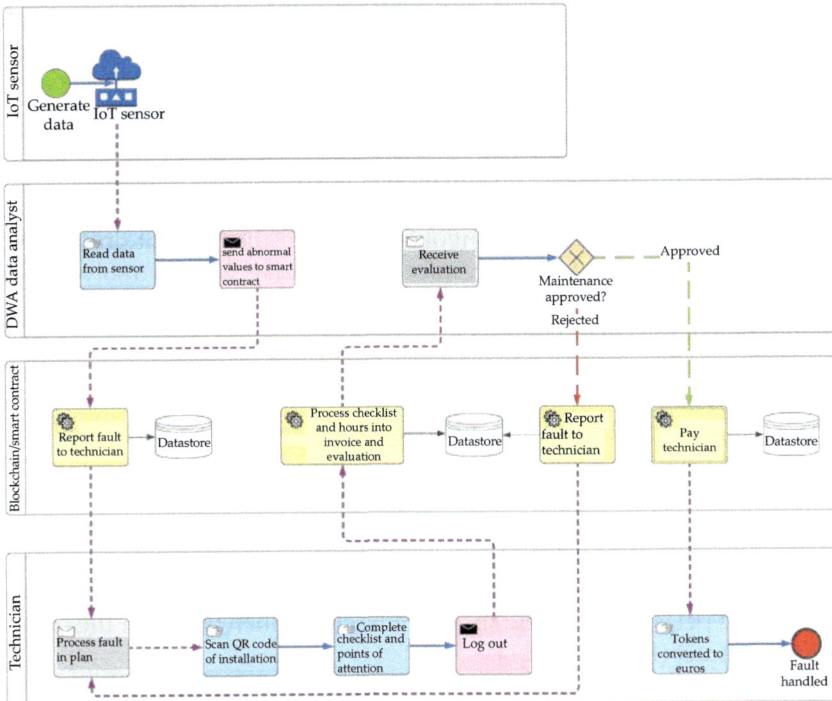

Figure 6.7. Smart maintenance (Franken).

4.2 *Smart contract as a maintenance contract*

Smart contracts can serve as legitimate contracts to replace a physical contract (Pal, 2018). In certain cases, it is laid down by law that the contract must be in writing (Steerneman, 2021). This is the case, for example, with a purchase agreement for a house. In most cases, there is freedom of the contract, whereby the parties are free to determine how the contract is drawn up. A contract drawn up on a beer mat could even be a binding agreement. What is subsequently stated in the contract must not be in violation of the law. A contract may therefore also be written in a programming language. It must also be clear to the parties in advance what is described in the contract and what kind of agreement they have entered. In order to achieve this clarity, a grammatical explanation in written language can be added to the contract. This applies, for example, if one of the parties does not speak or only moderately speaks the language in which the contract was drawn up (Steerneman, 2021).

Article 6:217 of the Dutch Civil Code (General Section of Contract Law) states the following in Article 217 1 about the conclusion of contracts. *"An agreement is concluded through an offer and its acceptance. 2. Articles 219–225 shall apply unless otherwise provided in the offer, in another legal act or in a custom"*. Article 218 then states: *"An offer shall be valid, void or voidable in accordance with the rules applicable to multilateral legal acts"*. Finally, Article 6:227 stipulates that *"the obligations assumed by the parties must be determinable"*.

A smart contract via the Ethereum blockchain is written in the solidity coding language (Entriken, 2020). This coding language could legally be used for the contract. There is therefore a risk that uninformed counterparties may be able to invoke an error if they do not understand the contract and are not properly informed (Zondag, 2021). To solve this, a grammatical explanation in written language can be added to the contract in the code of the smart contract.

An annual contract evaluation is conducted. The physical contract can be supplemented with new agreements for the coming year (Drissen, 2021). However, a blockchain smart contract can no longer be adjusted once it has been placed on the blockchain. In addition, the contract cannot be deleted (Morabito, 2017). This has the advantage that the contract cannot be manipulated or deleted by malicious parties. A self-destruct function must be placed in the code of the smart contract. The moment this function is triggered, the contract freezes and no more automated actions are performed. A new smart contract will then take over the frozen smart contract (Rongen, 2021).

The main legal problems are the immutability of contracts and the automatic nature of contracts. Due to these two facts, there is no room for the open standards of contract law (Vermeulen, 2021). Consider the Haviltex standard, unforeseen circumstances and, in the event of shortcomings, the reasonable term (Zondag, 2021). By means of a hybrid contract, a contract in which a part is physically written out and a part that is executed via the code on the blockchain, space can be made for reasonableness and fairness (Pal, 2018).

GDPR legislation has been in force since May 25, 2018 ? (Bart W. Schermer, 2018). A company that collects personal data must therefore, among other things, give someone the opportunity to be omitted, i.e., all their data will be deleted from that company. If the smart contract records personal data of, for example, a technician to check who has performed the work, these cannot be deleted due to the nature of the blockchain. This is against the law (Pal, 2018). Therefore, when drawing up the smart contract, there must be a method for storing the technician's identification in such a way that it cannot be traced back to this person by others. This includes cryptographic encryption, for example.

4.3 Summary

A smart contract is a coded application that can be programmed on the blockchain. A smart contract does not have to work via the blockchain. In addition, a smart contract is not "smart" because it is a set of pre-programmed codes that generates a predefined output for certain inputs. A smart contract also does not have to be a contract.

A smart contract via the blockchain is already used in practice to make and keep processes and information flows transparent. Due to the decentralized nature of the blockchain, the information is accessible to everyone and no one owns the data. Everything that the smart contract performs can be traced back via the blockchain. Various practical examples prove that a smart contract can indeed be used to provide insight into and improve the maintenance process. However, smart contracts differ from one situation to another, which means that multiple contracts must be linked to each other in order to achieve this. The DAO that is formed in this way can entirely automate a building with respect to monitoring and maintenance processes.

From a legal point of view, a smart contract can and may be used as a replacement for the current form of contract. From a legal point of view, there are some loopholes in making an agreement completely autonomous. In order to avoid obstacles, the smart contract must be framed properly. In addition, it must be checked whether an autonomous smart contract is desirable or whether a hybrid form is created by keeping part of the contract in the current way and allowing suitable, well-framed components to run via a smart contract.

Finally, a smart contract can be used to improve the maintenance process by refining the data requirements on the blockchain via the smart contract. Depending on the needs of stakeholders, a desired output can be generated based on input values.

5. The application

5.1 The added value

Increasing developments in the field of smart contracts mean progress in terms of efficiency, effectiveness, and the economy (Andersen, 2016). Disadvantages could also appear from this progress. In the development of smart contracts and in the field of digitization and automation, it is important to consider the significance of these contracts and their use in relation to ethics (Werf, 2017). The specific stakeholders differ according to the situation. Overall, the stakeholders in a maintenance process are as follows.

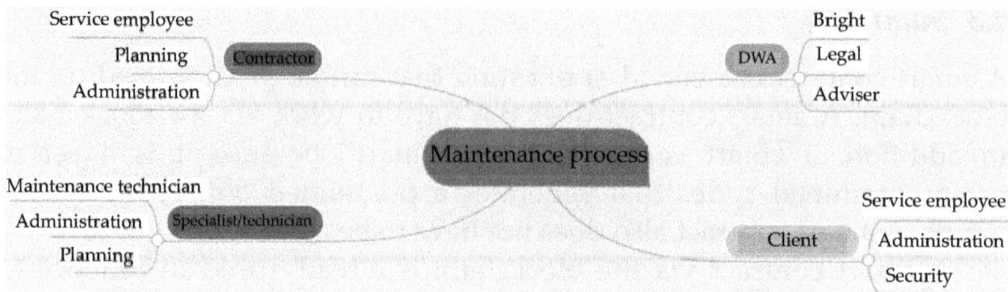

Figure 6.8. Stakeholders in the maintenance process (Franken, Stakeholders Onderhoudsproces).

Iwaarden has applied the concept of a smart contract to the maintenance of a coffee machine. It emerged that the smart contract will save time for various stakeholders (planning, service desk, etc.) (Iwaarden, 2021). For example, his analysis shows that the work of the service desk is eliminated completely. In addition, the planning work is almost completely discarded. The total time saved in the process is 60%. However, this does not mean that the associated jobs will be affected immediately. Iwaarden has indicated that the work of this maintenance process lies in secondary activities. For these employees, this time saving reduces the workload on the primary processes because they can spend more time on the primary work processes. (A smart contract is custom work, and these savings may vary depending on the situation.)

5.2 *Practical objections*

When applying smart contracts, resistance can arise from maintenance parties. If a client has decided to work through smart contracts, the maintenance party must also agree to this. The smart contract only works when all parties cooperate (Erkelens, 2021). For the maintenance party, this means stricter control of the work, which can appear to them as distrust. However, various maintenance parties have indicated that they look at this differently (Drissen, 2021). The maintenance party currently faces the administrative burden of providing evidence that the KPIs have been met (Out, 2021). These obstacles are removed by making the work transparent through automation. Partly for this reason, the maintenance parties are willing to cooperate in this new way of working.

In addition to the necessary consensus, the environmental impact of some new technologies is an issue. The entire Bitcoin network consumes 80 terawatt hours per year (1, × 109 Kilowatt [kW]). This is as much as a country like of Chile consumes (a Dutch household consumes an average of 2,741 kilowatt hours (kWh) of electricity per year). Ethereum is doing considerably better at around 26 terawatt hours per year, equivalent to 2.5 million households (Digiconomist, 2021). With the advent of Ethereum

2.0, this energy consumption will be reduced by 99%, according to Buterin (Fairley, 2019).

5.3 *A user story*

A smart contract is a set of promises specified in digital form, including protocols within which the parties fulfil these promises. A smart contract is therefore actually nothing more than an if-this-then-that algorithm, i.e., an algorithm that generates a certain output value based on a certain input value.

Building maintenance: the practice

As an example, one could look at the practice with Alice and Bob. She is the manager of an office with a heat pump system that is under a maintenance contract with Bob, the maintenance party. The contract stipulates that Bob performs preventive maintenance on the system several times a year.

Alice has no or limited insight into the work performed by Bob. However, there are problems, such as the system regularly malfunctioning. Furthermore, energy consumption is much higher than previously assumed. Bob sends her an invoice that is higher than Bob's original tender. However, it is not transparent to Alice why the invoice is higher.

Alice pays the invoice, but later than agreed, and she asks Bob a lot of questions about each invoice. This costs Bob a lot of time, while he could have worked on other jobs in that time. He also notes that Alice is keeping the building open much longer than previously stated. The maintenance process is starting to take more and more time, and the annoyance is increasing. In short, the trust between Alice and Bob is beginning to crumble, rightly or wrongly.

Data

The example is somewhat black and white and at the same time familiar. If one deploys the theory of smart contracts for building maintenance, then building maintenance, based on the example of Alice and Bob, can be well captured in a set of promises. Just like with the candy machine, but with one condition: data.

More and more data are becoming available, and more and more meaning is being given to data. This includes data from building management systems, sensors, energy meters, etc. For example, reports are made on how a building and its assets perform and whether the KPIs included in the contract are achieved. These data would gain added value if the data were combined with a smart contract for maintenance. But how does that work?

Fiction or reality

Back to Alice and Bob. They now use a smart contract for the maintenance contract. Essentially, the maintenance is done in a predefined period, at an x number of maintenance times and based on use and data. How does that work in practice?

- Alice's heat pump system has sensors, and the data from these can be used to track the system's performance.
- The smart contract describes the KPIs that this system must meet (the set of pre-programmed promises).
- The smart contract establishes that there is a certain underperformance or that an x number of operating hours has been reached based on the data (if this).
- The smart contract reports as output that there is work to be done for Alice (then that).
- Bob receives the same notification and will perform maintenance based on the data (then that).
- Bob registers at the building, performs maintenance and then logs out (if this).
- The smart contract sends Alice a report of the improved performance, including the actual number of working hours and the materials used (then that).
- The smart contract automatically pays Bob on time, without any questions, based on pre-programmed promises, such as hourly wage, parts price, etc. (then that).

The benefit of this method is that by means of a smart contract one can make the entire maintenance process more transparent: from no or limited insight to maximum transparency and timely payment. An important advantage is that information is automatically shared with the parties involved and payments are automatically processed. This can also reduce the costs of the process (invoices, questions about invoices, etc.), during maintenance.

Hassle versus focus

The use of smart contract technology is not yet a fait accompli. In any case, it does invite consideration (and imagination). Imagine if what we now encounter in maintenance were a thing of the past and that we could talk to each other about what really matters. Such as focusing on your core business or thinking about how your building will meet future obligations around energy, for example (Paris Proof). Instead of checking invoices and asking questions that are not answered. Or pursuing payment of invoices that should have been paid long ago. Not to mention a shortage of employee hours.

5.4 *Summary*

Each stakeholder has a different interest in improving the maintenance process. The maintenance process can be improved by means of smart contracts. As this technology automates information sharing, people are no longer required. These people can therefore be deployed more efficiently within the companies where they work. In the current process, the maintenance process takes too much time for the stakeholders. With a smart contract, this time can be spent on the primary work processes, resulting in a lower workload.

6. Overall summary

The current maintenance process differs per party and per building and depends on the building and its assets. The maintenance process in general consists of two different phases: policy and operational. In the policy phase, a gap analysis is drawn up containing the wishes and needs of the client. A suitable maintenance contractor is then selected to take care of the maintenance of the assets. In the operational phase, the actual maintenance is done, monitored, and evaluated. A lack of insight into the work performed by the technicians creates mistrust and dissatisfaction. For this reason, clients are currently asking contractors to comply with strict KPI values in order to monitor this process. However, this gives the contractors a lot of administrative work and hinders them in performing the primary work processes. In addition to the insight, both parties spend a lot of time providing each other with information.

Smart contracts via the blockchain can process work operations on a blockchain. The smart contract does not have to be used as a maintenance contract and can work as support in the maintenance process. The advantage of this is that the processes via the smart contract are always clear to the stakeholders.

However, the autonomous smart contract also has disadvantages compared to the current situation. As processes are automatically processed by the smart contract, there is no possibility for human judgement. In addition, the smart contract is coded on the blockchain so that it can no longer be modified or deleted without this being considered in advance. A smart contract can also work as a replacement for the current contract, but this presents legal challenges that may not be desirable.

In most cases, smart contracts work via the Ethereum blockchain. These smart contracts are written in the solidity coding language. This coding language can be learned through a course. There is also the option of hiring an external company to code a smart contract. The costs for this are comparable to those of a freelancer.

Various stakeholders in real estate operations benefit from improving the maintenance process via a smart contract on the blockchain. Various stakeholders' employees will be relieved of the work involved in the maintenance process and can thus be used more efficiently for the primary process of the companies. It should be noted, however, that blockchain technology consumes a particularly high amount of energy, which is contradictory in the context of sustainability. There are alternatives in development that save up to 99% of energy consumption, so that this will no longer be a hindrance in the future.

In short, the information sharing of the maintenance process can be improved by smart contracts if a further investigation is carried out for each situation in order to find out where the added value of smart contract technology lies. By recording wishes and needs in the coding together with the client and contractor, several smart contracts can be used per component. This could be, for example, making the technician's work transparent.

It is advisable to first improve the current processes in terms of transparency and automating the information requirement, in contrast to the smart contract method. For this purpose, it is first possible to create a standard per installation that makes it possible to scale up to a smart contract blockchain method in the future.

When these standards are in place, the information needs are automated and the work is clearly logged digitally, then a smart contract can be created on the blockchain that replaces these processes. The necessary information is therefore already available digitally and can be used as input for the smart contract. Depending on the transactions, the costs of smart contracts via a blockchain can increase considerably. It is therefore advisable to determine the purpose of the generated data. If fewer data points need to be loaded onto the blockchain, this will also affect the operating costs of the smart contract. If necessary, a cloud environment can be used instead of the blockchain. A cloud application could be developed with the operation of a smart contract (if this, then that). The required information can then be automatically stored in the correct folders in the SharePoint environment. Worklists can be digitized for the technician by means of QR codes for the installations. The application could record the time required by the technician to perform maintenance on the installation and thus draw up an invoice. With this information, the invoice contains an overview of the number of hours and the work performed. The client then has an insight into the maintenance history of the installation. The parties can print out reports and advise the client on recommendations based on the available data.

Bibliography

(2021, 03 15). Retrieved from bloxy.info: https://stat.bloxy.info/superset/dashboard/smart_contracts/?standalone=true.

Algemeen Nederlands woordenboek. 2021, 05 24. Retrieved from ensie.nl: https://www.ensie.nl/anw/setpoint.

Alharby, A.v. 2017. Blockchain-Based Smart Contracts A Systematic Mapping Study. Computer Science & Information Technology.

Andersen, N. 2016. Getting smart about smart contracts. Deloitte.

Ante, L. 2020. Smart Contracts on the Blockchain – A Bibliometric Analysis and Review. Blockchain Research Lab.

Arshdeep Bahga, V.K. 2016. Blockchain Platform for Industrial Internet of Things. Georgia Institute of Technology.

Bahga, V.K. 2016. Blockchain Platform for Industrial Internet of Things. Georgia Institute of Technology.

Bart W. Schermer, D.H. 2018. Handleiding Algemene verordening gegevensbeschermingen Uitvoeringswet Algemene verordening gegevensbescherming. Ministry of Justice and Security.

Beck, J. 2020, 12 1. The Ethereum 2.0 Beacon Chain is here. Now what? Retrieved from consensys.net: https://consensys.net/blog/blockchain-explained/the-ethereum-2-0-beacon-chain-is-here-now-what/.

Beyer, D.S. 2019, 08 23. Blockchain Before Bitcoin: A History. Retrieved from Blockchaintelegraph: https://blocktelegraph.io/blockchain-before-bitcoin-history/.

Bhardwaj, C. 2018, 06 18. Explained: What are Smart Contracts and Their Applications. Retrieved from appinventiv: https://appinventiv.com/blog/smart-contract-guide/#3.

Bitcoin koers. 2021, 2 25. Retrieved from Bitcoinkoers.org: https://www.bitcoinkoers.org/.

Block 0. 2021, 2 24. Retrieved from Blockchain.com: https://www.blockchain.com/btc/block/000000000019d6689c085ae165831e934ff763ae46a2a6c172b3f1b60a8ce26f.

bloxy.info. 2021. retrieved from :https://stat.bloxy.info/superset/dashboard/smart_contracrs/?standalone=true.

Blygold. 2021, 5 18. Technische vs economische levensduur. Retrieved from Blygold: https://www.blygold.nl/blog/technische-vs-economische-levensduur/.

Buitenhuis, H. 2021, 4 26. Onderhoud WKO. (D. Franken, Interviewer).

Businessinsider. 2018, 12 19. Een hypotheek afsluiten via de blockchain? Zo staan we er nu voor. Retrieved from Business Insider: https://www.businessinsider.nl/een-hypotheek-afsluiten-via-de-blockchain-zo-staan-we-er-nu-voor-davinci/.

CFI. 2021, 3 12. Smart contracts. Retrieved from CFI: https://corporatefinanceinstitute.com/resources/knowledge/deals/smart-contracts/.

Chay Lin Lim, A. J. (2020). Blockchain Basisboek. De Boekdrukker Amsterdam.

Christidis, M.D. 2016. Blockchains and Smart Contracts for the IoT. IEEE.

Coingeek.com. 2021, 03 03. A QUICK GUIDE TO BITCOIN SMART CONTRACTS. Retrieved from coingeek: https://coingeek.com/bitcoin101/bitcoin-smart-contracts/.

Conway, L. 2021, 01 19. The 10 Most Important Cryptocurrencies Other Than Bitcoin. Retrieved from investopedia: https://www.investopedia.com/tech/most-important-cryptocurrencies-other-than-bitcoin/.

Cryptografisch geld. 2021, 05 24. Retrieved from dfbonline.nl: https://www.dfbonline.nl/begrip/15096/cryptografisch-geld.

Cryptonews. 2021. Wie heeft Ethereum gemaakt? Retrieved from Cryptonews: https://nl.cryptonews.com/guides/wie-heeft-ethereum-gemaakt.htm.

Cryptopedia. 2021, 01 27. What Was The DAO? Retrieved from Cryptopedia: https://www.gemini.com/cryptopedia/the-dao-hack-makerdao.

cryptozombies. 2021, 5 11. Retrieved from cryptozombies: https://cryptozombies.io/.

Digiconomist. 2021, 03 12. Ethereum Energy Consumption Index. Retrieved from Digiconomist: https://digiconomist.net/ethereum-energy-consumption.

Dilmegani, C. 2021, 1 18. Smart Contracts in 2021: What it is & Why it matters? Retrieved from research.aimultiple: https://research.aimultiple.com/smart-contracts/#what-are-the-leading-smart-contract-development-companies.

Drissen, R. 2021, 3 19. Onderhoudsproces DWA algemeen. (D. Franken, Interviewer).

DWA.nl. 2021, 2 8. Retrieved from DWA: https://www.dwa.nl/.

EatTheBlocks. 2020, 7 16. Learn Solidity: Full Course For Beginners. Retrieved from Youtube: https://www.youtube.com/watch?v=d_Rynes-SvI&ab_channel=EatTheBlocks.

ecoomischwoordenboek. 2021, 05 24. Retrieved from economischewoordenboek.nl: https://www.economischwoordenboek.nl/?zoek=technische%20levensduur.

encyclo. 2021, 05 24. Retrieved from encyclo.nl: https://www.encyclo.nl/begrip/integraal_beheer.

Entriken, W. 2020, 11 30. Smart contract. Retrieved from Ethereum: https://ethereum.org/en/developers/docs/smart-contracts/.

Erik Weitenberg, M.E. 2020. Smart Governance for Smart Contracts. Dutch Blockchain Coalition.

Erkelens, J. 2021, 3 10. Smart contract in lift onderhoud. (D. Franken, Interviewer).

Ethereum.org. 2021, 03 12. Ethereum 2.0. Retrieved from Ethereum.org: https://ethereum.org/en/eth2/vision/.

Fairley, P. 2019, 01 2. Ethereum Plans to Cut Its Absurd Energy Consumption by 99 Percent. Retrieved from spectrum IEEE: https://spectrum.ieee.org/computing/networks/ethereum-plans-to-cut-its-absurd-energy-consumption-by-99-percent.

Flower, T. 2020, 05 21. How Many Computer Programming Languages Are There? Retrieved from career karma: https://careerkarma.com/blog/how-many-coding-languages-are-there/.

Frank, S.S. 2019, 02 13. Vitalik Buterin created one of the world's largest cryptocurrencies in his early twenties — here's how he did it and why. Retrieved from Business insider: https://www.businessinsider.nl/vitalik-buterin-created-ethereum-one-of-the-worlds-three-largest-cryptocurrencies-2019-1?international=true&r=US.

Franken, D. (sd). 2021. Onderhoudsproces DWA. Onderhoudsproces in het algemeen.

Franken, D. (sd). 2021. Stakeholders Onderhoudsproces.

Franken, D. (sd). 2021. WKO Installatie. WKO installatie.

Frankenfield, J. 2021, 02 12. Decentralized Applications – dApps. Retrieved from Investopedia: https://www.investopedia.com/terms/d/decentralized-applications-dapps.asp.

Funda. 2020, 1 15. Wordt dit het jaar van de blockchain in de vastgoedsector? Retrieved from Funda in business: https://www.fundainbusiness.nl/meer/artikel-fib/wordt-dit-het-jaar-van-de-blockchain-in-de-vastgoedsector/.

Fungeren. 2021, 5 24. Retrieved from woorden.org: https://www.woorden.org/woord/fungeren.

Geronion, D. 2020, 12 16. Top 12 Smart Contract Use Cases. Retrieved from 101blockchains: https://101blockchains.com/smart-contract-use-cases/.

Giuseppe Antonio Pierro, R.T. 2020. An Organized Repository of Ethereum Smart Contracts' Source Codes and Metrics. MDPI.

Golem network. 2021, 3 1. Retrieved from golem.netwerk: https://www.golem.network/#the-network.

GoodFirms. 2021, 5 13. Retrieved from Top Smart Contract Development Companies: https://www.goodfirms.co/directory/services/list-blockchain-technology-companies/smart-contract-development.

grafische bergippen. 2021, 05 24. Retrieved from encyclo: https://www.encyclo.nl/lokaal/10223.

Grider, S. 2021, 5 12. Ethereum and Solidity: The Complete Developer's Guide. Retrieved from udemy: https://www.udemy.com/course/ethereum-and-solidity-the-complete-developers-guide/?LSNPUBID=vedj0cWlu2Y&ranEAID=vedj0cWlu2Y&ranMID=39197&ranSiteID=vedj0cWlu2Y-FpW44_kvp.VsoZdfv588ow&utm_medium=udemyads&utm_source=aff-campaign.

Grit, R. 2019. Informatiemanagement. *In*: Grit, R.(ed.). Informatiemanagement (p. 198). Noordhoff.

Guido Ongena, K.S. 2018. Blockchain-based Smart Contracts in Waste Management: A Silver Bullet? University of Maribor Press.

Gürsoy, G.B. 2020. Using Ethereum blockchain to store and query pharmacogenomics data via smart contracts. BMC Medical Genomics, 13.

Haber, S. &. 1991. How to Time-Stamp a Digital Documents. Morristown: Journal of Cryptology.

Hajee, B. 2021, 3 3. Data kwaliteit. (D. Franken, Interviewer).

Hamers, L. 2019. Smart Contracts in the Operation and Maintenance Industry. Eindhoven University of Technology.

Hirsh, S. &. 2020. Blockchain. In S. &. Hirsh, Blockchain (p. 1). ALA Neal-Schuman.

Hoe KPI's bepalen voor je organisatie? 2021, 05 24. Retrieved from bztrs.nl: https://bztrs.nl/blog/hoe-kpis-bepalen-organisatie/#:~:text=Zoals%20hierboven%20staat%20beschreven%2C%20staat,worden%20ook%20wel%20kengetallen%20genoemd.

Hollander, L. 2019, 01 29. The Ethereum Virtual Machine — How does it work? Retrieved from Medium: https://medium.com/mycrypto/the-ethereum-virtual-machine-how-does-it-work-9abac2b7c9e.

Horst, H.v. 2020, 9 18. Omscholen kan maar effe omscholen niet. Retrieved from Joop: https://joop.bnnvara.nl/opinies/omscholen-kan-maar-effe-omscholen-niet.

Husneara Sheikh, R. M. (2019). Smart Contract Development, Adoption and Challenges: The Powered Blockchain. International Research Journal of Advanced Engineering and Science.

Internet der dingen. 2021, 05 24. Opgehaald van. Retrieved from Wikipedia: https://nl.wikipedia.org/wiki/Internet_der_dingen.

iOlite. 2021, 03 12. Problems & Costs of Smart Contract Development. Retrieved from Medium: https://medium.com/@iolite/problems-costs-of-smart-contract-development-649d88eedd1f#:~:text=A%20simple%20smart%20contract%20with,contract%20on%20the%20main%20net.

Ir. Olivier Rikken, M.S. 2016. Smart contracts als specifieke toepassing van de. Dutch Blockchain Coalition.

Iwaarden, K.v. 2021, 3 30. Edge smart contract koffiemachine. (D. Franken, Interviewer).

Jacqui Frank, S. S. 2019, 02 13. Vitalik Buterin created one of the world's largest cryptocurrencies in his early twenties—here's how he did it and why. Retrieved from Business insider: https://www.businessinsider.nl/vitalik-buterin-created-ethereum-one-of-the-worlds-three-largest-cryptocurrencies-2019-1?international=true&r=US.

Jennifer Li, M.K. 2020. A blockchain and smart contract-based framework to increase traceability of built assets. Information Technology for Construction Conference.

John Ream, Y.C. 2016. Upgrading blockchains: Smart contract use cases in industry. Deloitte.

Li, M.K.J. 2020. A Proposed Framework for Blockchain and Smart Contract-Based Automation of Maintenance and Repairs During Operation of Built Assets. Newcastle, UK.

Liftinsight. 2021, 2 15. SMART CONTRACTS: NEXT LEVEL IOT. Retrieved from Liftinsight: https://www.liftinsight.com/nl/publicaties/blogs/smart-contracts-next-level-iot/.

Lim, A.J. 2020. Blockchain Basisboek. De Boekdrukker Amsterdam.

Liu, K.W. 2019. Permissionless versus Permissioned Blockchain. America: American Accounting Association.

Luzuriaga, P. 2019. Smart contracts and Transaction Costs Economics. Tilburg Law and Technology Institute; Business Law Departament.
Maher Alharby, A.v. 2017. BLOCKCHAIN-BASED SMART CONTRACTS A SYSTEMATIC MAPPING STUDY. Computer Science & Information Technology.
Manlu Liu, K.W. 2019. Permissionless versus Permissioned Blockchain. America: American Accounting Association.
Manning, C. 2021, 02 03. INTRODUCTION TO DAPPS. Retrieved from Ethereum: https://ethereum.org/en/developers/docs/dapps/.
Marcus, J. 2020, 09 12. Waarom Ethereum 2.0 een gamechanger kan worden voor blockchain. Retrieved from BTCdirect: https://nieuws.btcdirect.eu/ethereum2-0/.
Mark Horvath, D.M. 2019. Innovation Insight for Blockchain Security. Gartner.
Markteffect. 2021, 05 24. Retrieved from markteffect.nl: https://www.markteffect.nl/meer/kennisbank/GAP-analyse.
Mearian, L. 2019, 12 30. 10 top distributed apps (dApps) for blockchain. Retrieved from computerworld: https://www.computerworld.com/article/3510457/10-top-distributed-apps-dapps-for-blockchain.html.
Missie en Visie. 2021, 2 8. Retrieved from DWA.nl: https://www.dwa.nl/missie-en-visie/.
Morabito, V. 2017. Business Innovation Through Blockchain. Springer International Publishing.
Moulakhnif, R. 2019, 09 3. Is Vyper a good alternative to Solidity? Retrieved from Meduim: https://medium.com/coinmonks/is-vyper-a-good-alternative-to-solidity-ac89c33a1d43.
Nakamoto, S. 2009. Bitcoin: A Peer-to-Peer Electronic Cash System.
NEN2767. 2019, 4 1. Retrieved from NEN.nl: https://www.nen.nl/nen-2767-1-c1-2019-nl-256366.
Opschoor, S. 2021, 3 18. Data kwaliteit. (D. Franken, Interviewer).
Opschoor, S. 2021, 4 23. WKO Schiphol. (D. Franken, Interviewer).
Out, W. 2021, 4 7. Smart contract. (D. Franken, Interviewer).
Pal, L.C. 2018. De juridische duiding van een smart contract naar Nederlands privaatrecht. Universiteit van Amsterdam.
Plas, W.v. 2021, 2 8. Introductie. (D. Franken, Interviewer).
Qualm, M. 2021, maart 7. Onderhoudsproces algemeen. (D. Franken, Interviewer).
Ream, Y.C. 2016. Upgrading blockchains: Smart contract use cases in industry. Deloitte.
Richards, S. 2021, 01 20. INTRO TO ETHEREUM. Retrieved from Ethereum: https://ethereum.org/en/developers/docs/intro-to-ethereum/.
Rijmenam, M.v. 2018. A Distributed Future: Where Blockchain Technology Meets Organisational Design and Decision-making. Sydney: University of Technology Sydney.
Rikken, M.S. 2016. Smart contracts als specifieke toepassing van de. Dutch Blockchain Coalition.
Rongen, R. 2021, 4 1. Smart contract mogelijkheden. (D. Franken, Interviewer).
Rongen, R. (sd). Smart contract voorbeeld. 2Bsmart.
Rosic, A. 2021, 02 1. What is Ethereum Gas? [The Most Comprehensive Step-By-Step Guide Ever!]. Retrieved from Blockgeek: https://blockgeeks.com/guides/ethereum-gas/.
Rotkiewicz, K. 2020, 10 15. Best smart contract platforms. Retrieved from Ulam labs: https://www.ulam.io/blog/smart-contract-platforms/.
Schermer, D.H. 2018. Handleiding Algemene verordening gegevensbeschermingen Uitvoeringswet Algemene verordening gegevensbescherming. Ministry of Justice and Security.
Semrush.com. 2018. cryptocurrencies study: search volume trends. semrush.com.
Sharma, T. K. 2021. 5 BEST USE CASES OF ETHEREUM SMART CONTRACTS. Retrieved from Blockchain council: https://www.blockchain-council.org/blockchain/5-best-use-cases-of-ethereum-smart-contracts/.

Sheikh, R. M. 2019. Smart Contract Development, Adoption and Challenges: The Powered Blockchain. International Research Journal of Advanced Engineering and Science.

Smokers, A.P.K. 2020, 4 13. Beheerplan energiecentrale stadskantoor Delft.

Smokers, K. 2021, 4 23. Onderhoud WKO standskantoor Delft. (D. Franken, Interviewer).

Staking. 2021, 03 15. Retrieved from Ethereum.org: https://ethereum.org/en/eth2/staking/.

Stallings, J.R. 2000. Netwerkbeveiliging en cryptografie : beginselen en praktijk. Schoonhoven: Academic Service informatica.

Steerneman, B. 2021, 4 9. Juridische zaken rondom onderhoudscontracten. (D. Franken, Interviewer).

Suiker, P. 2018, 06 21. Dapps - wat zijn het en hoe gebruik je ze? Retrieved from Allesovercrypto: https://allesovercrypto.nl/blog/dapps-zijn-gebruik.

Suiker, P. 2018, 10 19. Hoe kan ik blockchain integreren in mijn bedrijf? Retrieved from allesoverblockchain: https://allesovercrypto.nl/blog/blockchain-integreren-mijn-bedrijf.

Szabo, N. 1994. Smart Contracts: Building Blocks for Digital Markets.

Szabo, N. 2016. Smart Contracts: 12 Use Cases for Business & Beyond. Chamber of Digital Commerce.

Tardi, C. 2021, 03 2. Gwei. Retrieved from investopedia: https://www.investopedia.com/terms/g/gwei-ethereum.asp.

Techopedia. 2021, 3 11. Software Bug. Retrieved from Techopedia: https://www.techopedia.com/definition/24864/software-bug-.

transactie. 2021, 05 24. Retrieved from Vandale.nl: https://www.vandale.nl/gratis-woordenboek/nederlands/betekenis/transactie#.YKzAlqgzY2w.

Vallivaara, V. 2019. Asset Tracking With Smart Contracts. VTT Technical Research Centre of Finland Ltd.

Van Dale betekenis asset. 2021, 05 24. Retrieved from vandale.nl: https://www.vandale.nl/gratis-woordenboek/engels-nederlands/vertaling/asset#.YKtYY6gzY2w

Vermeulen, L. 2021, 4 28. Smart contractg als contracten. (D. Franken, Interviewer)

Wackerow, P. 2020, 12 23. PROOF-OF-STAKE (POS). Retrieved from ethereum.org: https://ethereum.org/en/developers/docs/consensus-mechanisms/pos/

Wat is een QR code. 2021, 5 24. Retrieved from kliksafe.nl: https://www.kliksafe.nl/blogs/online-risicos/wat-is-een-qr-code/#:~:text=De%20afkorting%20QR%20betekent%20Quick,verwijzing%20naar%20iets%20op%20internet.

Weitenberg, M.E. 2020. Smart Governance for Smart Contracts. Dutch Blockchain Coalition.

Wenbo Wang, D.T. 2019. A Survey on Consensus Mechanisms and Mining Strategy Management in Blockchain Networks. IEEE.

Werf, P.v. 2017. DE ETHISCHE KANT VAN DE DIGITALE TRANSFORMATIE. RATHENAU INSTITUUT.

Westra, D. 2018, 03 20. Smart contracts uitleg – Wat zijn smart contracts? Retrieved from alles over crypto: https://allesovercrypto.nl/blog/smart-contracts-uitleg-zijn-smart-contracts#voordelen.

William Stallings, J. R. (2000). Netwerkbeveiliging en cryptografie : beginselen en praktijk. Schoonhoven: Academic Service informatica.

WKO-systeem. 2021, 5 24. Retrieved from enerso.nl: https://enerso.nl/wko-systeem/#:~:text=WKO%20is%20een%20vorm%20van,te%20slaan%20in%20de%20bodem.

Wood, D.G. 2021. ETHEREUM: A SECURE DECENTRALISED GENERALISED TRANSACTION LEDGER.

woorden.org. 2021, 05 24. Retrieved from Woorden.org: https://www.woorden.org/woord/repetitief.

Zondag, N. 2021, 4 16. Smart contracten juridische kwesties. (D. Franken, Interviewer).

Chapter 7
Blockchain Technology for Decentralized Energy Production and Consumption
The Case of an Emerging Economy

Ridoan Karim[1,*] and *Imtiaz Sifat*[2]

1. Introduction

Recently energy industries, all over the world are increasingly concerned with environmental efficiency, reliability, transparency, accountability, social responsibility, or social inclusiveness and so on. These stated attributes are now more relevant than ever since COVID-19 wreaked havoc in the socio-political world order. The world has been forced to contribute to social and environmental causes and promote sustainability. Besides, many developing countries are carving new strategies and policies and attempts to attract new investments, including small or SME investors (Gómez-Bolaños et al., 2020).

Nevertheless, missing opportunities to attract new or foreign investors are rampant in the energy sector of developing countries due

[1] School of Business, Department of Business Law & Taxation, Monash University, Malaysia.
[2] Institute for Management Research, Radboud University, Netherlands.
* Corresponding author: ridoan.karim@monash.edu

to the challenges stemming from corruption, obscurity, technological uncertainty, and political instability (Baloch et al., 2020). Furthermore, the lack of transparency in the power industry associated with the demand and supply and the security of energy supply is a pressing matter for many countries, including Brazil, India, Indonesia, Bangladesh, Pakistan and many nations in Africa (Debnath and Mourshed, 2018). The conventional trends and the regulations between the Government and stakeholders in the above-mentioned countries have failed to safeguard the interests of the investors and significantly disarray the economic consequences.

Economical and stable electricity supply are often central to the economic development of a nation. The advent of new disruptive technologies offers a deciding environment if used correctly can handle major perils lingering to the energy sector. New innovations not only technically change the system but also the strategies of economic development by safeguarding the environment and protecting the expectations of the stakeholders (Debnath and Mourshed, 2018).

Blockchain, as a disruptive technology, creates various opportunities and challenges to traditional business standards, including the energy industry (Oh et al., 2017). Hence, this is of interest to examine the opportunities and challenges of blockchain technology in the energy industry to date and evaluate the existing examples and cases where blockchain is utilized in the energy sector. A Bangladeshi start-up company ME Solshare is currently offering its energy supports through blockchain. An in-depth overview of the potential opportunities and challenges relevant to blockchain in the energy sector will help to understand its application in different parts of the world. Hence, this study attempts to shed light on potential opportunities and associated industry challenges of blockchain applications in the energy industry.

Technological development in a specific industry requires strategy, regulatory and policy reforms. In the case of Bangladesh, blockchain in the energy industry can be a very prospective option where transparency is required amid the issues relating to corruption, backlogs, and ineffective management. Again utilization of blockchain in the energy industry of Bangladesh promises to track the sustainable energy mix of the country through promoting energy production by renewable means. It can be said that the consistent ascent in the costs of oil, coal, petroleum products and the absence of natural gas reserve holds the struggle for Bangladesh to supply the ever-increasing demand for energy. As of now, the vast energy demand of the nation is provided through petroleum and natural gas, with the additional support from some coal-based power plants. Nevertheless, the ecological effect of the use of petroleum derivatives is also an adjoining challenge for the government of Bangladesh. Hence, renewable energy, especially solar power plants, seems to be an attractive choice for Bangladesh to decrease non-renewable energy source utilization, provide a sufficient supply of energy and keep the earth clean from the ozone-depleting substance emanations.

ME Solshare, being an energy company promoting the use of solar power plants through blockchain application, promises to deliver many opportunities for the overall energy industry in Bangladesh, Nevertheless, there are challenges that need to be addressed. Challenges can be broadly categorized into legal, regulatory, technical, economic, social, and political which are, by its nature, are also connected with the public policies of the government. Without a proper business and regulatory framework, the government or the industry players are most likely to encounter difficulties associated with blockchain applications. Therefore, this chapter, promises to bring different perspectives that policymakers and companies might reflect before utilizing the blockchain as its contemporary forms in the energy industry.

2. Why blockchain in the energy industry ?

Concerns over sustainability, environmental efficiency, social inclusion, and transparency have been mounting around the world, and Bangladesh is no exception. Recently the country has pledged towards sustainable developments through active policymaking and regulatory pursuit of foreign funds into the nation's budding and foreign-dependent energy sector (Ahmed, 2019). A combination of inadequate pre-existing legal framework and lax enforcement are thought to be key contributors to these concerns (Karim et al., 2019). This resulted in an opportunity for the existing energy-sector players to shirk their environmental responsibilities and chase the accounting bottom line (Karim et al., 2019). Understanding this, the government has of late promised more rigor in handling matters in a bid to both attract more inward investment and simultaneously benefit the small and medium enterprises. Whether these initiatives have yielded the desired outcomes remains an open question. Both structural and operational factors contribute to the slow pace of progress.

Blockchain technology has been largely confined to finance and cryptocurrency. The distributed ledger system's relevance in other areas of business is slowly coming to light. Peer-to-peer energy trading is a specific use case that allows one to deep-dive into the real value added of blockchain technology. ME Solshare, a blockchain startup operating in Bangladesh, is connecting houses with solar panels in order to improve people's livelihood and market participation (UNFCCC, 2020). Access to electricity has major implications for alleviating poverty including prolonging the hours that people can be productive, whether for work or education. In Bangladesh, if people have an identity, they can get a loan from their bank to purchase a solar panel. They are able to use energy generated from this clean and consistent electricity source in places where it was not previously accessible. After consuming what they need, the user can sell their extra energy to their neighbors, creating a community microgrid. Microgrids also improve the community's resilience against black- and brownouts, where the central electricity grid may not be reliable. There are sixty-five million in Bangladesh that currently do not have access to the centralized grid (UNFCCC, 2020).

Despite such a promising application of blockchain in the energy industry, the company on several occasions has confronted challenges in the industry as well. One major limitation of blockchain technology is that it is still evolving. Due to only a few production-ready blockchain systems in the energy industry world-wide, there is always the risk of locking the product (a blockchain system) (Andoni et al., 2019). The adoption of a fully open-source technology for energy industry can also be detrimental as there remain sensitive issues which need to be addressed with privacy. Additionally, the scalability of major public blockchain systems is not satisfactory. In theory, the private blockchain systems seem to offer better scalability. However, there is no conclusive proof of their scalability as it is not well documented so far for any large-scale adoption. Hence, it is of interest to discover the scalability of blockchain applications of ME Solshare in the energy industry of Bangladesh (Rhydwan et al., 2020).

Additionally, there are organizational challenges of blockchain applications in the energy industry. The energy industry or the entreprenuers in the energy sector of Bangladesh are not aware of the advantages of the private blockchain technology, which can bring changes for their businesses. Many regard cryptocurrencies as the only application for blockchain and hence they treat these two synonymously (Hasan et al., 2018). The lack of expertise and local resources also play a key role to demotivate an organizsation towards a blockchain-based solution in the energy industry (Rhydwan et al., 2020). All this makes it challenging for these organizations to adopt blockchain to transform business models in the energy sector. The organizational acceptability and readiness for blockchain technology will depend on several factors: their understanding of blockchain technology and the advantages it might bring to them, the motivation to adapt to changes accordingly, access to technical expertise and the blockchain-friendly government incentives and policies (Albrecht et al., 2018). The lack of a combination of these factors creates a challenge to embrace blockchain technology in the energy industry. Hence, it is important to find both academic and practical solutions to this major challenge.

Simultaneously, there also remain certain legal challenges. Legal concerns vary from private to public international law, financial to energy laws and regulations, based on the nature and scope of blockchain applications. As finance transactions will move from energy providers or banks to a peer-to-peer system, the question appears who is accountable for securing each financial transaction's settlement (Penzo and Selvadurai, 2021). Such a duty of care could not only be levied on energy users and providers. Instead, an individual body or a network operator should be formed to conform to the requirements of financial services in compliance with banking laws and regulations.

Hence, the governance of any blockchain system is a critical issue which is often overlooked. How a blockchain is governed defines its success and adoption in many ways. Interestingly, different aspects of a blockchain governance are analog to how an organization or a consortium or organization distribute responsibilities among themselves (Karim and Sifat, 2022). Each organization/industry must understand this before they decide to adopt blockchain for their solutions. This calls for a new governance model which itself might be challenging.

3. Blockchain in the energy industry: usage & practice

Due to the speculative bubbles in the cryptocurrency markets, modern citizens consider blockchain synonymous to applications in finance, banking, and FinTech industries. In other words, the payment and mode of exchange applications of blockchain grab the highest number of headlines (Upadhyay, 2019). Nonetheless, with cryptocurrencies exhibiting enough independence in their pricing and market dynamics behavior, the controversy over whether they are an independent asset class is ceasing (Sifat, 2021). The novelty aspect of cryptocurrencies is effectively fading. This makes possible greater propagation of news to the public about the myriad applications and extensions of blockchain-based initiatives. The nature of blockchain technology has changed the fintech industries because of its high performance, fast and stable nature of transactions. Besides, blockchain is claimed to be able to enable financial trades, breaking down national currency frontiers (Chakravarty et al., 2020). Additionally, blockchain is said to reduce the burden of audits on every financial ledger (Queiroz et al., 2019).

Nevertheless, blockchain has its implications beyond digital currencies. In fact, there are various uses of this technology ranging from land and property registration to property possession, and trade protection (George et al., 2019). It can also be used, for international cash payment, fund transfer, and recording intellectual property rights and copyrights for different industries (Chang et al., 2019). As for payment systems, blockchain technology is the smartest application with greater accessibility, a more agile platform, less prone to errors, and smoother transfers than that of the other existing payment and settlement processes. In addition to the fintech industry, blockchain has a potent future in the energy industry. For the energy market, however, blockchain can be a very expensive data storage tool (Hou et al., 2019). Unfortunately, it is an undeniable fact that blockchain has always been widely underestimated in sectors outside the financial industry (Hald and Kinra, 2019).

Regulatory bodies grasp it even less, or probably not at all (Rennock et al., 2018), which means that the energy market (for good reasons is a heavily regulated market) will not be a suitable choice for the proliferation of decentralized blockchain technologies. Given this, it is still true that in addition to enabling money exchange, blockchain technology will be able to accommodate complex tasks such as tracking activity, property recordkeeping and exchanges, transfers of environmental and social goods, etc. As of the first quarter of 2021, another innovation of blockchain-enabled technology has gained momentum—nonfungible tokens. These tokens are exhibiting limitless power of blockchain technology in not only storing memory but also keeping accurate records and historical snapshots. There have already been certain implementations of blockchain in the energy industry. The focus here is on the possibilities that blockchain can bring in the energy industry.

3.1 Peer-to-peer energy trading

A recent paper by the German Energy Agency (DENA) reveals that the executives of the German energy sector opine that blockchain technology's blueprint holds promises for creating an effective, accessible, and—most crucially—a sustainable infrastructure of power generation and distribution (Mika and Goudz, 2020). Most industry practitioners also believe that eventual expansion of this sector is highly likely—as per the latest DENA survey (Burger et al., 2016). The existing views of market leaders today may be largely influenced by the internet buzz and new prospects around the consultancy sector. Due to the still embryonic nature of this technology's prospects, there are no ill precedents of blockchain technology creating accidents or making unsavory headlines to dissuade analysts' attitude towards a technological transition to a more sustainable energy infrastructure.

It appears that the uncertainty surrounding the way blockchain technology will eventually transform the industry is not large enough to discourage the quick adoption. Indeed, several consortiums have already been formed to bring together multiple industries to further this technology's reach and accelerate its adoption. The Energy Web Foundation is expected to partner with players of the blockchain working groups in the energy sector around the world to create a flexible, open-source platform targeted directly toward the demands of energy industry and design it to be energy efficient (Burger et al., 2016). Singularity (a well-known startup in the energy industry) is in collaboration with the Rocky Mountain Institute (American Energy Company) to create a partnership for the energy industry with the vision to make blockchain more productive to encourage more efficient operations in the energy sector (Bürer et al., 2019). The new partnership seeks to pursue R&D in blockchain and energy to help utilities or investors, technology creators, consumers, and green energy firms realize how current market structures may be assisted, undermined, or transformed.

Bloomberg New Energy Finance (BNEF) has published one case of a company using blockchain solutions to attract new consumers (McCrone et al., 2019). BNEF estimated that Tokyo Electric Power Co. would like to regain the customer's trust and confidence by restoring transparent information structure in the domestic market (McCrone et al., 2019). Japan's largest power provider has developed a company called Trende, which attempted to enter into solar energy production and enable peer-to-peer power purchases of solar technologies via blockchain (Martin, 2018).

Smaller companies or new entrants to the energy sector are increasingly evolving with peer-to-peer trading of energy models and utilities. Such trading through blockchain can bring a possible technological change. These changes can eventually lead to conceivably more profitable business models for certain types of customers (Martin, 2018). Consequently, blockchain could shape the prospective future of peer-to-peer power trading, since the energy start-ups are looking forward to offering competitive deals through innovative technologies. Nevertheless, it is yet be understood how such peer-to-peer transactions can be coordinated on a scalable level, thus maintaining improvements in the infrastructure that facilitates such power trading is quintessential. The peer-to-peer blockchain trade is implemented on a pilot scale in most countries.

3.2 Managing energy supply and demand in real-time

Electricity markets are constantly forced to balance supply and demand. Such a balance is a challenge for both renewable and fossil-fuel-based energy generation. In the transition process from fossil-fuels to renewable sources, many countries are in dire need of new flexible systems to accurately forecast the power demand and match the supply accordingly into the system. Hence, a transparent data structure (backed by blockchain technology) is also essential to evaluate energy sources and prepare them for quick adaption in times of scarcity.

Blockchain (theoretically), is the technology that can offer stable, real-time data transmission and allow effective monitoring and maintenance of electricity-industry infrastructures. The technology can also provide quicker response times (again, in theory) in an emergency

(Siemon et al., 2020). Data is expected to be protected and accessed by each stakeholder. Blockchain is anticipated to add a security and collaboration layer to the existing digital pilots by allowing quick, reliable data collection and connectivity between equipment vendors, infrastructure maintenance, and emergency response teams. In order to serve this purpose, Tennet TSO GmbH (Germany) is now partnering with battery manufacturers International Business Machines Corp. and Sonnen GmbH to establish a virtual transmission line using blockchain to use surplus electricity extracted from wind turbines and store power by disbanding into thousands of household batteries in the northern part of the world and unleash electricity in the south (Höhne and Tiberius, 2020). These actions could reduce the need for new power lines on which utilities depend on returns and efficient management of the supply chain of the energy industry (Höhne and Tiberius, 2020). The UK-based corporation Electron is also planning a new breakthrough in terms of the supply-chain model by utilizing blockchain technology (Goranovic et al., 2017). The company is also using blockchain to build (via versatility marketplace) a framework to maintain the power demand and supply. This event is dubbed as Energy eBay because of its tremendous role and prospects of stimulating widespread industry participations (Goranovic et al., 2017).

Developing countries, still undergoing the ultimate hurdle of ensuring sufficient energy supply, can implement blockchain-powered applications to make the demand forecasting strong and accurate via real-time data analytics from the system. Such exposure of information can help regulators to effectively manage the supply of electricity following its economic mandates. Real-time demand signals emitting from a blockchain-based ledger include the ability to transact between all the assets demanded and supplied, therefore, helps to make effective decisions (Dong et al., 2018).

3.3 *Promoting investments in energy industries*

According to Crunchbase (a multinational start-up database), at this time, 140 companies are coordinating toward the blockchain-empowered energy sector (Andoni et al., 2019). Start-ups appear to be the leading advancement in transforming the business models in the electricity industry to make use of blockchain-based applications (Deign, 2017). Blockchain technology offers transparency to investors. Governments are aiming to form strategic alliances with the energy start-ups with a view of employing the blockchain technology for quicker responses and incorporating trust in the system to break the conventional model of the slow licensing process (Andoni et al., 2019).

Start-ups can act as a potent player transforming the energy market through blockchain-enabled technologies. Nonetheless, to be successful for the energy revolution, there is a crying need for serious commitments and support from governments. Risks and incentives to achieve priorities such as climate change and energy transformation targets must be carefully considered when working with the appropriate grid infrastructure. Blockchain technology can trace the energy investments in different electricity sources and promote sustainable energy solutions.

US-based company TransActive Grid, Power Ledger, and Singularity from Australia, Ideo CoLab, etc., are some of the start-ups in the energy industries that are efficiently utilizing blockchain technology (Wang et al., 2017). These companies have connoted that specific usage of blockchain technology increases the efficiency in supply analyses of the energy industry, helps in pricing and project profits, assists in electricity sharing, provides options for automated power plants, and does microgrid management (German Energy Agency, 2016). In the meantime, such innovations can also be exploited to trade renewable energy certificates. Known as RECs, these are typically given to producers of solar energy based on the anticipated production demands rather than actual figures. Several innovative ventures are already occupied in designing grids and systems to facilitate power production to be able to get these certificates. One such firm, Volt Markets, supplies energy and monitors a trade network built on smart contracts underpinned by Ethereum's technology (Henderson et al., 2018).

3.4 Increasing energy access in developing countries

In the energy sector, blockchain can also retain its originality and be used as the cryptocurrency for monetary transactions, in fact, some companies have already begun this campaign; for instance, SolarCoin, Bankymoon, and BlockCharge, to name a few (Kumar, 2018). In terms of blockchain usage, start-ups are still involved while applications are catching up. Others would go for joint ventures and co-operations as a viable option. Hence, the value blockchain proposes would be the removal of the broker as intermediaries in between parties.

In principle, a complete decentralization of the energy sector through blockchain implementation may be accomplished if financial transactions are removed from central control. These advances may further allow room for inventions that over time would increase access to electricity in developing countries. Taking Smart prepaid meters as an example, a technology, that only releases power to residential consumers after they have updated their accounts and moved money to their energy supplier (Chitchyan and Murkin, 2018).

This program could be advantageous for high inflation countries like the BRICS economies or South Asian nations. Conceptualizations of the technology came from a South African enterprise—Bankymoon—which leverages Bitcoin's network to enable remote payment systems (Dogo et al., 2019). For poor economies which suffer from a lack of economic resources, such innovations bode well. As for the altruists who want to donate in helping these schools carry on their activities, they can bypass the traditional restrictions and dive right into crypto-based systems to contribute to the school's smart meter. Consequently, the schools will receive power credit and instantaneously achieve energy self-sufficiency without unnecessary difficulties from intermediaries (Henderson et al., 2018).

Blockchain can also do crowd-funding in the energy sector and increase energy access in developing countries (Arnold et al., 2019). Numerous solar panel schemes are still left unfunded in many parts of Africa, most of them are worth less than USD 1 million (Brilliantova and Thurner, 2019). Crowd-financing could fill-in this funding gap, where people around the world would be able to buy the photovoltaic cells that will make up the solar panels in African homes (Higgins, 2016). The solar panels can only be installed when enough solar cells are pre-purchased. Throughout the crowd-sale duration (a certain finite amount of days), the total an investor wants to pay is assigned to the number of solar cells he can get for it (because of the bitcoin's volatility) (Brilliantova and Thurner, 2019). These mentioned cells provide African households with electricity, and households, in turn, pay investors a rental income in bitcoin for several years. The blockchain platform is used in this case to fund access to electricity.

3.5 *Regulatory reporting and compliance*

Regulators constantly expect energy and resource firms to have large volumes of data that can be evaluated to identify non-compliance with legal and regulatory requirements (Diestelmeier, 2017). Collecting and analyzing the necessary data is a big challenge for the latest technology and applications. There is also a substantial danger of the data falling into the wrong hands and being misused, exposing confidential business information, and placing a company at a strategic disadvantage.

Blockchain could theoretically solve many of these problems, facilitating accountability and encouraging regulators to access safe, transparent data safely at source and encouraging businesses to keep a tight control over what information is accessible and who can access it (Diestelmeier, 2017). A significant additionally advantage of having such a forum to exchange knowledge with regulators is that it will establish the industry-standard data format, which is impossible at present (Bürer et al., 2019).

Energy companies are particularly worried about trade secrets. Private blockchain networks offer pre-approved parties' authorization for data and limited consortium entry. Private and cooperative blockchains offer an intermediate alternative before the required privacy features of business demand can be introduced by the public blockchains (Bürer et al., 2019). Blockchain's core focuses on the electricity market are cost reduction, sustainable development, and increased accountability without sacrificing privacy, which can bring a paradigm shift to the whole energy sector of a developing country within a short span.

4. Methods

This study used the qualitative method, collecting data through semi-structured interviews with a purposive sample of seven participants, consisting of three industry players, two academicians, one government employee and one legal expert. The thematic analysis framework of Braun and Clarke (2006) has been utilized to analyze the collected data.

Newman and Benz (1998) emphasized designing the methodology depending on the research questions. In general, qualitative approaches could be time-consuming and complicated (Saunders et al., 2016); nevertheless, the method can ensure the robustness of research through engaging experts' opinions. Whereas a quantitative methodology utilizes statistical analysis tools to theorize findings, a qualitative method aims to uncover new insights and to highlight the experience of experts (Saunders et al., 2016; Creswell, 1999), as well as to gain an overall knowledge of the research perspective by enabling the researcher to collect data from reality (Braun and Clarke, 2014). As this research aims to explore blockchain utilization in the energy industry, adopting a qualitative method seemed appropriate. The blockchain technology is still in a nascent stage in Bangladesh; hence, empirical elements such as field survey were not considered in this research.

4.1 Sampling method and sample size

In this study, the energy experts of the blockchain energy industry, energy companies/industry players (three), government bodies (two), academics (one) and legal expert (one) who have active participation in implementing blockchain projects in Bangladesh are taken as experts for the interview, because they can share firsthand information on the study's aims. The lack of experts on blockchain technology in Bangladesh proceeded as a challenge in devising a suitable sampling frame. Despite the unavailability of experts, 120 individuals in the energy and blockchain field have been identified to generate an accurate list. Furthermore, as the topic 'blockchain in the energy industry' is broad, specialists from many fields cannot be brought together without first comprehending their backgrounds.

Purposive sampling was used to collect data from the participants. According to Saunders et al. (2016), a common difficulty in business research is the lack of an appropriate sample frame, which encourages the use of non-probability sampling. According to Schindler and Cooper (2006) "*Participants for individual depth interviews are usually chosen not because their opinions are representative of the dominant opinion but because their experiences and attitudes will reflect the full scope of the issue under study.*" It cannot be denied that non-probability sampling has the risk of a researcher's subjective choices and can affect the sample; nevertheless, such a sampling can be utilized if a researcher has limited resources (e.g., workforce and time). The advantage of non-probability sampling is that it allows the researcher to concentrate on people with specific expertise with the relevant knowledge necessary to obtain the study's objectives (Etikan et al., 2016).

The sampling method was undertaken using heterogeneous sampling (Etikan et al., 2016), which included 120 experts—based on competence in 'energy' and 'blockchain technology.' Participants were chosen from a number of educational backgrounds and with diverse levels of experience in the field. The study participants were chosen and approached personally by the researcher. All the people who were approached consented to take part in the study.

Hence, the study found a sample frame of seven blockchain and energy experts for this study.

The sample size of the study is substantiated since it was already established that only five interviewees are sufficient to conduct a study

Table 7.1. Sample frame of seven blockchain and energy experts.

Field	List	Sector or Experience	Interview Date
Industry	Participant 1	Blockchain and Peer-to-Peer energy trading	October 24, 2021
Industry	Participant 2	Blockchain and Peer-to-Peer energy trading	October 22, 2021
Industry	Participant 3	Blockchain and Peer-to-Peer energy trading	October 25, 2021
Government (BPDB)	Participant 4	Energy Industry	October 28, 2021
Government (Engineer)	Participant 5	Blockchain	October 29, 2021
Academic (Lecturer)	Participant 6	Blockchain and Big Data	November 1, 2021
Legal Expert (Advocate in Bangladesh)	Participant 7	Energy Consultancy	November 5, 2021

(Krueger et al., 2012). The experts as interviewees included one software engineer, one technical analyst, one senior manager/engineer from ME Solarshare, a company promoting blockchain applications in the energy industry of Bangladesh. Additionally, one deputy general manager and one engineer from the Bangladesh Power Development Board (BPDB), one academician and one legal expert participated in the interviews for this project. With seven interviews and evaluating all the themes that have been identified through literature review, the sample size is deemed sufficient.

4.2 Data collection

To achieve the objective of the study, the mode of data collection was completed through semi-structured interviews. Qualitative interviews required the participant's responses to be interpreted, affecting the results due to the interviewer›s subjective biases (Saunders et al., 2016). However, the method has several benefits as the qualitative interviews highlight the experts' perspectives on a particular field (Rubin and Rubin, 2012), and scholars contended that this method is best suited to exploring real experiences (Denscombe, 2009). A semi-structured interview style allows to explore new topics or go further into concerns pointed out by the participants (Patton, 1980).

Nevertheless, the method was determined after weighing the inherent advantages and drawbacks as it suits best to achieve the study's objective. However, to improve the study's validity and reliability, the methodological flaws have been carefully considered. The recommendations from Saunders et al. (2016) and Newman and Benz (1998) were assessed carefully to review the interview questions and the participant's answers. The data was gathered using Kallio et al. (2016) approach for qualitative semi-structured interviews. In order to clarify the questions and increase the quality of the data collection, a pilot interview was conducted prior to the main interviews, and minor changes to the interview guide were made.

The interview questions were developed based on the subjects discovered through literature review. The interview guide provided the foundation for the interviews, but the participants were

Note: Adapted from Kallio et al. (2016).

encouraged to go more indepth. They were continuously asked to speak out about any problems or success factors they experienced relating to blockchain implementation in the energy industry. Video conferencing was used for the interviews. Before starting the interviews, sound and video tests were undertaken to verify that there were no technical issues that might impede the interview process. Before starting the interviews, all participants consented that they would be recorded. The project was discussed with the participants prior to the start of the study.

4.3 Data analysis

To discover, evaluate, and define the subjects in the collected material, the study used Braun and Clarke's (2006) qualitative analytical approach. Six primary processes were performed with the data, creating initial codes, exploring the themes, reviewing themes, defining and labeling themes, and finally producing the report with the data.

All interviews were transcribed. When the data was sorted and analyzed, it was discovered that all the identified prospects and challenges of utilizing blockchain technology in the energy industry could be categorized into five key subjects: peer-to-peer energy trading; managing energy supply and demand in real-time; promoting investments in energy industries; increasing energy access in developing countries; and regulatory reposting and compliance.

4.4 Ethical considerations

Before starting of this consultancy report, the London Graduate School assessed the proposal and granted ethical approval. During this research, special attention was paid to the following points:

Participants were made aware about the study and given the opportunity to provide the consent in writing (Silverman, 2005). All the research participants received a letter notifying them of the study's background, their ability to withdraw from the study, the importance of voluntary participation, and safeguarding the identity of the participants. At the time of the interview, the information was reiterated. None of the participants elected to stop taking part in the research. The identity of the participants was kept hidden. Special care was made in disclosing facts about the participants and publishing quotes because their professions were specified.

5. Findings and analysis

The participants' choices of prospects and challenges on blockchain adoption in Bangladesh's energy industry showed a high level of consistency. During the analytical process and the literature study, five primary subjects emerged. Although the participants were frequently encouraged to address any topic they wanted throughout the interviews, they all did so within the context of one of the five primary issues. As a result, the researcher believes that saturation has been reached.

5.1 Peer-to-peer energy trading in Bangladesh

The attraction of blockchain in the energy sector is yet to be discovered and understood, so from the above analysis, it can be postulated that blockchain caters immense possibilities for the energy sector of a developing country that faces challenges of instability, corruption, and lack of electricity supply. The blockchain can introduce and transform a well-functioning business model, and reduce risks of investments in the energy market. It can take care of the regulatory risks associated with investments, since risks in investments remain a major concern for corporate players.

Energy industry decision-makers and utility firms have stated that blockchains may solve some of the industry's problems. The advent of dispersed energy resources and information and communication technology is causing energy systems (ICT) transition. Blockchains can provide a viable solution for controlling and managing increasingly decentralized complex energy systems and microgrids.

Some utilities and their services in Bangladesh may be smart enough to obtain blockchain technology at its present state and can offer transparency and liberalization towards energy stakeholders at different levels.

> *"Blockchain-based communication system surely offers appealing characteristics. Blockchain can adequately respond to numerous obstructions found in the energy sector of Bangladesh. It can also cater to the corresponding requirement of the local trade in electricity production and consumption from a particular vantage point to provide the necessary shortage to the power grid." (Participant 3)*

In Bangladesh, blockchains can help regulate decentralized energy systems and microgrids. Community energy markets, which are facilitated by localized P2P energy trading or distributed platforms, can considerably boost energy self-production and self-consumption, which can impact revenues and rates. Blockchains have the potential to be utilized for smart device connection, data transfer, and storage. Smart meters, sophisticated sensors, network monitoring equipment, control, and energy management systems, as well as smart home energy controllers and building monitoring systems are all examples of intelligent devices in the smart grid. Smart grid applications can benefit from data standardization provided by blockchain technology in addition to safe data transport.

> *"Blockchains in the energy industry of Bangladesh, has the potential to start a new era of decentralised energy networks. I have explained in several conferences and showed empirical evidences on how blockchain can be a cost-effective option in energy management scenario flexibility services or asset management." (Participant 1)*

Nevertheless, one major limitation of blockchain technology is that it is still evolving. Due to only a few production-ready blockchain systems in the energy industry world-wide, there is always the risk of locking a product (a blockchain system). The adoption of a fully open-source technology for energy industry can also be detrimental as there remain sensitive issues which need to be addressed with privacy. Additionally, the scalability of major public blockchain systems is not satisfactory. In theory, the private blockchain systems seem to offer better scalability. However, there is no conclusive proof of their scalability as it is not well documented so far for any large-scale adoption.

> *"A private blockchain system does not allow everyone to access the blockchain data, only authorised users can access it. Nevertheless, it must be noted that anyone, who has access to the blockchain network, can access every single piece of data in the blockchain, unless special measures are taken. This may undermine the privacy of different organisations who are part of the same private blockchain network, but do not want to share sensitive information with one another." (Participant 6)*

The existence of different blockchain systems provide a wide-range of options for organizations. It also offers an opportunity for them to select the appropriate one for their special use-cases. On the other hand, the inadvertent side-effect of this is the creation of blockchain silos that might need to be inter-connected in the future. However, the lack of interoperability and compatibility among these blockchain systems will be a major hurdle to bridge these disconnected silos. The energy industry requires interoperability and compatibility to perform efficiently. Additionally, it seems Bangladesh has scarcity of blockchain experts. Without understanding the full effect of blockchain in the energy industry, participant 2 believes the country should not transform the energy transitions into this platform immediately.

> *"Every new technology faces a shortage of expertise, especially during its evolving period. Blockchain technology is no exception; there is an acute shortage of blockchain experts all over the world. This is even more true in case of the energy industry. In addition, the lack of knowledge*

> *about blockchain and its benefits among the practitioners, both in private and government organisations in Bangladesh, is a major challenge for a wide-scale blockchain adoption. Because of the lack of required technical expertise or lack of other technical resources, many organisations are hesitant to explore the ways a blockchain system can help them. This is prohibiting them from harnessing the potential benefits of any blockchain system, especially in the energy industry." (Participant 2)*

5.2 *Managing energy supply in Bangladesh*

The attraction of blockchain in the energy sector is yet to be discovered and understood, it can be postulated that blockchain caters immense possibilities for the energy sector of a developing country that faces challenges of instability, corruption, and lack of electricity supply. However, blockchain can introduce and transform a well-functioning business model, and reduce risks of investments in the energy market. Not to mention, blockchain can take care of the regulatory risk associated with investments since risks in investments remain a major concern for corporate players.

> *"For me, some utilities and their services in Bangladesh may be smart enough to obtain blockchain technology at its present state and can offer transparency and liberalization towards energy stakeholders at different levels. At this juncture, the review of prospects and challenges connected to the application of blockchain technologies in the energy sector of Bangladesh is elaborated." (Participant 7)*

The participants saw a need to make more organizational acceptability and readiness for blockchain technology. The energy industry or the entreprenuers in the energy sector of Bangladesh are not aware of the advantages of the private blockchain technology, which can bring changes for their businesses. Many regard cryptocurrencies as the only application for blockchain and hence they treat these two synonymously. The lack of expertise and local resources also play a key role to demotivate an organization towards a blockchain-based solution in the energy industry. All this makes it challenging for these organizations to adopt blockchain to transform the business models in the energy sector. Hence, one interview differed from the rest; here the participant described that a blockchain adoption for any organization in the energy sector can implicate a new model of thinking which would require to transform their business model.

> *"If a drastic transformation is required, many business organisations and NGOs in the energy industry of Bangladesh will be unwilling to adopt any blockchain system soon. Risk estimation is an intrinsic process for*

any organisation when it decides to adopt a new technology which would require significant business model transformation." (Participant 4)

Several participants pointed out that clarifying the blockchain utilization is a long-term, systematic work that needs to be established and mained within the energy industry, which could take time.

"The adoption of a fully-open source technology for energy industry can also be detrimental as there remains sensitive issues which need to be addressed with privacy. Additionally, the scalability of major public blockchain systems is not satisfactory. In theory, the private blockchain systems seem to offer better scalability. However, there is no conclusive proof of their scalability as it is not well documented so far for any large-scale adoption." (Participant 3)

Bangladesh is still undergoing the ultimate hurdle of ensuring sufficient energy supply, thus it can implement blockchain-powered applications to make the demand forecasting strong and accurate via real-time data analytics from the system. Such exposure of information can help the regulators to effectively manage the supply of electricity following its economic mandates. Real-time demand signals emitting from a blockchain-based ledger include the ability to transact between all the assets demanded and supplied, therefore, helps to make effective decisions.

The blockchain technologies in the power sector can improve the power-metering market. In Bangladesh, blockchain has the potential to finally either break the monopoly regime or partly bring the competitive bidding into the system which is currently missing. Blockchain-enabled smart metering services can enhance the value creation, while it should be done with a strict observation of accepted standards in order to secure transactional trust. For Bangladesh, the future of the economy is largely reliant on the energy industry. Blockchain technologies can be the enabler to render an energy management. As participant 3 said:

"I believe, the energy industry of Bangladesh can drastically change if it is embedded with blockchain." (Participant 3)

5.3 *Promoting investments in energy industries*

Blockchain in the energy industry of Bangladesh can bring prospective investments. Smaller companies or new entrants to the energy sector of Bangladesh can increasingly involve with peer-to-peer trading of energy models and utilities. While Bangladesh still faces a challenge to ensure sufficient energy supply, it can introduce blockchain to understand the real-time electricity demand. Such exposure of information can help the regulators of the country to effectively manage the supply of electricity by understanding its economic mandates. Blockchain can also help via crowd-funding in the energy sector of Bangladesh, especially in the renewable energy industry. Such an option of crowd-funding may increase access to energy in this vicinity. For Bangladesh, blockchain can solve the pressing issues of the energy sector relating to corruption, transparency, and accountability.

> *"I believe, for a developing economy like Bangladesh, Blockchain certainly has the answers to numerous challenges regarding the decentralized energy-production scenario. It can further aid the policymakers of the country to discern the energy demand and deviations in real-time through grid simulations. For the policymakers, blockchain is also helpful to make the demand planning and accompany all the other considerations through the implementation of this technology. As an aftermath, the costs of electricity would be open to all the stakeholders, including utilities owned and/or managined the power distribution grid." (Participant 1)*

In Bangladesh's wholesale energy markets complicated operations with the involvement of third-party intermediaries such as brokers, trading agents, exchanges, price reporters, logistics providers, banks, and regulators exist. To integrate information kept independently by each phase of the transaction, available techniques entail manual post-processing and additional communications. As a result, present procedures are sluggish and time-consuming, as the transactions in Bangladesh must be checked and reconciled many times from the start to finish. Blockchain can play a massive role here to diminish such intermediaries.

Nevertheless, participant 7 has introduced some challenges in such aspects as well:

> *"As finance transactions will move from energy providers or banks to a peer-to-peer system, it comes to the question of who is accountable for securing each financial transaction's settlement. Such a duty of care should not only be levied on energy users and providers. Instead, an individual body or a network operator could be formed to conform to the requirements of financial services in compliance with the banking laws and regulations." (Participant 7)*

Hence, a perfect blockchain paradigm should allow for a mechanism that totally operates without a responsible central authority. But a legal personality is not defined in blockchain applications. In case of any damages appearing, the existing liability laws and regimes are not sufficient to deal with the compensations. This constitutes a series of legal problems. Hence, specific liability laws relating to blockchain in energy industries are needed to guarantee the legal responsibilities of the parties involved. Specific laws are needed to administer the liability principles in payment defaults, technological breakdowns, or deliberate non-performance, etc. As the energy industry typically entails using vital infrastructure, the stakeholders need an emergency plan to specify the protocols in case of a disaster.

5.4 Increasing energy access in Bangladesh

Several participants described that the blockchain start-ups, like ME Solshare could help to increase the energy access in rural areas. Bangladesh, with an exceptional track record of growth and development, is on course to becoming a higher middle-income nation in the upcoming years, and has become a global role model for growth and development. However, Bangladesh still confronts several obstacles that must be adequately handled for the country to continue its path to achieving the SDGs by 2030 and being a developed nation by 2041. The access to energy is something that Bangladesh is still struggling with. It is undeniable that proper use of cutting-edge technology, such as blockchain technology in the energy industry, will play a significant role to mitigate the challenges associated with the energy crisis.

> *"One of the key obstacles of Bangladesh is the lack of accountability and transparency that is common for the energy sector. For the sustainable development of a country, it is imperative to adopt mechanisms that will increase accountability and transparency in energy. Ensuring accountability and transparency has added advantages. For example, it increases trust and instills confidence in the Government and public sectors. That is why it is imperative that the Government adopts mechanisms by which trust can be increased. I believe, this trust can increase when people receive their right to energy access." (Participant 3)*

The participants from ME Solshare believe numerous solar panel schemes are still left unfunded in Bangladesh. Crowd-financing could fill this funding gap, where people around the world would be able to buy the photovoltaic cells that will make up the solar panels on Bangladeshi homes. The solar panels only get installed when enough solar cells are pre-purchased. Throughout the crowd-sale duration (a certain finite number of days), the total an investor wants to pay is assigned to the number of solar cells he can get for it (because of the bitcoin's volatility). These mentioned cells provide Bangladeshi households with electricity, and households, in turn, pay investors a rental income for several years.

> *"The blockchain platform can be used in this case to fund access to electricity." (Participant 5)*

5.5 *Regulatory reporting and compliance: issues relating to laws of Bangladesh*

All the participants have accepted that blockchain can identify non-compliance with legal and regulatory requirements in the energy industry. Nevertheless, they have mentioned the biggest challenge of blockchain implementation in the energy industry of Bangladesh lies with law and policy. Bangladesh has always considered blockchain-based cryptocurrencies as "hostile." As per the Foreign Exchange Regulation Act, 1947, and the Money Laundering Prevention Act, 2012, the Bangladesh Bank finds bitcoin and other cryptocurrencies illegal. There is, however, considerable controversy about the legality of utilizing the blockchain technology itself, other than its crypto aspects.

> *"I think although the government is recently introducing several aspects of blockchain applications for upholding the motto of "Digital Bangladesh," the policy-makers seem to have no clue how to regulate the blockchain technology." (Participant 7)*

Most of the energy-related blockchain applications so far are held in public blockchains. All transactions in public blockchains are easily accessible. Nevertheless, transactions in public blockchains do not indicate that the identity of the parties is always understandable. For example, the parties in a bitcoin transaction can participate anonymously. This, therefore, can be an added advantage for cryptocurrency situations; nevertheless, it contributes to difficulties for energy industries, both politically and philosophically.

Hence, money laundering on ETS markets, or market theft due to confidentiality, will then remain as a persisting challenge in the energy market even though blockchain applications are introduced. Therefore, the existing situation of market exploitation and uneven competition by large energy vendors and suppliers cannot be easily changed through blockchain applications. This will affect the integrity of the relevant traditional economy, except for implementing blockchain applications that can identify the parties in energy transactions. Consequently, a range of regulatory reforms have been developed relating to blockchain applications, especially in the financial sector. While there are expert arguments on the blockchain recognition/identification of electronic profiles, such access to identity remains unanswered due to technical and regulatory barriers.

> *"I think unidentifiability will lead to a situation where the stakeholders cannot identify the real problem or hold any authority responsible for a wrong, which stands against the core philosophy of introducing blockchain in the energy industry." (Participant 6)*

One of the basic features of blockchain contradicts the personal data laws. Most of the laws relating to data protection state that personal data must be deleted after they have served their purpose. Many practitioners and academic observers have argued that blockchain technology is incompatible with privacy laws like the EU General Data Protection Regulation, or GDPR. The blockchain's original goal was to allow peer-to-peer transactions without the need for a central data possessor. No party takes responsibility for the availability or protection of a specific blockchain network in a permissionless public blockchain system. All users of the system have access to the data on the network. In the case of sensitive data in the energy industry, blockchain certainly breaches several privacy principles, such as "Rights of Data Subjects", "Security Principle", "Retention Principle" and "Right to be Forgotten".

> *".......it is important to note that Bangladesh does not have any specific legislation relating to data protection. The Technology Act and Digital Securities Act provides legal recognition for electronic certificates and transactions carried out employing electronic data interchange, in addition to other means of electronic communication, which involve the use of alternative or paper-based methods of communication, and storage of information to facilitate electronic filing of documents with government agencies. It is regardless to say that the government requires specific legislation comprising with specific clauses of blockchain and data privacy if the technology needs to be utilized in the energy industry." (Participant 7)*

6. Discussion and recommendations

Blockchain technologies are deemed to be one of the most forthcoming pathways to expedite the entrance of various energy sources. Nevertheless, there are a lot of challenges associated with it. One major limitation of the blockchain technology is that it is still evolving. Due to only a few production-ready blockchain systems in the energy industry world-wide, there is always the risk of locking to the product (a blockchain system).

The energy industry or the entreprenuers in the energy sector of Bangladesh are not aware of the advantages of the private blockchain technology, which can bring changes for their businesses. Many regard cryptocurrencies as the only application for blockchain and hence they treat these two synonymously. The lack of expertise and local resources also play a key role to demotivate an organization towards a blockchain-based solution in the energy industry. All this makes it challenging for these organizations to adopt blockchain to transform the business models in the energy sector.

Additionally, with every dramatic transition of new technologies, blockchain poses a range of legal concerns. These vary from private to public international law, financial to energy laws and regulations, based on the nature and scope of blockchain applications.

Most of the energy-related blockchain applications so far are held in public blockchains (Mika and Goudz, 2020). All transactions in public blockchains are easily accessible. Nevertheless, transactions in public blockchains do not indicate that the identity of the parties is always understandable (Feng et al., 2019). Unidentifiability will lead to a situation where the stakeholders cannot identify the real problem or hold any authority responsible for a wrong, which stands against the core philosophy of introducing blockchain in the energy industry.

Hence, money laundering on ETS markets, or market theft due to confidentiality, will then remain as a persisting challenge in the energy market even though blockchain applications are introduced. Therefore, the existing situation of market exploitation and uneven competition by large energy vendors and suppliers cannot be easily changed through blockchain applications. This will affect the integrity of the relevant traditional economy, except for implementing blockchain applications that can identify the parties in energy transactions (Corrales et al., 2019). Therefore, a range of regulatory reforms have been developed relating to blockchain applications, especially in the financial sector. While there are expert arguments on the blockchain recognition/identification of electronic profiles, such access to identity remains unanswered due to technical and regulatory barriers.

The chapter has identified prospects and challenges of blockchain implementation in the energy industry. Based on the findings, four recommendations are made which Bangladesh could follow:

6.1 *Establishing governance through laws and policies*

The governance of any blockchain system is a critical issue which is often overlooked. How a blockchain is governed defines its success and adoption in many ways (Zachariadis et al., 2019). Interestingly, different aspects of a blockchain governance are analog as to how an organization or a consortium or organizations distribute responsibilities among themselves. Each organization/industry must understand this before they decide to adopt blockchain for their solutions. This calls for a new governance model which itself could be challenging.

A regulatory framework surrounding any novel technology instills confidence among the adopters. On the contrary, the lack of any such framework creates uncertainties. This is why a blockchain-friendly regulatory framework can be an effective tool to overcome many challenges within an industry.

Since it is possible for the nodes of a decentralized (particularly public) ledger to span multiple locations around the world, it becomes hard to establish a specific application of jurisdictions' laws and regulations (Corrales Compagnucci et al., 2020). But the risk of a transaction of an industry representing every jurisdiction remains. This results in an overwhelming number of rules and regulations that can be applicable on transactions in a blockchain based system, even in the energy sector. The laws that might apply to transactions of public blockchain systems have to be considered beforehand so that necessary measures can be taken to mitigate the risks. On the contrary, in a private or permissioned blockchain the process is quite easy because it has the provision of creating a form of legal framework and internal governance structure.

It is obvious that law and enforcement would work as a significant determinant to either open the market or close them for good. The fast development of proactive regulation remains a challenge to the regulators. And devising this environment would make sure of consumer protection and guarantee a system with significant details for a well-functioning society, for instance, the secure and reliable supply of electricity. Further, it is important to recognize this systematic stability without obstructing the disruptive potential of blockchain technology. Besides, an absence of law or regulation regarding blockchain could make investors skeptical about funding. Before investing in new technologies, it is usual for the energy industry to be patient and wait for a long time for technology to catch up, the same also applies for the emergence of policies.

6.2 *Creating human resources and technical experts*

Blockchain is a cutting-edge technology which is full of technical jargon which even the seasoned tech enthusiasts and programmers find hard to grasp (Höhne and Tiberius, 2020). For any successful adoption of any blockchain-based service in the energy industry of Bangladesh, it is imperative that the usability of such service is analyzed so that all kinds of consumers can use it effectively.

6.3 *Securing financial transactions*

Protection of transactions and security can benefit from cryptographic techniques in Bangladesh, although the application of crytocurrency is still legally prohibited. It can cut the intermediaries of the wholesale energy market, enhancing the direct transactions between the producer and consumer. For a developing economy like Bangladesh, blockchain certainly has the answers to numerous challenges regarding the decentralized energy production scenario. It can further aid the policymakers of the country to discern the energy demand and deviations in real time through grid simulations. For policymakers, blockchain is also helpful to create demand planning and accompany all the other considerations through the implementation of this technology (Kiviat, 2015). As an consequence, the costs of electricity would be open to all the stakeholders, including utilities owning and/or managing the power distribution grid.

6.4 *Increase public acceptance*

The organizational acceptability and readiness for blockchain technology will depend on several factors: their understanding of blockchain technology and the advantages it might bring to them, the motivation to adapt to changes accordingly, access to technical expertise and the blockchain-friendly government incentives and policies (Kouhizadeh et al., 2021). The lack of a combination of these factors imposes a challenge to embrace blockchain technology in the energy industry. Hence, there is a need for positive promotion of blockchain utilization through different campaigns implemented by the Government.

7. Conclusion

Embarking on blockchain has the power to unite the fragmented systems in order to generate insights and assess the value of care properly. In the long run, a nationwide blockchain network to keep the energy records may enhance efficiencies and bolster better investments. However, blockchain technology has neither reached the maturity stage nor the silver bullet to an instant solution. Several organizational, technical, and behavioral economic challenges need to be approached before adopting blockchain in the energy sector of Bangladesh.

Therefore, though this technology has tremendous potentials, it is very important to note that such technology should be dealt with sincerity. To achieve the government's vision toward a 'Digital Bangladesh', the government should regulate such technologies to achieve the maximum growth surrounding the energy industry. In addition, a pilot project on the energy sector can also be introduced in order to understand the capability of blockchain technology and to use it to the fullest in order to enjoy the maximum benefit for the country.

This chapter has identified the main challenges and prospects of blockchain implementation in the energy industry of Bangladesh. This study contributed to existing research by collecting qualitative data on blockchain implementation in the energy industry. Collecting in-depth qualitative data in the context of Bangladesh had not been done before.

The study confirmed results of earlier studies which also emphasized the importance of utilizing blockchain in the energy industry, especially in the developing country context. It also contributed to existing research by identifying a particular challenge to the implementation of blockchain technology in the context of Bangladesh. This finding had not been emphasized in earlier studies. Future researchers may focus on each aspect of this research findings in more detail and use quantitative research tools to answer different research questions.

References

Ahmed, B. 2019. Environmental governance and sustainable development in Bangladesh: millennium development goals and sustainable development goals. Asia Pacific Journal of Public Administration 41(4). doi: 10.1080/23276665.2019.1698930.

Albrecht, S., S. Reichert, J. Schmid, J. Strüker, D. Neumann and G. Fridgen. 2018. Dynamics of blockchain implementation—a case study from the energy sector. In Proceedings of the 51st Hawaii International Conference on System Sciences. doi: 10.24251/hicss.2018.446.

Andoni, M., V. Robu, D. Flynn, S. Abram, D. Geach, D. Jenkins, P. McCallum and A. Peacock. 2019. Blockchain technology in the energy sector: A systematic review of challenges and opportunities. Renewable and Sustainable Energy Reviews. doi: 10.1016/j.rser.2018.10.014.

Arnold, L., M. Brennecke, P. Camus, G. Fridgen, T. Guggenberger, S. Radszuwill, A. Rieger, A. Schweizer and N. Urbach. 2019. Blockchain and initial coin offerings: blockchain's implications for crowdfunding. In Business Transformation through Blockchain. doi: 10.1007/978-3-319-98911-2_8.

Baloch, Z.A., Q. Tan, N. Iqbal, M. Mohsin, M. Alharthi, W. Iqbal and I.S. Chaudhry. 2020. Trilemma assessment of energy intensity, efficiency, and environmental index: evidence from BRICS countries. Environmental Science and Pollution Research. doi: 10.1007/s11356-020-09578-3.

Braun, V. and V. Clarke. 2006. Using thematic analysis in psychology. Qualitative Research in Psychology 3(2): 77–101. ISSN 1478-0887 Available from: http://eprints.uwe.ac.uk/11735. doi: 10.1097/00005053-199205000-00001.

Braun, V. and V. Clarke. 2014. What can "thematic analysis" offer health and wellbeing researchers?. International Journal of Qualitative Studies on Health and Well-being 9(1): 26152.

Brilliantova, V. and T.W. Thurner. 2019. Blockchain and the future of energy. Technology in Society. doi: 10.1016/j.techsoc.2018.11.001.

Bürer, M.J., M. De Lapparent, V. Pallotta, M. Capezzali and M. Carpita. 2019. Use cases for Blockchain in the Energy Industry Opportunities of emerging business models and related risks. Computers and Industrial Engineering. doi: 10.1016/j.cie.2019.106002.

Burger, C., A. Kuhlmann, P. Richard and J. Weinmann. 2016. Blockchain in the energy transition. A survey among decision-makers in the German energy industry. German Energy Agency.

Chakravarty, S.R. and P. Sarkar. 2020. Applications of blockchain. In an Introduction to Algorithmic Finance, Algorithmic Trading and Blockchain. doi: 10.1108/978-1-78973-893-320201021.

Chang, S.E., Y.C. Chen and T.C. Wu. 2019. Exploring blockchain technology in international trade: Business process re-engineering for letter of credit. Industrial Management and Data Systems. doi: 10.1108/IMDS-12-2018-0568.

Chitchyan, R. and J. Murkin. 2018. Review of blockchain technology and its expectations: Case of the energy sector. arXiv.

Corrales Compagnucci, M., T. Kono and S. Teramoto. 2020. Legal aspects of decentralized and platform-driven economies. In Perspectives in Law, Business and Innovation. doi: 10.1007/978-981-15-1350-3_1.

Corrales, M., P. Jurcys and G. Kousiouris. 2019. Legal Tech, Smart Contracts and Blockchain, Legal Tech, Smart Contracts and Blockchain, Perspectives in Law, Business and Innovation.

Creswell, J.W. 1999. Mixed-Method Research: Introduction and Application. In Handbook of Educational Policy (pp. 455–472). Academic Press.

Debnath, K.B. and M. Mourshed. 2018. Challenges and gaps for energy planning models in the developing-world context. Nature Energy. doi: 10.1038/s41560-018-0095-2.

Deign, J. 2017. 15 Firms Leading the Way on Energy Blockchain, Greentech Media.

Denscombe, M. 2009. Ground Rules for Social Research: Guidelines for Good Practice. McGraw-Hill Education (UK).

Diestelmeier, L. 2017. Regulating for blockchain technology in the electricity sector: Sharing electricity-and opening Pandora's Box? In 16th Annual Conference in Science, Technology, and Society Studies.

Dogo, E.M., A.F. Salami, N. Nwulu and C. Aigbavboa. 2019. Blockchain and Internet of Things-Based Technologies for Intelligent Water Management System. in. doi: 10.1007/978-3-030-04110-6_7.

Dong, Z., F. Luo and G. Liang. 2018. Blockchain: a secure, decentralized, trusted cyber infrastructure solution for future energy systems. Journal of Modern Power Systems and Clean Energy. doi: 10.1007/s40565-018-0418-0.

Etikan, I., R. Alkassim and S. Abubakar. 2016. Comparision of snowball sampling and sequential sampling technique. Biometrics and Biostatistics International Journal 3(1): 55.

Feng, Q., D. He, S. Zeadally, M.K. Khan and N. Kumar. 2019. A survey on privacy protection in blockchain system. Journal of Network and Computer Applications. doi: 10.1016/j.jnca.2018.10.020.

George, R.P. et al. 2019. Blockchain for business. Journal of Investment Compliance. doi: 10.1108/joic-01-2019-0001.

German Energy Agency. 2016. Blockchain in the energy transition. A survey among decision-makers in the German energy industry. Berlin. Available at https://www.dena.de/file admin/dena/Dokumente/meldungen/dena/ESMT studies_blockchain_englisch.pdf.

Gómez-Bolaños, E., N.E. Hurtado-Torres and B.L. Delgado-Márquez. 2020. Disentangling the influence of internationalization on sustainability development: Evidence from the energy sector. Business Strategy and the Environment. doi: 10.1002/bse.2360.

Goranovic, A., M. Meisel, L. Fotiadis, S. Wilker, A. Treytl and T. Sauter. 2017. Blockchain applications in microgrids: An overview of current projects and concepts. In Proceedings IECON 2017 - 43rd Annual Conference of the IEEE Industrial Electronics Society. doi: 10.1109/IECON.2017.8217069.

Hald, K.S. and A. Kinra. 2019. How the blockchain enables and constrains supply chain performance. International Journal of Physical Distribution and Logistics Management. doi: 10.1108/IJPDLM-02-2019-0063.

Hasan, M.G., K.I. Sharif and M.H. Miraz. 2018. Supply chain management for garments industries using blockchain in Bangladesh. Journal of Business Management and Economic Research. doi: 10.29226/tr1001.2018.54.

Henderson, K., M. Rogers and E. Knoll. 2018. What every Utility CEO should know about Blockchain. McKinsey & Company.

Higgins, S. 2016. How Bitcoin Brought Electricity to a South African School, CoinDesk.

Höhne, S. and V. Tiberius. 2020. Powered by blockchain: forecasting blockchain use in the electricity market. International Journal of Energy Sector Management. doi: 10.1108/IJESM-10-2019-0002.

Hou, W., L. Guo and Z. Ning. 2019. Local electricity storage for blockchain-based energy trading in industrial internet of things. IEEE Transactions on Industrial Informatics. doi: 10.1109/TII.2019.2900401.

Kallio, H., A.M. Pietilä, M. Johnson and M. Kangasniemi. 2016. Systematic methodological review: developing a framework for a qualitative semi-structured interview guide. Journal of Advanced Nursing 72(12): 2954–2965.

Karim, M.A., R. Karim, M.T. Islam, F. Muhammad-Sukki, N.A. Bani and M.N. Muhtazaruddin. 2019. Renewable energy for sustainable growth and development: An evaluation of law and policy of Bangladesh. Sustainability (Switzerland) 11(20). doi: 10.3390/su11205774.

Karim, R. and I. Sifat. 2022. Blockchain technology in the energy industry: a review on policies and regulations. pp. 109–125. *In*: Sonali Vyas et al. (eds.). Blockchain Technology: Exploring Opportunities, Challenges, and Applications. Boca Raton: CRC Press. doi: 10.1201/9781003138082-7.

Kiviat, T.I. 2015. Beyond Bitcoin: Issues in regulating blockchain transactions. Duke Law Journal.

Kouhizadeh, M., S. Saberi and J. Sarkis. 2021. Blockchain technology and the sustainable supply chain: Theoretically exploring adoption barriers. International Journal of Production Economics. doi: 10.1016/j.ijpe.2020.107831.

Krueger, T., T. Page, K. Hubacek, L.C. Smith and K.M. Hiscock. 2012. The role of expert opinion in environmental modelling. Environmental Modelling and Software 36: 4–18. doi: 10.1016/j.envsoft.2012.01.011.

Kumar, N.M. 2018. Blockchain: Enabling wide range of services in distributed energy system. Beni-Suef University Journal of Basic and Applied Sciences. doi: 10.1016/j.bjbas.2018.08.003.

Martin, C. 2018. How Blockchain Is Threatening to Kill the Traditional Utility. Bloomberg.com.

McCrone, A. et al. 2019. Global Trends in Renewable Energy Investment 2019. Bloomberg New Energy Finance.

Mika, B. and A. Goudz. 2020. Blockchain-technology in the energy industry: blockchain as a driver of the energy revolution? With focus on the situation in Germany. Energy Systems. doi: 10.1007/s12667-020-00391-y.

Newman, I. and C.R. Benz. 1998. Qualitative-Quantitative Research Methodology: Exploring the Interactive Continuum. SIU Press.

Oh, S., M. Kim, Y. Park, G. Roh and C. Lee. 2017. Implementation of blockchain-based energy trading system. Asia Pacific Journal of Innovation and Entrepreneurship. doi: 10.1108/apjie-12-2017-037.

Patton, M.Q. 1980. Qualitative Evaluation Methods.

Penzo, S. and N. Selvadurai. 2021. A hard fork in the road: developing an effective regulatory framework for public blockchains. Information and Communications Technology Law. doi: 10.1080/13600834.2021.1959729.

Queiroz, M.M., R. Telles and S.H. Bonilla. 2019. Blockchain and supply chain management integration: a systematic review of the literature. Supply Chain Management. doi: 10.1108/SCM-03-2018-0143.

Rennock, M.J.W., A. Cohn and J.R. Butcher. 2018. Blockchain technology regulatory and investigations. The Journal Litigation.

Rhydwan, A.H.M., M.S. Choyon, M.N. Iftekhar, A.M.H. Sad and D. Nandi. 2020. Smart grid implementation with consortium blockchain: a proposed model for Bangladesh. In ETCCE 2020 - International Conference on Emerging Technology in Computing, Communication and Electronics. doi: 10.1109/ETCCE51779.2020.9350911.

Rubin, H.J. and I.S. Rubin. 2012. Qualitative Interviewing: The Art of Hearing Data. SAGE Publications.

Saunders, M., P. Lewis and A. Thornhill. 2016. Research Methods for Business Students. 7th ed. New York: Pearson Education.

Schindler, P.S. and D.R. Cooper. 2006. Marketing Research. Tata McGraw-Hill Education.

Siemon, C., D. Rueckel and B. Krumay. 2020. Blockchain technology for emergency response. In Proceedings of the 53rd Hawaii International Conference on System Sciences. doi: 10.24251/hicss.2020.075.

Sifat, I.M. 2021. On cryptocurrencies as an independent asset class: Long-horizon and COVID-19 pandemic era decoupling from global sentiments. Finance Research Letters 43: 102013. https://doi.org/10.1016/j.frl.2021.102013.

Silverman, D. 2005, September. Instances or sequences? Improving the state of the art of qualitative research. In Forum Qualitative Sozialforschung/Forum: Qualitative Social Research (Vol. 6, No. 3).

UNFCCC. 2020. ME SOLshare: Peer-to-Peer Smart Village Grids | Bangladesh, United Nations Framework Convention on Climate Change.

Upadhyay, N. 2019. Transforming Social Media Business Models Through Blockchain, Transforming Social Media Business Models Through Blockchain. doi: 10.1108/9781838672997.

Wang, J., Q. Wang, N. Zhou and Y. Chi. 2017. A novel electricity transaction mode of microgrids based on blockchain and continuous double auction. Energies. doi: 10.3390/en10121971.

Zachariadis, M., G. Hileman and S.V. Scott. 2019. Governance and control in distributed ledgers: Understanding the challenges facing blockchain technology in financial services. Information and Organization. doi: 10.1016/j.infoandorg.2019.03.001.

Index

About the Editor

Dr. Jan Veuger MRE FRICS MSV is a Scientist in Blockchain and Real Estate, and Professor (appointed from 2019–2022), School of Finance and International Business, Saxion University, the Netherlands; and Institute for Business Hanze University Groningen, the Netherlands (2012–2019). Jan graduated as a doctor from the Erasmus University Rotterdam, the Netherlands, one of Europe's top business schools for education and in the top three for research. Besides being a professor, Jan is co-promoter of several PhD candidates, Chairman of the Committee of quality certificates (CKV) at Quality Center Social Housing Corporations (2013–2022) and has substantial expertise as a member of the Supervisory Board of Commissioners for different organizations (2,000 employees).

Furthermore, member of the supervisory committee for research into 'New virtual money flows and the detection of criminal monies' of Ministry of Justice and Security, Scientific Research and Documentation Centre (WODC), member of the RICS Netherlands & Department Research and Innovation, Fellow of the RICS, Member Academic Board FIBREE, author of many (e)book(chapters), international scientific and professional publications, syllabi, research reports and has given many guest lectures. https://www.linkedin.com/in/dr-ing-jan-veuger-mre-frics-11112617/.

9781032152400